School Teachers

PETER LANG
New York • Washington, D.C./Baltimore • Bern
Frankfurt am Main • Berlin • Brussels • Vienna • Oxford

School Teachers

Professional and Demographic Characteristics

Jianping Shen

Van E. Cooley, Chia-lin Hsieh, Xuejin Lu,
Nancy B. Mansberger, Louann Bierlein Palmer,
Sue Poppink, Gary L. Wegenke, Huilan Yang

PETER LANG
New York • Washington, D.C./Baltimore • Bern
Frankfurt am Main • Berlin • Brussels • Vienna • Oxford

Library of Congress Cataloging-in-Publication Data

Jianping Shen.
School teachers: professional and demographic characteristics /
Jianping Shen.
p. cm.
Includes bibliographical references and index.
1. Teachers—Certification—United States.
2. Teachers—Professional relationships—United States.
3. Education—Demographic aspects—United States. I. Shen, Jianping.
LB1771.S36   371.120973—dc22   2009018339
ISBN 978-0-8204-9736-5

Bibliographic information published by **Die Deutsche Bibliothek**.
Die Deutsche Bibliothek lists this publication in the "Deutsche
Nationalbibliografie"; detailed bibliographic data is available
on the Internet at http://dnb.ddb.de/.

The paper in this book meets the guidelines for permanence and durability
of the Committee on Production Guidelines for Book Longevity
of the Council of Library Resources.

© 2009 Peter Lang Publishing, Inc., New York
29 Broadway, 18th floor, New York, NY 10006
www.peterlang.com

All rights reserved.
Reprint or reproduction, even partially, in all forms such as microfilm,
xerography, microfiche, microcard, and offset strictly prohibited.

Printed in the United States of America

CONTENTS

Foreword   vii

Acknowledgments   xi

Section 1. Teacher Qualification and Certification

Chapter 1. Are teachers qualified? A national study of secondary
public school teachers using SASS 1999–2000   3
Xuejin Lu, Jianping Shen, and Sue Poppink

Chapter 2. The certification characteristics of the public school
teaching force: National, longitudinal,
and comparative perspectives   30
Jianping Shen and Sue Poppink

Chapter 3. Has the public teaching force become more diversified?
National and longitudinal perspectives on gender,
race, and ethnicity   45
Jianping Shen, Gary L. Wegenke, and Van E. Cooley

Section 2. Inequitable Distribution of Public School Teachers

Chapter 4. Teacher quality and students placed at risk:
Results from the Baccalaureate and Beyond
Longitudinal Study 1993–97   61
Jianping Shen, Nancy B. Mansberger, and Huilan Yang

Chapter 5. The distribution of the quality of the public
teaching force: Results from multiple waves of schools
and staffing surveys   72
Jianping Shen

Section 3. Alternative Certification

Chapter 6. Has the alternative certification policy materialized
its promise? A comparison between traditionally and
alternatively certified teachers in public schools   91
Jianping Shen

Chapter 7. Alternative certification, minority teachers,
and urban education   104
Jianping Shen

Chapter 8. Alternative certification and math and science teachers   115
Jianping Shen

Section 4. Teacher Attrition

Chapter 9. Inadequate Preparation Does Impact Teacher Attrition   125
    Jianping Shen and Louann Bierlein Palmer
Chapter 10. Teacher retention and attrition in public schools:
    Evidence from the 1990–91 Schools and Staffing Survey   141
    Jianping Shen

Section 5. Teacher Preparation

Chapter 11. Improving the professional status of teaching:
    Perspectives of future teachers, current teachers,
    and education professors   163
    Jianping Shen and Chia-lin Hsieh
Chapter 12. Student teaching in the context of a school-university
    partnership: A case study of a student teacher   178
    Jianping Shen
Chapter 13. A study of contrast: Visions of preservice teacher education
    in the context of a professional development school   199
    Jianping Shen

Index   219

FOREWORD

John I. Goodlad

Many years ago, when I was a professor at the University of Chicago, I taught a class each winter quarter intended to be primarily for school-based teachers and principals studying toward the M.A. or Ph.D. degree. A small percentage of these graduate students were engaged in full-time studies at the University. The enrollment each year was quite large. It soon became apparent to me that many of those in the class hoped to qualify, on earning their degrees, for teaching in universities. Early on, we discussed what would be expected of them for advancement through the ranks from assistant to full professor. They would be required, I said, to engage in a steady stream of research, an activity demanding the ability to write well enough to gain publication in professional journals.

Rather foolishly, given the size of these classes, I expressed my willingness to read and comment on papers they were writing or might write during the weeks of the class. Even though only about a quarter of the group took advantage of my offer, they kept me busy with papers, which I read and returned with written comment.

I recommended two pieces for reading that I thought might be helpful in the improvement of their writing: educator Ralph Tyler's syllabus entitled *Basic Principles of Curriculum and Instruction*, first published by the University of Chicago Press in 1950, and Ernest Hemingway's classic, *The Old Man and the Sea*. Tyler's is a very straightforward syllabus for developing curricula for educational institutions at any level. He often began his writing or presentation by introducing his message with the words "There are three things here," and then with clarity and precision briefly describing the three elements. Hemingway's *The Old Man and the Sea* is a masterpiece of superb prose. I had read it twice, years before, the second time with the intent of finding a paragraph or a sentence or perhaps even a word I would want to change. I found none.

I would now add another book to the two I recommended. It is this one that you are about to read. It should be read by educational researchers (and researchers in other fields) whether or not they are interested in teaching, teachers, or teacher education. Indeed, if you are not very interested in the topic, you might profit nonetheless from reading just a chapter or two because of its superb execution. Just as Tyler had the precision to introduce and explain the one, two, three, four, or five components of the phenomena he was addressing, Jianping Shen and his colleagues present at the outset a clear and precise description of what will follow in their text and then proceed with the comprehensiveness and clarity that should be characteristic of research reports but all too often are not.

Over the years, I have served on the review boards of several educational journals. With one of these in particular, I read many of the articles submitted that closed with the statistical significance of their findings. Again and again, I recommended that the paper be returned to its author with a request that it address the economic, political, or social implications of the findings as well. After a couple of years of this, the editor wrote me a very nice letter noting the frequency with which I suggested further work on the part of an author when the other readers approved publication. In answering, I drew from John Dewey, who is one of the few prominent educators of decades ago who educational scholars commonly cite.

Every educational researcher should read Dewey's little book entitled *The Sources of a Science of Education*, published about eight decades ago (probably most available today in *The Later Works of John Dewey, Volume 5, 1925–1953*, edited by Jo Ann Boydston, first published by Southern Illinois University Press in 1984). He wrote that educational research should arise out of practice, and then, after careful inquiry, the outcomes of the research should be returned to practice. This challenges the researcher to figure out how best to render the research accessible to practitioners. Clearly, publishing it in academic journals read by specialists in the field falls far short of this goal. It is more likely to contribute to the academic advancement of the author than into the work of practitioners. Getting it into the hands of schoolteachers and administrators is a challenge. But is this not a major responsibility of educational researchers?

What Jianping Shen and his colleagues have provided is a handbook, a compendium, a reference book for a wide range of potential readers. They provide, with supporting data, the kind of information that every school board member, every school administrator, every local, state, and federal official making educational policy should have when entering into the decisions that are now largely undergirded by ideology rather than evidence. This is the book that pundits like George Will should read before they write anything about teachers and their qualifications and role in the education of children and youths.

Again and again, I read reviews of books that close with the recommendation that what they just finished reading should be on every person's or educator's bookshelf. This book should not be on the shelf of the recommended readers I listed above; it should be on their desks as a basic reference to be drawn upon in checking the validity of statements about schoolteachers—their qualifications, the distribution of qualified teachers in our communities, alternative teacher certification, the relationship between teacher preparation and student accomplishment, and much more.

If we are to have good schools, we must have good, well-qualified teachers. If we are to have good teachers and good schools, we must have a populace that is well informed about both. This book provides an important part of what we must know about the present in order to deal wisely with the future. For those readers who are educational researchers, I repeat my observation that there is much to be learned in the pages that follow about the structure and comprehensiveness of reporting their findings, conclusions, and implications to those they want to influence.

ACKNOWLEDGMENTS

We want to thank the publishers and organizations for the permission to use the materials in the following sources:

Lu, X., Shen, J., & Poppink, S. (2007). Are teachers qualified? A national study of secondary public school teachers using SASS 1999-2000. *School Leadership & Policy, 5* (4), 129–152.

Shen, J., & Poppink, S. (2003). The certification characteristics of the public school teaching force: National, longitudinal, and comparative perspectives. *Educational Horizons, 81*, 130–137.

Shen, J., Wegenke, G. L., & Cooley, V. E. (2003). Has the public teaching force become more diversified: National and longitudinal perspectives on gender, race, and ethnicity. *Educational Horizons, 81*, 112–118.

Shen, J., Mansberger, N. B., Yang, H. (2004). Teacher quality and students placed at risk: Results from the Baccalaureate and Beyond Longitudinal Study 1993-97. *Educational Horizons, 82*, 226–235.

Shen, J. (1997). Has the alternative certification policy materialized its promise? A comparison between traditionally and alternatively certified teachers in public schools. *Educational Evaluation and Policy Analysis, 19* (3), 276–283.

Shen, J. (1998). Alternative certification, minority teacher, and urban education. *Education and Urban Society 31* (1), 30–41.

Shen, J., & Palmer, L. B. (2005). Attrition patterns of inadequately prepared teachers. In J. R. Dangel & E. M. Guyton (Eds.), *Research on alternative and non-traditional education (Teacher Education Yearbook XIII)* (pp. 143–157). Lanham, MD: Scarecrow.

Shen, J. (1997). Teacher retention and attrition in public schools: Evidence from SASS91. *Journal of Educational Research, 91* (2), 81–88. Reprinted with permission of the Helen Dwight Reid Educational Foundation. Published by Heldref Publications,1319 Eighteenth St., NW, Washington, DC 20036-1802. Copyright © 1997.

Shen, J., & Hsieh, C. (1999). Improving the professional status of teaching: Perspectives of future teachers, current teachers, and education professors. *Teaching and Teacher Education, 15* (3), 315–323.

Shen, J. (2002). Student teaching in the context of school-university partnership: A case study of a student teacher. *Education, 122* (3), 564–580

Shen, J. (1996). A study of contrast: Visions of preservice teacher education in the context of a professional development school. *The Professional Educator, 18* (2), 45–58.

SECTION 1

Teacher Qualification and Certification

CHAPTER ONE

Are Teachers Highly Qualified?
A National Study of Secondary Public School Teachers Using SASS 1999–2000

Xuejin Lu, Jianping Shen, and Sue Poppink

Introduction

In the last 15 years, interest in the impact of teacher qualifications on student achievement has grown among education policymakers and researchers. Research shows that teacher qualifications are one of the key factors associated with student performance (Darling-Hammond, 2000; Ferguson, 1991; Goldhaber & Brewer, 2000; Laczko-Kerr & Berliner, 2002; Monk, 1994; Sanders & Rivers, 1996). Yet, a growing body of research reveals that a large number of the nation's teachers, especially teachers in secondary schools and in high-need schools, are lacking preparation and content background in the subjects they teach (Ingersoll, 1996; Seastrom, Gruber, Henke, McGrath, & Cohen, 2002). The concern about students' performance and the condition of teacher qualifications is so great that the No Child Left Behind (NCLB) legislation signed into law in 2002 contains provisions that mandate all teachers be highly qualified by 2006. In brief, under NCLB, a highly qualified secondary teacher must (a) have at least a bachelor's degree, (b) obtain full state certification or licensure, and (c) demonstrate subject area competence in each of the academic subjects taught.[1] Obviously, this policy focuses on improving teacher qualifications to address the issue of teacher quality.

A document from the U.S. Department of Education argued the importance of teacher quality: "Conceptually, measuring teaching quality ought to be a high priority of any examination of teaching and learning, since, literally defined, it represents the direct effect on students by teachers as they create their classroom magic" (1999, p. 1). According to Lewis and colleagues (1999), teacher quality refers to two broad categories: teacher qualifications and teaching practices, a position that a document from the U.S. Department of Education supported (1996). While teacher qualifications such as postsecondary education and certification are among the inputs teachers bring to schools, teaching practices involve the quality of teaching that teachers exhibit in their classroom. Stronge (2002) argued that teacher qualifications may not directly address the quality of teaching and student learning, but that they are a necessary prerequisite of effective teaching. Some well-established indicators of teacher qualifications—such as teachers' education credentials, including their background in the subject matter and the certification they hold—inform researchers and policymakers as to how well prepared teachers are to take on their teaching assignments (Lewis et al., 1999; Mandel, 1996). A growing body of research concerning teacher quality suggests that both teacher qualifications and teaching practices matter in terms of student achievement (Stronge, 2002). In this study, we use a nationally representative data set—the Public Teacher Questionnaire of the Schools and Staffing Survey (SASS) 1999–2000—to inquire into teacher qualifications, but not into teaching practices.

Literature Review

In this section, we first review literature on teachers with high qualifications, particularly in subject-shortage areas such as math and science. Then, we review literature on the distribution of teachers with high qualifications among schools that serve high proportions of at-risk students. Finally, we present literature on the relationship between teacher qualifications and student achievement.

Teachers with High Qualifications

Many have argued that teacher qualifications are positively related to student achievement (Darling-Hammond, Berry, & Thoreson, 2001; Ferguson, 1991; Goldhaber & Brewer, 2000; Laczko-Kerr & Berliner, 2002; Monk, 1994); therefore, it isn't surprising that education policymakers as well as school administrators and researchers have turned their attention to this important topic. This attention is focused on teachers' postsecondary degrees, including their majors and certification. Ravitch (1998) criticized teachers' subject matter knowledge and argued that education students should have academic majors rather than general education degrees. In addition, certification policies have drawn criticism. A growing number of the nation's teachers are entering classrooms with emergency or temporary certification (Riley, 1998; Shen & Poppink, 2003). Finally, at the secondary level, research attention is increasingly directed toward teaching assignments—that is, teachers assigned to teach subjects that do not match their preparation or education (U.S. Department of Education, 1996). Such mismatches are commonly referred to as out-of-field teaching. Therefore, in recent years a significant number of studies focused on the qualifications of secondary teachers and the distribution of qualified teachers across different schools (Ingersoll, 1994, 1996, 1999; Kaplan & Owings, 2002; Shen & Poppink, 2003; Seastrom et al., 2002).

According to the 1998 Fast Response Survey System (FRSS), virtually all teachers in American public schools had a bachelor's degree and nearly half (45%) had a master's degree, however, only 66% of high school teachers had an undergraduate or graduate major in an academic field that they teach (Lewis et al., 1999). In a study of 8th- and 10th-graders' math and science achievement, Goldhaber and Brewer (1998) had similar findings. They found that, depending on the subject, only 68% to 76% of teachers had at least a bachelor's degree in their subject areas, and a lower proportion of math and science teachers than of English and history teachers had bachelor's degrees in the subject areas they taught.

In terms of teacher certification, Lewis and colleagues (1999) reported that most teachers (92% and 93% for departmentalized and general elementary respectively) were fully certified in the fields of their main teaching assignments, the fields in which they taught the most courses. However, when exploring the certification characteristics of the public school teaching force nationwide, Shen and Poppink (2003) found that, over a twelve-year period (1987–88 to 1999–2000), the percentage of teachers uncertified in their main teaching assignments increased from 2.7 to 5.7.

In order to find out the extent to which public secondary students (grades 7–12) are taught core academics by out-of-field teachers (teachers without at least a college minor in the field they teach), Ingersoll (1996) analyzed national data—the Schools and Staffing Survey (SASS)—and found that many students were taught by out-of-field teachers: 20% in English classes, 25% in mathematics, 39% in life science or biology, 56% in the physical sciences, and over 50% in history or world civilization. Analyzing data from different waves of SASS, Seastrom and colleagues (2002) confirmed the continuous prevalence of out-of-field teaching between 1987 and 2000. Seastrom and colleagues (2002) also provided subject-specific estimates of out-of-field teaching. They reported that at the high school level in the 1999–2000 school year, a minimum of six out of every 10 students enrolled in physical science classes (including those in the subfields of chemistry, geology/earth/space science) had teachers who did not have certification and a major in the subject taught. Approximately

30% of those enrolled in mathematics, English, and social science classes had out-of-field teachers.

Mathematics classrooms are of particular concern. Blank and Langesen (2001) found that though the number of high school mathematics teachers in U.S. public schools increased by 22,000 between 1990 and 2000 to a total of 134,000, the percentage of teachers certified to teach high school mathematics among those assigned to teach the subject has decreased from 90% in 1990 to 86% in 2000. The Council of Great City Schools (2000) reported that 95% of urban school districts nationwide are in immediate need of high school mathematics teachers. In addition, the shortages in high-minority and high-poverty schools were particularly distressing. In schools with over 50% minority enrollment in grades 7-12, 24% of mathematics teachers taught out-of-field. For high-poverty schools, in which 60% or more of the students qualified for free or reduced-price lunch programs, 31% of mathematics teachers had neither an undergraduate nor graduate major nor a minor in mathematics (Clewell & Forcier, 2001). These studies show that the need to find qualified mathematics teachers for the nation's schools is critical.

Distribution of Teachers with High Qualifications

Providing highly qualified teachers, as defined by NCLB, to schools that serve high proportions of at-risk students has been a challenge for many school districts. Previous studies on the distribution of qualified teachers showed that students in high-need schools—high-poverty and high-minority student population schools, and those with students who perform low on achievement tests—are less likely than other students to be taught by teachers with high qualifications (Ansell & McCabe, 2003; Ingersoll, 2002; Lavigne, 1992; Shen & Poppink, 2003). These high-need schools were associated with having more teachers who taught out-of-field, lacked certification, or did not have appropriate certification.

Shen and Poppink (2003) reported that in comparison to suburban and rural schools, urban schools had higher percentages of uncertified teachers and of teachers with weaker certification (temporary certificates, emergency certificates, and waivers) in their main teaching assignments. Similarly, Lavigne (1992) observed that among New York City public schools, high-poverty schools and those with high percentages of minority students had significantly fewer certified teachers than low-poverty and low-minority enrollment schools.

Using the attributes of school poverty and percentage of minority students, Ingersoll (1998) did a nationwide analysis of out-of-field teaching and found that low-income schools had higher levels of out-of-field teaching than did more affluent schools. Using data from the National Center for Education Statistics, Harris and Ray (2003) examined the distribution of teacher quality in Michigan's public schools by analyzing teacher certification status. They found that teachers in urban schools are less likely to meet the NCLB certification requirements for highly qualified teachers in their main teaching assignment than their counterparts in suburban and rural areas. About three times as many urban school teachers did not meet the NCLB certification requirements for their main assignment when compared to suburban or rural teachers. Shen and colleagues (2004) reported that many urban school districts have been forced to employ underqualified teachers due to teacher shortages and the class-size reduction movement. In New York City, for example, more than 9,000 teachers were teaching on temporary or emergency license, compared with 1,185 in the rest of the state in the 1997–1998 school year (Darling-Hammond, 2002).

Teacher Qualifications on Student Achievement

In recent years, researchers have conducted an increasing number of studies seeking to understand whether teachers with high qualifications can make a difference in students' learning (Chaney, 1995; Darling-Hammond, Berry, & Thoreson, 2001; Ferguson & Womack, 1993; Fuller, 1999; Hawk, Coble, & Swanson, 1985; Monk, 1994; Monk & King, 1994; Rowan, Chiang, & Miller, 1997; Strauss & Sawyer, 1986). Monk's (1994) study of the relationship between teacher preparation and student achievement indicated that both subject content courses and subject-specific pedagogy courses in a teacher's preparation were positively related to student achievement. Other available evidences demonstrated that teachers with subject-specific preparation or with a major in their subjects taught had a significantly positive impact on student achievement, particularly in math and science (Chaney, 1995; Goldhaber & Brewer, 1998; Rowan, Chiang, & Miller, 1997; Weglinsky, 2000). Analyzing the data from the National Assessment of Educational Progress (NAEP), Weglinsky (2000) observed that, in math and science, students whose teachers majored or minored in the subject they taught outperformed peers whose teachers did not have a major or minor in their subject by 40% of a grade level. Studies have also shown that students taught by teachers certified in the subject performed better than those who were not (Goldhaber & Brewer, 2000; Hawk, Coble, & Swanson, 1985), and students taught by regularly certified teachers outperformed students taught by undercertified teachers (Laczko-Kerr & Berliner, 2002). Laczko-Kerr and Berliner (2002) found that students taught by regularly certified teachers made about 20% more academic progress per year than did students taught by undercertified teachers.

In a multivariate analysis using data from 1993–1994 SASS and the National Assessment of Educational Progress (NAEP), Darling-Hammond (2000) found that the most consistent, highly significant predictor for student achievement in the subjects of reading and mathematics in all years and at all grade levels was the variable of well-qualified teachers (teachers with full certification and a major in the subject they teach). Her study revealed that the combination of strong subject content knowledge (a major in the subject taught) and strong pedagogical content knowledge (full certification in the subject taught) was by far the most important determinant of student achievement. Darling-Hammond's study highlights the critical influence of highly qualified teachers on student learning.

Some recent studies that focused their attention on the impact of teacher qualification on disadvantaged students' achievement revealed that disadvantaged students' achievement is especially sensitive to the qualification of their teachers (Nye et al., 2004; Sanders & Rivers, 1996). For example, Nye and colleagues (2004) found that teacher effects are much larger in low-Social Economic Status (SES) schools than in high-SES schools. Olson (2003) also found that having a highly qualified teacher for four or five years in a row could fundamentally close the gap in student achievement between students from low-income families and those from high-income families. Sanders and Rivers (1996) found that disadvantaged students with the most effective teachers gained over 50 percentile points in their test scores, while those with the least effective teachers gained 14 percentile points. In the book *Qualities of Effective Teachers,* Stronge (2002) defined effective teachers as individuals who have teacher preparation and qualifications as well as skills in classroom management, planning, and teaching, and who monitor student progress. These studies suggest that teachers with strong teacher qualifications can help disadvantaged students close the achievement gap.

Ansell and McCabe (2003) pointed out that if one wants to understand the root of the achievement gap, he or she should first understand the teacher gap that exists between the skill levels of teachers. Therefore, to end the achievement gap between minority and non-minority students and between those with different economic backgrounds, an article in *Education Week* urged states to end the teacher gap, stating that providing well-qualified teachers for those who need them most is a starting point for closing that gap ("To Close the Gap," January 9, 2005). However, according to Ansell and McCabe (2003), in addition to the existing student achievement gap and teacher quality gap, there was also a policy gap nationwide: few states track and inform the public about the distribution of qualified teachers across different types of schools and few states or districts try to match highly qualified teachers with high-need schools.

Purpose of the Study

The purpose of this study is to provide valuable information about the availability of highly qualified teachers and the distribution of these teachers in public secondary schools. Specifically, the purpose of this study is threefold. First, we inquire into secondary teachers' qualifications by investigating whether or not teachers are highly qualified in their *main* teaching assignment. Specifically, we observed teacher qualifications by (a) all main teaching assignment fields,[2] (b) core academic fields (i.e., English, social studies, math, and science), and (c) the subfields of science (i.e., chemistry, physics, earth, life, and physical science).

Second, we examine whether or not teachers are highly qualified in *each* subject taught,[3] that is, in each of the individual subjects that teachers are assigned to teach during the school day. Again, we focus our attention on (a) core academic subjects and (b) the subfields of science.

Third, we inquire into whether there are significant differences in the distribution of teachers who are highly qualified in the field of their main teaching assignment by school locations (urban, suburban, and rural)[4] and by levels of minority student enrollment (less than 5%, 5% to 19%, 20% to 49%, and 50% or more).[5]

Significance of the Study

Our study of teacher qualifications by the characteristics of highly qualified teachers is unique for several reasons. First, it is timely in light of the increasing concern about the qualifications of teachers, especially in specific subject areas, and the distribution of teachers with high qualifications across different types of schools. By using a national data set, we are able to add valuable information to the existing knowledge base on the conditions and distribution of highly qualified teachers at the secondary level nationwide by subject matter and across schools. This helps us understand the challenges that lie ahead as educational organizations implement the NCLB's highly qualified teacher provisions. In addition, this study can provide information to those who are preparing to reauthorize the Elementary and Secondary Education Act of 1965, which in its present form is the

NCLB. Second, to date few studies have inquired into teacher qualifications by focusing on the NCLB's definition of a highly qualified teacher. By combining data on teachers' degrees, including both certification and major areas of study, we provide new empirical information to the discussion of teacher qualifications. Many of the previous studies on teacher qualifications tended to investigate certification and postsecondary majors separately, but the legislation makes no such distinctions. Finally, we analyzed highly qualified teachers not only by main teaching assignments but also by each subject taught, providing new angles of analysis. In addition, we offer data on the distribution of highly qualified teachers by school locations and minority student enrollments.

Method

Data Source

The data for this study were extracted from the Schools and Staffing Survey (SASS) public-use data file. SASS is the largest survey of K–12 educators in the United States. Data were periodically collected by the National Center for Education Statistics (NCES), beginning in the 1987–1988 school year. We used the 1999–2000 SASS data collected from the secondary public school teachers. The use of this NCES data set has many advantages. First, the SASS is a major source of data regarding teacher qualifications in the United States. Second, the SASS collected data on the broadest range of teacher qualification measures, such as teachers' educational backgrounds and teaching assignments. In the area of teachers' educational backgrounds, the SASS collected data on all degrees earned (from associates to doctorates), the subject field of these earned degrees, whether teachers were certified in their fields of assignment, and the type of certification they held in those fields. In the area of teacher assignments, the survey collected data on main and secondary subject fields of assignments, and, for secondary school teachers, on the subject fields they taught for each period of the school day (U.S. Department of Education, 1994).

Sample and Sampling Weight

The primary sampling unit of the SASS is the school. Once schools are selected, teachers are subsequently selected from those schools to include in the SASS school sample frame.[6] The sample size of public secondary school teachers (9–12) in the 1999–2000 SASS public teacher data file was 21,493. Because the SASS sampling involves stratification, disproportionate sampling of certain strata, and clustered probability sampling, the subsample of secondary school teachers was not a representative one. Therefore, weights were applied to approximate the population.[7] Weights can adjust for differential selection probabilities and non-response and, therefore, can compensate for not collecting data from the entire population. As a result of this adjustment, the final weighted sample of secondary school teachers was 895,327. The weighted sample was nationally representative of secondary public school teachers, allowing us to generalize to the national population of secondary public school teachers.

In this study, relative sample weights were used in the data analysis. Because of the relative weighting, the total sample of secondary school teachers was reduced from 21,493 to 12,624. Relative sample weights, rather than final sample weights, were used because when conducting chi-square tests, the larger final sample weights would inflate the statistics, which in turn would lead to a higher Type I error rate—an erroneous rejection of the null hypothesis when it is true (Charles, 1998). After the application of the relative weights, the findings of the study are generalizable to the national population. The relatively weighted sample size for the study was 12,624, which represented an estimated national population of 895,327 secondary school teachers.

Measurement

In the area of teachers' educational backgrounds, the SASS contains data on all degrees earned (from an associate degree to a doctorate), the subject field of these degrees, whether teachers were certified in their fields of assignment, and the type of certification they held in those fields. In the area of teacher assignments, the survey collected data on main and secondary subject fields of assignment, and, for secondary school teachers, on the subject fields they taught for each period of the school day.

To aid research on in-field and out-of-field teaching, NCES staff created composite variables for measuring each of the two types of teaching.[8] In the 1999–2000 SASS data file, in-field or out-of-field teaching were defined as containing two elements of teacher qualifications: state certification status (that is, the extent to which a teacher's certification matches the subject the teacher teaches) and postsecondary education (Tourkin et al., 2004; Seastrom et al., 2002).[9]

The SASS data also provide four approaches to measure in-field or out-of-field teaching: teachers in-field by main assignments, teachers in-field by each subject taught, classes taught by in-field teachers, and students taught by in-field teachers. The focus of this study is on the first two measures for teachers: teacher in-field by main teaching assignments and teacher in-field by each subject taught. The "main teaching assignment" measure was captured by the extent to which teachers' qualifications matched the subject area in which they taught the most classes. A major strength of the main assignment measure is that it can be calculated for all teachers. Teachers' main assignments and their qualifications were directly matched since it is relatively straightforward to ask teachers to report their main assignments and then compare their qualifications against their main assignments.

However, this main assignment measure did not capture teaching that occurs outside of teachers' main assignments. In reality, many teachers teach one or more classes outside their main assignments. Therefore, we also used an "each subject taught" measure. It captured the extent to which teachers' qualifications match their assignments in each subject area they teach. For example, with this measure, we can report that among all secondary teachers teaching at least one math course, what percentage of those teachers was teaching in-field. In this study, we adopted both measures for teachers—a teacher's main assignment and each subject taught—to estimate the extent to which public secondary school teachers meet the requirements to be highly qualified.

Highly Qualified Teacher Variable Featured in This Study

Indicators of a highly qualified teacher used in this study include teachers who have

1. at least a bachelor's degree. Teachers who received a "regular" or "standard" certificate to teach a specific subject and grade level are required by all states to have at least a bachelor's degree that includes subject matter as well as pedagogical studies (Seastrom et al., 2002).
2. a full state certification. In various states, a teacher can obtain (a) a regular or standard state certificate or advanced professional certificate, (b) a probationary certificate, (c) a provisional or alternative certificate, (d) a temporary certificate, or (e) an emergency certificate or waiver. A full state certification in this study refers to the awarding of standard or regular, advanced or probationary certificates. According to Seastrom and colleagues (2002), in many states, a "probationary" certificate is provided to new teachers who have completed all the requirements of the standard certificate except for the completion of the probationary period. These new teachers will earn the standard certificate in due time through full-time teaching in the school (usually two or three years after beginning teaching).
3. a major in the subject taught.

Therefore, operationally, teachers who meet these three criteria are identified as highly qualified and those who do not are identified as not having the requirements. According to NCLB, secondary school teachers can demonstrate subject-matter competency in several different ways. Due to the complexity of the law and its implementation, we recognize that the definition of "highly qualified teachers" in this study is a simple one; nonetheless, it allows us to examine highly qualified teachers across states.

Data Analysis

Corresponding to the purpose of this study, the writing below presents three analyses of teacher qualifications using the Schools and Staffing Survey. Each analysis differs in the focus it brings to the issue of teacher qualifications. The first analysis focuses on teacher qualifications based on their main teaching assignment field. We identify and describe the percentages of secondary public school teachers who are highly qualified by (a) main teaching assignments (a composite variable that was calculated by combining all the main teaching assignment fields reported by secondary teachers) (b) core subjects, and (c) the subfields of science.

The second analysis focuses not on main teaching assignments, but on teacher qualifications in each subject a teacher teaches. That is, this second analysis examined whether a teacher is highly qualified in all subject areas they were assigned to teach. We also present and explain the percentages of teachers highly qualified in the core subjects and in the subfields of science.

The third analysis focuses on the distribution of highly qualified teachers. We apply chi-square for goodness of fit tests to examine if the proportion of highly qualified teachers is the same for schools in different locations and for schools with different levels of minority student enrollment. The chi-square tests applied here are considered to be appropriate since they explore the proportion of cases that fall into the various categories of a single variable and compare these with hypothesized values (Gravetter & Wallnau, 2000). Relative weights were applied when conducting chi-square tests and the frequency analysis .

Results

In the following, we first present findings on highly qualified teachers in their main teaching assignments, then in each subject taught, and finally on the distribution of highly qualified teachers by school locations and minority student enrollments.

Highly Qualified Teachers by Main Teaching Assignment

Highly Qualified Teachers by All Main Teaching Assignment Fields

We first examined what percentage of secondary school teachers were highly qualified in their main teaching assignment for the 1999–2000 school year. Table 1.1 displays the results related to teacher qualifications in all main teaching assignments. Of the 12,624 secondary teachers we studied, 11,790 reported their main teaching assignment fields. The result indicates that 72.8% of the teachers were highly qualified and shows that more than one-fourth of secondary teachers did not meet highly qualified teachers' requirements in their main teaching assignment field.

Table 1.1 Highly Qualified Teachers by All Main Teaching Assignment Fields

Secondary teachers who reported main teaching assignments (all subject fields)	N	%
Highly qualified	8,582	72.8
Not highly qualified	3,208	27.2
Total	11,790	100

Highly Qualified Teachers by Core Fields of Their Main Teaching Assignments

After observing the overall pattern of teachers who were highly qualified in their main teaching assignments, we inquired into the percentage of teachers who are highly qualified in the core fields. Table 1.2 shows that the percentage of highly qualified teachers in each of these four core fields was higher than the percentage of highly qualified teachers in the overall main assignment fields, which was only 72.8%. That is, 75.7% of English, 73.2% of mathematics, 75.4% of science, and 79.1% of social studies teachers are highly qualified in their main teaching assignments. However, it is important to note that, in comparison with other core subjects, the percentage of teachers who were highly qualified in mathematics was the lowest.

Table 1.2 Highly Qualified Teachers by Core Academic Fields of Their Main Teaching Assignments

Core Subjects	N	Highly Qualified (%)	Not Highly Qualified (%)
English	1,847	75.7	24.3
Math	1,590	73.2	26.8
Science	1,411	75.4	24.6
Social Studies	1,393	79.1	20.9

Highly Qualified Teachers by Subfields of Science of Their Main Teaching Assignments

According to NCLB, high school science teachers must be highly qualified in each subfield of science taught. In this part of analysis, we investigated what percentage of secondary school teachers was highly qualified in the subfields of science. The results revealed that the percentages of highly qualified teachers in the individual subfields of science were much lower (see Table 1.3) than overall percentages and those in the core subjects. That is, in chemistry 42.5%, earth science 31%, life science 60.1%, physical science 41.6%, and physics 42.3% of the teachers were highly qualified. More than half of the secondary teachers who had their main teaching assignments in the subfields of science did not meet the highly qualified teachers' requirements, except those in the subfield of life science.

Table 1.3 Highly Qualified Teachers in the Subfields of Science of Their Main Teaching Assignments

Subfields of Science	N	Highly Qualified (%)	Not Highly Qualified (%)
Chemistry	302	42.5	57.5
Earth Science	114	31.0	69.0
Life Science	612	60.1	39.3
Physical Science	707	41.6	58.4
Physics	127	42.3	57.7

Note: In Table 1.2, a total of 1,411 science teachers is reported, while in Table 1.3, the total is 1,862—a difference of 451. This is due to the different ways of coding the teachers in the SASS data.[10] This does not affect the accuracy of the percentages of teachers in various fields and subfields who are highly qualified or not. The analyses reported in the paper are based on the coding system contained in the electronic coding book developed by the National Center for Education Statistics.

Highly Qualified Teachers by Each Subject Taught

The "each subject taught" measures capture the extent to which teachers' qualifications match the subject area in which they teach at least one class. In this case, the same teacher may teach in multiple fields. The teacher may be highly qualified in one subject area but may not be highly qualified in another subject area. This estimates the percentage of public secondary school teachers who are highly qualified in specific subjects.

Highly Qualified Teachers in the Core Subjects by Each Subject Taught

We examined the percentage of secondary school teachers highly qualified by core subjects. As Table 1.4 shows, 61.9% of English, 59.5% of mathematics, 65.2% of science, and 63.2% of social studies teachers were highly qualified in each subject taught. Not surprisingly, when the more stringent measure of highly qualified by "each subject taught" was applied, the percentages were lower than those of teachers who were highly qualified in their main teaching assignments. Again, the percentage of highly qualified math teachers was the lowest.

Table 1.4 Highly Qualified Teachers in Each of the Core Academic Fields

Core Subjects	N	Highly Qualified (%)	Not Highly Qualified (%)
English	2,201	61.9	38.1
Math	2,005	59.5	40.5
Science	1,659	65.2	34.8
Social Studies	1,817	63.2	36.8

Note: The N values are different in Table 1.2 and 1.4 because Table 1.2 focuses on the main teaching assignment and Table 1.4 on each subject taught.

Highly Qualified Teachers in the Subfields of Science by Each Subject Taught

Although the percentage of teachers who were highly qualified in the overall field of science was higher, at 65.2%, than other core subjects (see Table 1.4), the results of analyses based on the individual subfields of science showed that the percentage of highly qualified teachers in each subfield of science was much lower (see Table 1.5). The percentages of highly qualified teachers for each subfield of science ranged from 15.7% to 47.8%, with 15.7% in earth science, 23.4% in physics, 30.3% in physical science, 31.1% in chemistry, and 47.8% in life science. These indicate that there will be high demand for highly qualified science teachers in their subfields, much more so than in any core field.

Table 1.5 Highly Qualified Teachers in the Subfields of Science

Subfields of Science	N	Highly Qualified (%)	Not Highly Qualified (%)
Chemistry	447	31.1	68.9
Earth Science	250	15.7	84.3
Life Science	805	47.8	52.2
Physical Science	1,021	30.3	69.7
Physics	272	23.4	76.6

Note: The relationship between Tables 1.4 and 1.5 in terms of "science" and "subfields" is similar to that between Tables 1.2 and 1.3. Please see the note for Table 1.3. Furthermore, for Table 1.5 some teachers are counted more than once depending on how many of the subfields listed in Table 1.5 they teach.

Distribution of Highly Qualified Teachers

Finally, we investigated whether there was an equitable distribution of highly qualified teachers among schools that serve high proportions of students at risk of academic failure. There are many different variables available to address this issue. However, for this chapter, we chose to investigate how teachers highly qualified in their main teaching assignment fields were distributed, first by school locations and then by the percentage of minority student enrollment in schools.

Distribution of Highly Qualified Teachers by School Locations

A 2 x 3 chi-square test was applied to examine whether the proportion of highly qualified teachers was the same for the different school locations. Results revealed a statistically significant difference among different school locations, χ^2 = 16.58, p < .01, Cramer's V = .04. See Table 1.6 and Figure 1.1. The data indicated that urban and rural schools were less likely to be staffed with highly qualified teachers than their suburban counterparts with 70.6% in urban, 71.6% in rural, and 74.4% in suburban school districts.

Table 1.6 Distribution of Highly Qualified Teachers by School Location

Variable	N	School Location			χ^2	df	p	v
		Urban	Suburban	Rural				
Highly qualified teachers	8,582	70.6%	74.4%	71.6%	16.58	2	<0.01	0.04

Note. Percentages represent teachers who are highly qualified in their main teaching assignment field.

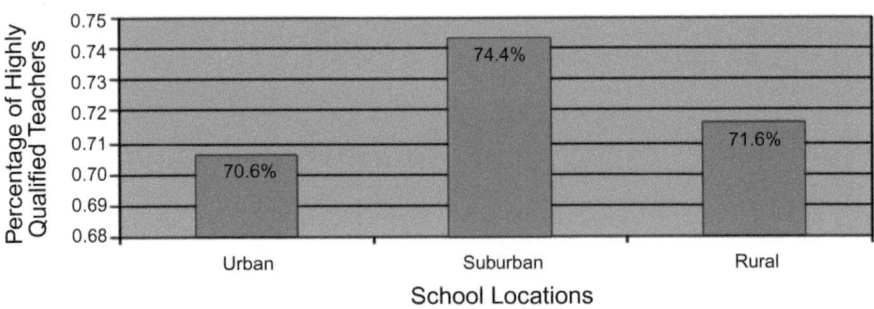

Figure 1.1 Distribution of Highly Qualified Teachers by School Locations

Distribution of Highly Qualified Teachers by Minority Student Enrollments

Another 2 x 4 chi-square test was applied to investigate whether the percentage of teachers who were highly qualified in their main teaching assignments were the same across schools with different percentages of minority student enrollment. The results indicate that the variation in the percentage of highly qualified teachers among schools with different levels of minority student enrollment was statistically significant, $\chi^2 = 101.91$, $p < .01$, Cramer's $V = .09$. See Table 1.7 and Figure 1.2.

The results also show that the higher the percentage of minority students in a school, the more likely that the school was served by teachers who did not meet the definition of highly qualified. As Figure 1.1 shows, schools comprised of fewer than 20% minority students had 76% highly qualified teachers, higher than the average for all schools of about 73%. In schools with 20–49% minority students, 73.3% of the teachers were highly qualified. Finally, in schools with greater than 50% minority students, only about 66% of the teachers were highly qualified. In schools with less than 20% minority student enrollment, the percentage of highly qualified teachers was 76%, whereas in schools with 50% or more minority students, the percentage of highly qualified teachers was only 65.9%—a 10% gap between the two types of schools.

Table 1.7 Distribution of Highly Qualified Teachers by Schools with Different Levels of Minority Student Enrollment

		Percentage of Minority Students							
Variable	N	< 5%	5–19%	20–49%	> 50%	χ^2	df	p	v
Highly qualified teachers	8,582	76%	76%	73.3%	65.9%	101.91	3	< 0.01	0.09

Figure 1.2 Distribution of Highly Qualified Teachers by Schools with Different Levels of Minority Student Enrollment

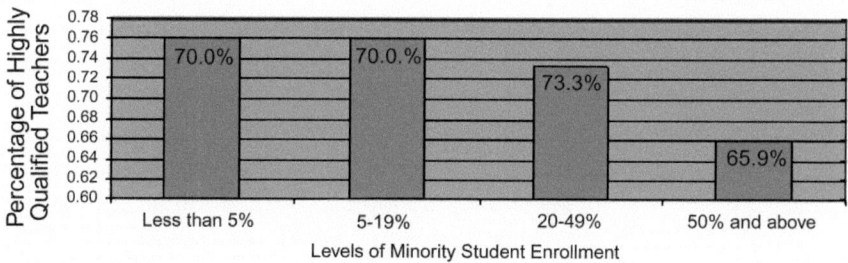

Conclusions and Discussions

Analyzing the 1999–2000 SASS data, we investigated the percentage of secondary school teachers who fit the highly qualified teacher definition. We also studied the distribution of such teachers by school location and by minority student enrollment. The following are the major findings and their implications.

First, we found that overall about 73% of secondary teachers were highly qualified in their main teaching assignments, the field in which they teach most of their classes. The percentages of highly qualified teachers in the core fields were between 73% and 79%. The percentage of highly qualified teachers in the subfields of science ranged from 31% to 60%. Overall one in four secondary teachers (27%) in public schools did not fit NCLB's highly qualified teacher definition in their main teaching assignments. The percentage of teachers who did not meet NCLB's highly qualified teacher requirements was even higher for subfields of science, ranging from 31% to 42.5%. Policymakers need to be aware of these low levels of qualifications.

When compared with the findings of earlier research on teachers' qualifications in their main teaching assignment field, the findings of this study suggest that most teachers fail to achieve the status of highly qualified because of the lack of a major in their subject taught, rather than the lack of a teaching certification. Previous studies on teacher qualifications showed that virtually all teachers had a bachelor's degree and most teachers (more than 92%) were fully certified in their main teaching assignments (Lewis et al., 1999). However, according to U.S. Department of Education (1994), in 1991, only 72.8% of teachers reported having a major in their main teaching assignment field.

Second, when the focus was shifted to examine highly qualified teachers in *each* subject taught, the percentages of highly qualified teachers dropped dramatically. The percentages of highly qualified teachers in the core subjects were between 59.5% and 65%, and in the subfields of science the percentages were between 16% and 48%. This finding indicates that in the subfields of science, a majority of secondary teachers teaching in these fields were not highly qualified by each course taught. Based on these results, there is no doubt that the mandate of highly qualified teachers under NCLB may affect many teachers, especially those teachers who are teaching science in secondary schools. These findings are in accordance with the study by Seastrom and colleagues (2002) who demonstrated that in the 1999–2000 school year one-third or fewer high school students in English, mathematics, and social science classes were taught by teachers who had neither a major nor a certification in the subject area taught. These figures were much higher for specific subfields of science, which ranged from 45% for biology/life science classes to 79% for geology/earth science. The results of this study imply that to ensure highly qualified teachers for all high school students, policymakers will need to find mechanisms for attracting and keeping mathematics and science teachers, particularly in the subfields of science.

Third, in terms of the percentage of highly qualified teachers in various subjects, the finding of this study is quite consistent with those reported by some of the previous studies on this topic. The results indicate that the percentages of highly qualified teachers in the area of math, and particularly in the subfields of science, were much lower in comparison with the areas of English and social studies. Given that previous research showed that in math and science, particularly at the secondary level, rigorous subject-area training and pedagogical training of teachers have a positive effect on students' achievement, more efforts should be made to improve the qualifications of secondary school teachers in these areas.

Finally, the investigation of highly qualified teachers in relation to school locations and minority student enrollment in schools revealed that urban and rural schools were disadvantaged in comparison with their suburban counterparts, and schools with higher levels of minority student enrollments were disadvantaged in comparison to schools with lower levels of minority student enrollments. These findings indicated that, in urban and rural schools and in schools with more minority students, there are fewer highly qualified teachers. The findings of this study were consistent with many other studies on the distribution of qualified teacher across different schools (Bishop, 2002; Ingersoll, 1996; Jerald, 2002; Shen & Poppink, 2003; Shen et al., 2004). In high-poverty and high-minority schools, students were much more likely to be assigned to a teacher who is not highly qualified (Jerald, 2002; Bishop, 2002). Urban schools, in comparison to suburban and rural schools, had a higher percentage of uncertified teachers (Shen & Poppink, 2003) and schools at risk had less-qualified new teachers (Shen et al., 2004). Such a situation deserves special concern among policymakers and researchers because students' achievement in these disadvantaged schools is very sensitive to the quality of their teachers (Sanders & Rivers, 1996). Again, these findings seem to raise a serious equity issue in staffing urban, suburban, and rural schools and schools with different levels of minority student enrollment. Facing the existing student achievement gap and the inequitable distribution gap of highly qualified teachers, Ansell and McCabe (2003) suggested that states and school districts should make efforts to track and inform the public about the distribution of qualified teachers across different types of schools and try to match highly qualified teachers with high-need schools .

Overall, the findings of this study are quite consistent with the findings of the previous studies on teacher qualifications in public secondary schools. Percentages of highly qualified teachers in the core fields and in each subfield of science in secondary public schools are far from satisfactory. In some of the subfields of science, the percentage of highly qualified teachers is extremely low. In addition, urban and rural schools as well as schools with high levels of minority enrollment have lower percentages of highly qualified teachers. The low percentage of teachers who fit the highly qualified teacher definition and the inequitable distribution of highly qualified teachers who meet these requirements among schools prior to NCLB pose a serious challenge that many states, districts, and schools face in implementing NCLB's highly qualified teacher requirements and improving teacher quality.

Notes

1. According to NCLB, secondary school teachers can demonstrate competence in subject knowledge in several ways: (a) a major in the subject they teach, (b) credits equivalent to a major in the subject, (c) passage of a state-developed test, (d) an advanced certification from the state, (e) a graduate degree, and (f) High, Objective, Uniform State Standard of Evaluation (HOUSSE). NCLB allows states to develop an additional way for current teachers to demonstrate subject-matter competency and meet highly qualified teacher requirements. Proof may consist of a combination of teaching experience, professional development, and knowledge in the subject taught garnered over time in the profession (U.S. Department of Education, 2004).
2. Main teaching assignments involved 21 subject fields in the SASS 1999–2000 data set, wherein these 21 subject fields were combined to create a new variable called "all main assignments."
3. In the area of teacher assignments, the Schools and Staffing Survey (SASS) for teachers collected data on main and secondary subject fields of assignment, and for secondary school teachers, on the subject fields they taught for each period of the school day (U.S. Department of Education, 1994).
4. In the SASS data file, the term "urban schools" refers to schools in large or midsize central city, "suburban schools" to schools in urban fringe of large or midsize city, and "rural schools" to the schools in small town or rural areas.
5. The percentage of minority students in a school refers to the percentage of students enrolled whose race or ethnicity is classified as one of the following: American Indian or Alaskan Native, Asian or Pacific Islander, black, or Hispanic, based on data in the 1995–96 Common Core of Data (CCD). In the 1999–2000 SASS data file, the percentage of minority students in schools is classified into four groups: less than 5%, 5% to 19%, 20% to 49%, and 50% or more.
6. Public schools were sampled to be representative at the national and state levels. The 1999–2000 SASS traditional public school sampling frame includes regular public schools, Department of Defense-operated military base schools, and special purpose schools such as special education, vocational, and alternative schools (Tourkin et al., 2004). Public charter schools were not included in the 1999–2000 SASS public school sampling frame. The term "public school teachers" refers to all the full-time or part-time teachers who teach any of the regularly scheduled classes in any of the K–12 grades. This includes administrators, librarians, and other

professional or support staff who teach regularly scheduled classes on a part-time basis. Itinerant teachers are included, as well as long-term substitutes who are filling the role of regular teachers on a long-term basis. Short-term substitute teachers and student teachers are not included (Tourkin et al., 2004).

7. The general purpose of the weighting is to produce population estimates from the SASS sample data. That process includes adjustments for nonresponse using respondents' data, and adjustments of the sample totals to reduce sampling variability (Tourkin et al., 2004). The final weight for public school teachers is the product of the following: Basic Weight, School Sampling Adjustment Factor, Teacher Sampling Adjustment Factor, School Noninterview Adjustment Factor, Teacher-Within School Noninterview Adjustment Factor, Frame Ratio Adjustment Factor, Teacher Adjustment Factor (Tourkin et al., 2004). The relative sample weight for public school teachers is based on the final weight for public school teachers (relative weight = teacher final weight * sample size/population size) (Shen, 1997).

8. Created variables are added to the file to aid analysis. One type of created variable is calculated using one or more survey variables, while the other type contains information from another source. There are approximately 500 variables that were derived, based on the SASS data file, mainly for use in analyzing out-of-field teachers (Tourkin et al., 2004).

9. In the SPSS program, we used the recode technique (based on the information provided in the SASS teacher data file about in-field and out-of-field teaching) to create a series of new variables labeled as "highly qualified teachers" in the subject taught (e.g., highly qualified teachers in math or science). The highly qualified teacher variables in this study were created by combining the following two categories of teachers in the SASS teacher data file as shown in Table A: (a) teachers with regular certification and a major, no minor and (b) teachers with regular certification and a major and a minor. The teachers who fall into either of these categories were identified as highly qualified teachers in the subject taught.

Table A. An Example of a Created Variable to Measure In-Field and Out-of-Field Teaching in Science, by Main Teaching Assignment

Variable Wording	Teacher taught classes in-field in main assignment—science
Variable	INF_M_SC
Description	Teachers in-field in main assignment—science
Category	Label
0	No regular certification, no major, no minor
1	No regular certification, no major, a minor
2	No regular certification, a major, no minor
3	No regular certification
4	Regular certification, no major, no minor
5	Regular certification, no major, a minor
6	Regular certification, a major, no minor
7	Regular certification, a major, a minor

Category 6 is straightforward; in it the teacher has a regular certification and a major in the subject taught. In Category 7, the teacher has a regular certification, and both a major and a minor in the subject taught (See Table B). This happens when a teacher teaches subjects such as social studies or general science. For example, in the subject field of social studies, a teacher may have a major in history and a minor in economics. As a result, the teacher has both a major and a minor in social studies (J. E. Kramer, personal communication, September 15, 2004).

Table B. An Example of the Created Variables of Highly Qualified Teachers

Category	Teacher taught classes in-field in main assignment—science	Highly qualified teachers in main assignment—science (Recoded)
0	No regular certification, no major, no minor	Not Highly Qualified Teachers
1	No regular certification, no major, a minor	
2	No regular certification, a major, no minor	
3	No regular certification	
4	Regular certification, no major, no minor	
5	Regular certification, no major, a minor	
6	Regular certification, a major, no minor	Highly Qualified Teachers
7	Regular certification, a major, a minor	

10. For Table 1.2, science teachers include those who teach "32. biology or life science," "33. chemistry," "34. earth/space science/geology," "35. general science," "36. physical science," "37. physics," and "38. other natural sciences." In Table 1.2, all these teachers are counted as science teachers. In Table 1.3, since the concept of "core subject taught" is utilized, National Center for Education Statistics recoded the data to be consistent with the subjects usually taught in schools. Therefore, in Table 1.3, teachers of "32. biology/life science," "33. chemistry," "34. earth/space science/geology," and "37. physics" are coded the same as teachers of "life science," "chemistry", "earth science," and "physics" respectively. However, teachers of "physical science" include those of "33. chemistry," "34. earth/space science/geology," "36. physical science," and "37. physics." In other words, teachers of "chemistry," "earth science," and "physics" are counted twice in Table 1.3. On the other hand, teachers of "general science" and "other natural sciences" are not counted in Table 1.3, because usually they are not listed as subfields of science. The analyses reported in the chapter are based on the coding system contained in the electronic coding book developed by the National Center for Education Statistics.

References

Ansell, S. E., & McCabe, M. (2003, January 9). Off target. *Education Week*, Retrieved May 20, 2005, from http://counts.edweek.org/sreports/qc03/templates/article.cfm?slug=17target.h22.

Bishop, T. M. (2002). *The distribution of teacher quality across public secondary schools and classrooms: A multi-level distributional analysis.* Unpublished doctoral dissertation. Maryland: University of Maryland College Park.

Blank, R. K., & Langesen, D. (2001). *State indicators of science and mathematics education, 2001: State-by-state trends and new indicators from the 1999–2000 school year.* Council of Chief State School Officers, Washington, DC (ERIC Document Reproduction Service No. ED463148).

Chaney, B. (1995, May). *Student outcomes and the professional preparation of eighth-grade teachers in science and mathematics.* Unpublished manuscript. Prepared for NSF Grant RED-9255255. Rockville, MD: Westat.

Charles, C. M. (1998). *Introduction to educational research* (3rd ed.). New York: Longman.

Clewell, B. C., & Forcier, L. B. (2001). Increasing the number of mathematics and science teachers: A review of teacher recruitment programs. *Teaching and Change, 8*(4), 331–361.

Council of Great City Schools (2000). *The urban teacher challenge: Teacher demand and supply in the Great City schools.* Washington, DC: Council of the Great City Colleges of Education (ERIC Document Reproduction Service No. 438340).

Darling-Hammond, L. (2002). Research and rhetoric on teacher certification: A response to "teacher certification reconsidered." *Educational Policy Analysis Archives, 10*(36). Retrieved January 30, 2004, from http://epaa.asu.edu/epaa/v10n36

Darling-Hammond, L. (2000). Teacher quality and student achievement: A review of state policy evidence. *Educational Policy Analysis Archives, 8*(1). Retrieved January 30, 2004, from http://epaa.asu.edu/epaa/v8n1

Darling-Hammond, L., Berry, B., & Thoreson, A. (2001). Does teacher certification matter? Evaluating the evidence. *Educational Evaluation and Policy Analysis, 23*(1), 57–77.

Elementary and Secondary Education Act of 1965 (1965). 20 USC 2701, 89th Congress

Ferguson, R. F. (1991). Paying for public education: New evidence on how and why money matters. *Harvard Journal on Legislation, 28*(2), 465–498.

Ferguson, P., & Womack, S. T. (1993). The impact of subject matter and education coursework on teaching performance. *Journal of Teacher Education, 44*(1), 55–63.

Fuller, E. J. (1999). *Does teacher certification matter? A comparison of TAAS performance in 1997 between schools with low and high percentages of certified teachers.* Austin: Charles A. Dana Center, University of Texas at Austin.

Goldhaber, D., & Brewer, D. (1998). When should we reward degrees for teachers? *Phi Delta Kappan, 80*(2), 134–138.

Goldhaber, D., & Brewer, D. (2000). Does teacher certification matter? High school certification status and student achievement. *Educational Evaluation and Policy Analysis, 22(2),* 129–145.

Gravetter, F. J., & Wallnau, L. B. (2000). *Statistics for the behavioral sciences* (5th edition). Belmont, CA: Wadsworth.

Harris, D., & Ray, L. (2003). *No school left behind? The distribution of teacher quality in Michigan's public schools* (Policy Report. No.16). East Lansing: Michigan State University, Education Policy Center.

Hawk, P. P., Coble, C. R., & Swanson, M. (1985). Certification: It does matter. *Journal of Teacher Education, 36(3),* 13–15.

Ingersoll, R. M. (1994). *Teacher shortages and teacher quality.* Paper presented at the Annual Meeting of the American Statistical Association (ERIC Document Reproduction Service No. ED415228)

Ingersoll, R. M. (1996). *Teacher quality inequality.* Paper presented at the Annual Meeting of the American Statistical Association, Chicago (ERIC Document Reproduction Service No. ED415230).

Ingersoll, R. M. (1998). The problem of out-of-field teaching. *Phi Delta Kappan, 79*(10), 773.

Ingersoll, R. M. (1999). The problem of under-qualified teachers in American secondary schools. *Educational Researcher, 28*(2), 26–37.

Ingersoll, R. M. (2002). Holes in the teacher supply bucket. *School Administrator, 59*(3), 42–43.

Jerald, C. (2002). *All talk, no action: Putting an end to out-of-field teaching.* Washington, DC: Education Trust (ERIC Document Reproduction Service No. ED468741).

Kaplan, L., & Owings, W. A. (2002). The politics of teacher quality: Implications for principals. *NASSP Bulletin, 86*(633), 22–41.

Laczko-Kerr, I., & Berliner, D. C. (2002, September 6). The effectiveness of "Teach for America" and other under-certified teachers on student academic achievement: A case of harmful public policy. *Education Pol-*

icy Analysis Achieves, 10(37). Retrieved February 13, 2004, from http://epaa.asu.edu/epaa/v10n37/.

Lavigne, J. E. (1992). Resource allocation and equity in school finance: An intradistrict analysis of the New York City public schools, 1980 to 1991. *Dissertation Abstracts International, 54*(03). (UMI No. 9319705)

Lewis, L., Parsad, B., Carey, N., Barfai, N., Farris, E., & Smerdon, B. (1999). *Teacher quality: A report on the preparation and qualifications of public school teachers* (NCES 1999-080). U.S. Department of Education, National Center for Education Statistics. Washington, DC: U.S. Government Printing Office.

Mandel, D. R. (1996). Teacher education, training, and staff development: Implications for national surveys. In *Conference proceedings. From data to information: New directions for the National Center for Educational Statistics,* G. Hoachlander, J. E. Griffith, & J. H. Ralph (Eds.). NCES 96-901. Washington, DC: U.S. Department of Education.

Monk, D. H. (1994). Subject area preparation and secondary mathematics and science teachers and student achievement. *Economics of Education Review, 13*(2), 125–45.

Monk, D. H., & King, J. A. (1994). Multilevel teacher resource effects on pupil performance in secondary mathematics and science: The case of teacher subject matter preparation. In *Choices and consequences: Contemporary policy issues in education,* E. G. Ehrenberg (Ed.), pp. 29–58. Ithaca, NY: ILR Press.

No Child Left Behind Act (2002). 20 USC 6301, 107th United States Congress.

Nye, B., Konstantopoulos, S., & Hedges, L. V. (2004). How large are teacher effects? *Educational Evaluation and Policy Analysis, 26*(3), 237–257.

Olson, L. (2003). Quality counts reveals national "teacher gap." *Education Week, 22*(16), 10.

Ravitch. D. (1998). Lesson plan for teachers. *The Washington Post,* August 10, p. A 17.

Riley, R. (1998). Our teachers should be excellent, and they should look like America. Federal initiatives. *Education and Urban Society, 31*(1), 18–29.

Rowan, B., Chiang, F., & Miller, R. J., (1997). Using research on employees' performance to study the effects of teachers on students' achievement. *Sociology of Education, 70*(4), 256–284.

Sanders, W., & Rivers, J. (1996). *Cumulative and residual effects of teachers on future student academic achievement.* Knoxville: University of Tennessee, Value-Added Research and Assessment Center.

Seastrom, M. M., Gruber, K. J., Henke, R., McGrath, D. J., & Cohen, B. A. (2002). Qualifications of the public school teacher workforce: Prevalence of out-of-field teaching 1987–88 to 1999–2000. *Education Statistics Quarterly, 4*(3), 12–19.

Shen, J. (1997). Teacher retention and attrition in public schools: Evidence from SASS91. *The Journal of Education Research, 9*(2), 81–88.

Shen, J., Mansberger, N., & Yang, H. (2004). Teacher quality and students placed at risks: Results from the Baccalaureate and beyond longitudinal study 1993–97. *Educational Horizons, 82*(3), 226–235.

Shen, J., & Poppink, S. (2003). The certification characteristics of the public school teaching force: National, longitudinal and comparative perspectives. *Educational Horizons, 81*(3), 130–137.

Strauss, R. P., & Sawyer, E. A. (1986). Some new evidence on teacher and student competencies. *Economics of Education Review, 5*(1), 41–48.

Stronge, J. H. (2002). *Qualities of effective teachers.* Alexandria, VA: Association for Supervision and Curriculum Development.

To close the gap, quality counts. (2003, January 9). *Education Week.* Retrieved May 20, 2005, from http://counts.edweek.org/sreports/qc03/templates/article.cfm?slug=17exec.h22

Tourkin, S. C., Pugh, K. W., Fondelier, S. E., Parmer, R. J., Cole, C., Jackson, B., Warner, T., Weant, G., & Walter, E. (2004) *1999–2000 Schools and Staffing Survey (SASS) Data file user's manual (NCES 2004-303).* U.S. Department of Education. Washington, DC: National Center for Education Statistics.

U.S. Department of Education. National Center for Education Statistics. (1994). *Qualifications of the public school teacher workforce: 1988 and 1991.* Statistical Analysis Report No. 95-665, by S. A. Bobbitt & M. M. McMillen. Washington, DC: U.S. Government Printing Office.

U.S. Department of Education. National Center for Education Statistics. (1996). *National assessments of teacher quality.* Working Paper No. 96-24 by Richard M. Ingersoll. Washington, DC: U.S. Government Printing Office.

U.S. Department of Education. National Center for Education Statistics. (1999). *Measuring teacher qualifications.* Working paper No. 1999-04, by Lara Fabiano. Project Officer, Dan Kasprzyk. Washington, DC: U.S. Government Printing Office.

U.S. Department of Education. *New No Child Left Behind flexibility: Highly qualified teachers.* (2004, March). Retrieved February 13, 2004, from http://www.ed.gov/nclb/methods/teachers/hqtflexibility.pdf.

Weglinsky, H. (2000). *How teaching matters. Bringing the classroom back into discussions of teacher quality. A policy information center report.* Princeton, NJ: Milken Family Foundation and Educational Testing Service.

CHAPTER TWO

The Certification Characteristics of the Public School Teaching Force
National, Longitudinal, and Comparative Perspectives

Jianping Shen and Sue Poppink

Introduction

How much and what kind of teacher preparation teachers need to improve the academic achievement of children is a central debate in the field of education today. On one side of the debate are those who argue that teaching ability is a function of innate talents and that teachers need very little preparation to teach (e.g., Ballou & Podgursky, 1993; Lasley, Bainbridge, & Berry, 2002). And on the other side of the debate are those who believe that teaching requires multiple forms of knowledge and skill that can be taught and learned, thus heightening the need for careful preparation. On this side of the debate, for example, Linda Darling-Hammond, writing for the National Commission on Teaching and America's Future, argued, "Reviews of more than two hundred studies contradict the long-standing myth that 'anyone can teach' and that 'teachers are born and not made'" (The National Commission on Teaching and America's Future, 1997, p.10).

Within the spectrum of this debate are policy options ranging from no formal teacher preparation to highly developed forms of preparation and ongoing professional development. In between are options responding to different configurations of the appropriate amount and kind of teacher preparation. There is the traditional four-year college preparation, and college preparation plus a fifth year internship. There are also programs such as Teach for America, which initially recruited students with strong undergraduate programs in various majors to go directly into schools; the program did, however, add some preparation immediately prior to placement in schools. There are alternative certification programs for those whose undergraduate programs did not certify them as teachers. Even within alternative certification programs, the amount and kind of preparation varies greatly.

With these many options opening up for entrance into the teaching labor force, data on exactly how teachers are entering the labor force and where they work within the educational system are helpful to the policy debate. For this chapter we asked what the trends are in terms of teacher preparation by looking at data from a national survey. We found that over a 12-year period a growing proportion of teachers had less preparation (1987–88 and 1999–2000) and that this was particularly true for recent entrants into the teaching force, those in urban schools and secondary schools.

The Debate on Holding the Educational System Accountable

Cochran-Smith and Fries (2001) argued that the

> highly politicized debates about reforming teacher education are embedded within two larger national agendas: the agenda to professionalize teaching and teacher education, ...and the movement to deregulate teacher preparation, which aims to dismantle teacher education institutions and break up the monopoly of the profession. (p. 3)

As they explain, at the heart of this debate are questions not about whether the educational system should be held accountable, but who within the system is to be held accountable and how that will be accomplished. Both those who would require high professional standards for entry into the teaching force and those who would deregulate the professional standards system argue that for too long entrance into the teaching force has been dependent on inputs such as the number of courses taken and passed, the number of hours spent in student teaching, and others. Each side, however, has differences of opinion about how best to hold the system accountable and determine its accountability.

Those who would professionalize teaching argue that accountability should be placed on those entering the teaching workforce to prove that they have reached professional status through demonstrations such as passing state teaching tests, showing their professional competence in their student teaching, and others. Those who would deregulate entrance into the teaching force argue that accountability ought to be placed on teachers already in the teaching force and that entry should be opened up to others in the labor force. That is, entrants need not necessarily have a formal teacher preparation program. Their accountability system would be to hold teachers responsible for students' achievement on standardized tests. These two lines of reasoning raise empirical questions about the current professional certification of teachers and of those entering the teaching labor force.

Teacher Certification and Student Achievement

Yet empirical studies point out the importance of teacher education for student achievement (Glass, 2008; Laczko-Kerr & Berliner, 2002). Recent empirical studies indicate that teachers' certification or licensing status is related to students' learning. Goldhaber and Brewer (2000) found that except for mathematics and science teachers with emergency certificates, fully certified teachers have a statistically significant positive impact on student test scores relative to teachers who are not certified in their subject area. Darling-Hammond, Berry, and Thoreson (2001), using the same data, later argued that even math and science teachers who have more teacher education training appear to do better in increasing student achievement. Furthermore, as cited by Darling-Hammond (2000), Fuller (1999) conducted a study indicating that when school districts have higher percentages of licensed teachers, students' pass rates on the Texas State Achievement Tests (TAAS) are significantly higher, even when holding constant some characteristics related to students' family backgrounds, schools, and teachers; and Fetler's (1999) research found that when the percentage of teachers with emergency certificates is higher, the average student score is significantly lower, after controlling for student poverty. Furthermore, Grossman's (1989a, b) in-depth qualitative studies of first-year English teachers indicated that those who entered teaching without teacher education experienced more difficulties than teachers with teacher education. The evidence on the importance of teacher education and certification is preponderant (Darling-Hammond, 2002).

Entering Teaching with or without Teacher Education

Yet the demand for teacher candidates across the nation is high and, as Stoddart and Floden (1995) have summarized, there has been a shortage of qualified teachers in urban schools and in subject areas such as math and science. This indicates that it may be necessary to open up the teaching labor force beyond traditional routes of certification. Some have pointed out that opening up the labor force attracts applicants who will make for a more diverse teaching force including older entrants and entrants from minority groups (e.g., Cornett, 1990; Stoddart, 1990) and that this is particularly true for urban schools (Natriello & Zumwalt, 1993; Stoddart, 1993).

However, others point out that opening up the teaching labor force hurts minority students in inner-city schools where teacher shortages occur more frequently (Darling-Hammond, 1990; 1994). When preparation requirements are relaxed for those teaching in inner-city schools, those students get less-qualified teachers (Darling-Hammond, 1990; Kirby, Darling-Hammond, & Hudson, 1989) for at least two reasons: (1) some teachers may have difficulty learning to teach by working on the job (Feiman-Nemser & Buchman, 1987; Kennedy, 1991; Zeichner, 1986) and (2) research suggests that pedagogical content knowledge—knowledge that enables teachers to connect their knowledge of subject matter with the students' knowledge (Shulman, 1987, 2002)—plays a very important role in teaching, and that teachers without traditional teacher education have more difficulties developing this knowledge base (Darling-Hammond, 1990; Grossman, 1989a, b; McDiarmid & Wilson, 1991; Shulman, 1987).

Despite the fact that some have found that opening up the teaching labor force does not live up to its expectations, the number of states accepting alternative certification increased from eight in 1983 to 18 in 1986, and to all states by 2007 (Feistritzer & Chester, 2000; Feistritzer, 2007). Shen and colleagues (Shen, 1997a, b, 1998, 2000; Shen & Palmer, 2005), using national data sets of Schools and Staffing Survey and the Baccalaureate and Beyond Survey, found that opening up the teaching force to nontraditional routes has mixed results in terms of diversifying the teaching force, attracting those having extensive experience outside of teaching, and reducing teacher shortage in math and science. Others have found that alternative certification fails to fulfill the promise that it will recruit those who have higher academic qualifications (Natriello, Hansen, Frisch, & Zumwalt, 1996). It is imperative to inquire further into whether and, if so, how the teaching workforce has changed due to the opening up of the force to those who have nontraditional certification. Therefore, this chapter also examines teachers who had temporary certificates, emergency certificates, or waivers.

Purpose and Methodology of the Study

Purpose of the Study

The purpose of the study was to inquire into how the certification characteristics of the public teaching force have evolved between 1987–1988 and 1999–2000. Therefore, we asked what percentage of teachers held teaching assignments in their primary teaching field. We examined whether this varied over time by all teachers, recent entrants into teaching, school location (urban, suburban, and rural), and school level (elementary and secondary). Then we examined the type of certificates teachers held, and whether this varied over time by all teachers, recent entrants into teaching, school location, and school level.

Marilyn Cochran-Smith and Mary Kim Fries (2001) provided context for this chapter in their article exploring the nature of the debate about whether teachers ought to be professionally prepared and certified, or whether schools ought to be staffed using a market-based approach. To help inform the policy debate surrounding these issues we asked some empirical questions about the status of professional certification over time.

Specifically, we asked four questions.

1. What percentage of all teachers and of recent entrants into the teaching force had teaching certificates in their primary teaching assignment over time?
2. What percentage of all teachers and new entrants into the teaching force had teaching certificates in their primary teaching assignment over time when examining them by location (urban, suburban, and rural) and school level (elementary and secondary)?
3. What percentage of public school teachers had a temporary certificate, emergency certificate, or waiver in their primary teaching assignment in 1993–94 and 1999–2000?
4. What percentage of public school teachers had a temporary certificate, emergency certificate, or waiver in their primary teaching assignment in 1993–94 and 1999–2000 by location and school level?

Sample, Data Source, and Weighting

We used data from the Schools and Staffing Survey (SASS) conducted by the National Center for Education Statistics—a national survey conducted over time of schoolteachers, school principals, and Local Education Authority (LEA) officials. Our study uses a component of the SASS, the Public School Teacher Survey (PSTS).

We had data for each of the three surveys from the PSTS (1987–88, 1993–94, and 1999–2000), allowing us to conduct what many refer to as a "trend study." In other words, by analyzing data from three nationally representative surveys, we were able to depict the trends of certification characteristics of the public teaching force.

We weighted the samples to approximate the population, making the sample nationally representative of public school teachers. Because the SASS sampling involved stratification, disproportionate sampling of certain strata, and clustered probability sampling, initially the resultant samples were not representative of the public school teaching force. Through weighting, the findings can be generalized to the national population of public school teachers. The achieved and weighted samples of the study are displayed in Table 2.1.

Table 2.1. Samples of the Three Surveys of Public School Teachers

	1987–1988	1993–1994	1999–2000
Achieved	40,593	47,105	44,933
Weighted	2,323,204	2,561,294	3,002,259

Results

Percentage of Public School Teachers Who Had Certification in Their Primary Teaching Assignment

Figure 2.1 shows that the percentage of teachers who had certificates in their primary teaching assignment decreased between 1987–1988 and 1999–2000, from 97.3% in 1987–1988 to 96.4% in 1993–94, and to 94.3% in 1999–2000. In other words, the percentage of teachers who did not have any kind of certificate in their primary teaching assignment increased from 2.7% to 5.7% between 1987–88 and 1999–2000, an increase of 3 percentage points. The trend is contradictory to the rhetoric of building a professionalized teaching force. Although 5.7% may not seem to be a particularly large percentage, it translates into about 171,100 teachers in public schools who do not have any type of certificate in their primary teaching assignment, which is substantial.

Another important way to examine the percentage of those with or without teaching certificates in their primary teaching assignment is to examine recent entrants in the teaching force, that is, those who have taught for less than three years. Examining characteristics of the recent entrants allows us to examine what the future might hold, and to examine the impacts of the most recent policies.

The trend for recent entrants shows that the teaching force is becoming even less professionalized over time. The data in Figure 2.1 indicate that the percentage of recent entrants who had certificates in their primary assignments decreased from 94.5% in 1987–88, to 92.6% in 1993–94, and to 86.0% in 1999–2000. In other words, 5.5% of the new teachers did not have any kind of certificate in their primary teaching assignment in 1987–88, and the percentage increased to 14% in 1999–2000, an increase of 8.5 percentage points between 1987–88 and 1999–2000. Whether teaching out-field or simply not possessing any kind of certificate, 5.7% of all teachers and 14% of recent entrants did not have any kind of certificate in their primary teaching assignment. And the trends indicated that this may only increase in the future. The teaching profession, the policy community, and the society at large are facing a serious issue.

Figure 2.1. Percentage of Public School Teachers Who Had Certification in Their Primary Assignment

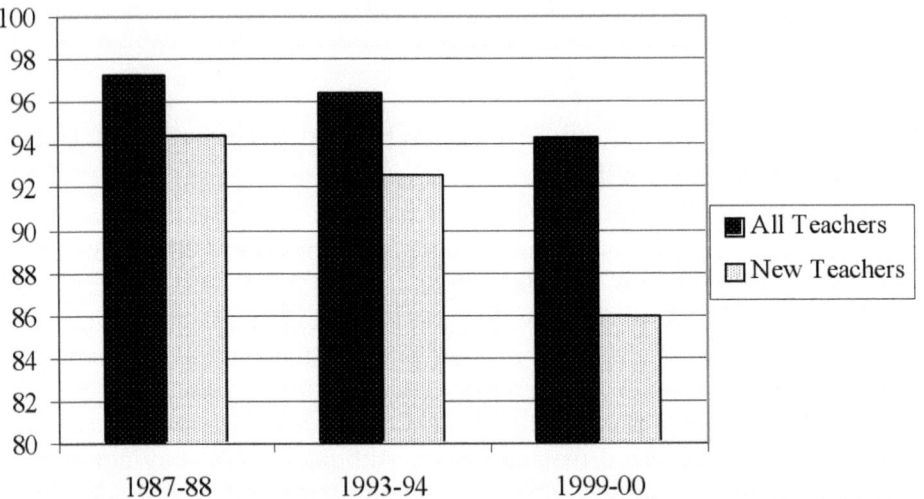

Variation in the Percentage of Public School Teachers Who Had Certification in Their Primary Teaching Assignment

Data in Table 2.2 show the percentage of teachers who had certification in their primary teaching assignment in relationship to their schools' locations (urban, suburban, and rural) and school level (elementary and secondary).

Table 2.2. Percentage of Public School Teachers Who Had Certification in Their Primary Teaching Assignment by All Teachers and Recent Entrants, and by Location and School Level, for School Years 1987–88, 1993–94 and 1999–2000

	1987–1988			1993–1994			1999–2000		
	Both	Elementary	Secondary	Both	Elementary	Secondary	Both	Elementary	Secondary
All Teachers									
Urban	95.7	96.0	95.3	94.9	95.4	94.3	93.3	94.2	92.2
Suburban	97.9	98.4	97.4	96.8	97.6	96.0	94.6	95.7	93.4
Rural	97.9	98.2	97.5	97.2	97.7	96.7	94.5	96.3	92.8
New Teachers									
Urban	91.0	92.0	89.3	89.0	91.5	85.7	81.6	84.3	78.2
Suburban	96.8	97.2	96.3	93.4	95.7	90.5	88.6	91.5	85.3
Rural	95.4	95.7	94.9	94.4	96.2	92.7	85.7	90.3	81.1

We found the following patterns. First, it is clear that in comparison to their suburban and rural counterparts, urban schools tended to have a lower percentage of teachers who had certificates in their primary teaching assignment. The pattern was consistent over the years. For example, during the 1987–88 school year, among all teachers, the percentage of those who had certificates in their primary teaching assignment were 95.7% in urban schools and 97.9% in suburban and rural schools. The pattern was similar during the 1999–2000 school year. In 1999–2000, among all teachers the percentage of those who had certificates in their primary teaching assignment was 93.3% in urban schools, and 94.6% and 94.5% in suburban and rural schools, respectively.

When we examined the data in relation to recent entrants, the finding was the same. It is more likely that recent entrants without any type of certificate in their primary teaching assignment were in urban schools rather than in suburban or rural schools. Urban students, who are more likely to be minority and economically disadvantaged than their rural and suburban counterparts, need teachers who can enable them to overcome economic disadvantage. Yet, they are more likely to have teachers who do not have any kind of certificate in their primary teaching assignment, as shown by data on both the entire teaching force and the new entrant teaching force.

Second, when school level is considered, the phenomenon of teaching without certificate in the primary teaching assignment is more prevalent at the secondary level than at the elementary level, a finding that was consistent over the years, across school locations, and for both all teachers and new teachers. Since secondary certificates are more specialized and there is a shortage of certified teachers in certain areas, it does not come as a surprise that teaching without a certificate in the primary teaching assignment is more common at the secondary level than at the elementary level. Another consistent pattern we found is that the percentage of teachers having certificates in their primary teaching assignment had been decreasing between 1987–88 and 1999–2000, the rate of decrease was greater at the secondary level than at the elementary level.

Third, the data in Table 2.2 give a finer grained picture of the findings represented in Figure 2.1. In Figure 2.1, we showed that the percentage of teachers who did not have a certificate in their primary assignment had increased between 1987–88 and 1999–2000 and that teachers with no certificate in their primary assignments were more prevalent among recent entrants, rather than all teachers. The disaggregated data in Table 2.2 confirm that the two findings are consistent across school locations and school levels.

Percentage of Public School Teachers Who Had Temporary Certificate, Emergency Certificate, or Waivers in Their Primary Teaching Assignment

The data in Figure 2.1 and Table 2.2 focus on whether the teachers have any kind of certificate in their primary assignment. Although it is important to know whether or not a teacher has a certificate in the primary assignment, it is also important to know what kind of certificate the teacher has in a primary assignment. The 1999–2000 Public School Teacher Questionnaire requested that respondents with a certificate in their primary teaching assignment choose from the following list of types of certificates: (a) regular or standard state certificate or advanced professional certificate, (b) probationary certificate, (c) provisional or other type given to persons who are still participating in what the state calls an "alternative certification program," (d) temporary certificate, and (e) emergency certificate or waiver. In this section, we explain data concerning those who had a temporary certificate and those with an emergency certificate or waiver. A technical note is needed before presenting the data. The typology of certificates in the 1987–88 survey does not allow for the separation of the provisional certificates from the temporary certificates, emergency certificates, and waivers. Therefore, the 1987–88 data could not be included in this section and only the data from the 1993–94 and 1999–2000 surveys were used.

The data in Figure 2.2 indicate that, in 1993–94, of all the teachers who reported having a certificate in their primary teaching assignment, 1.8% of them had temporary certificates, emergency certificates, or waivers. The statistics remained the same for the 1999–2000 school year. As to recent entrants, of those who reported having a certificate in their primary teaching assignment, in 1993–94, 8.3% had temporary certificates, emergency certificates, or waivers. The percentage decreased to 7.2% in 1999–2000. Therefore, the percentage of those having lower levels of certificates was much higher among new teachers than among all teachers. Given the career pattern of school teachers, this finding does not come as a surprise. The attrition rate among those having lower-level certificates is very high (Shen, 1997a, b; Shen & Palmer, 2005). Therefore, the revolving door keeps turning for teachers with lower-end certificates. Although the percentage of those having temporary certificates, emergency certificates, or waivers decreased from 8.3% in 1993–94 to 7.2% in 1999–2000, the corresponding statistic for all teachers remained at 1.8% for both 1993–94 and 1999–2000. The percentage of those who had temporary certificates, emergency certificates, or waivers was still high among new teaches and has not decreased for all teachers.

Figure 2.2. Percentage of Teachers Who Had Temporary Certificate, Emergency Certificate, or Waiver in Their Primary Assignment

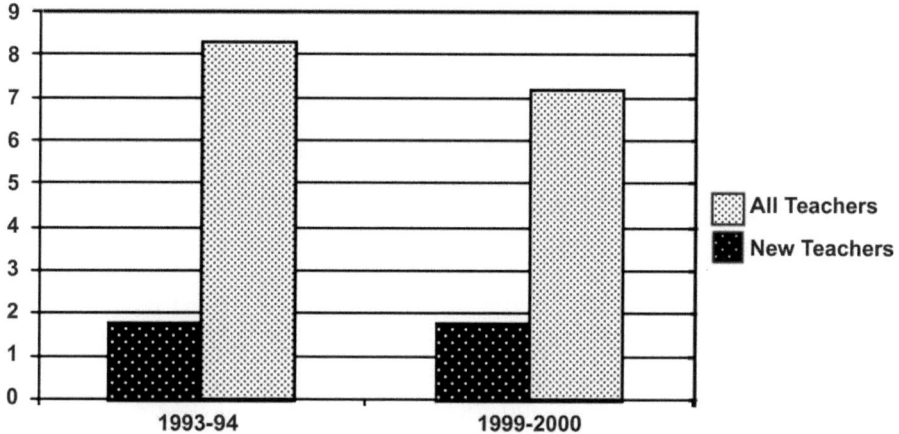

Variation in Percentage of Public School Teachers Who Had a Temporary Certificate, Emergency Certificate, or Waiver in Their Primary Teaching Assignment

Table 2.3 presents the disaggregated data on the percentage of public school teachers who had a temporary certificate, emergency certificate, or waiver in their primary teaching assignment in 1993-94 and 1999-2000. Again when we view the data from the perspective of school location, the percentage for urban schools was about 1.5 to 2 times higher than those for suburban and rural schools. In comparison to suburban and rural schools, urban schools appear to have a much higher percentage of teachers who had lower levels of certificates in their primary teaching assignment. As far as the school level is concerned, there appears to be no consistent patterns as to the percentage of elementary or secondary teachers who had a temporary certificate, emergency certificate, or waiver in their primary teaching assignment.

Table 2.3. Percentage of Public School Teachers Who Had a Temporary Certificate, Emergency Certificate, or Waiver in Their Primary Teaching Assignment by Location and School Level for School Years 1993-94 and 1999-2000

	1993-1994			1999-2000		
	Both	Elementary	Secondary	Both	Elementary	Secondary
All Teachers						
Urban	2.5	2.4	2.5	2.4	2.5	2.2
Suburban	1.2	1.2	1.3	1.7	1.5	2.0
Rural	1.7	1.6	1.7	1.3	1.3	1.4
New Teachers						
Urban	12.9	13.5	12.1	9.8	10.4	9.0
Suburban	6.1	4.9	7.5	6.7	5.7	7.8
Rural	7.0	7.2	6.9	5.0	4.3	5.9

Summary and Discussion

To better understand some of the statistics that underlie the debate between increasing the requirements for teacher certification and abolishing teaching certification altogether, it is important to know how the certification status of the public teaching force evolved over the years. Analyzing the data collected from the PSTS in 1987-88, 1993-94, and 1999-2000, we calculated the percentages of public school teachers who had certificates and inquired into the kind of certificate they had in their primary teaching assignment. We also investigated the possible variation between (a) all teachers and recent entrants into the teachers force, (b) urban, suburban, and rural teachers, (c) elementary and secondary teachers.

We found the following. First, among all public school teachers, the percentage of those who did not have any kind of certificate increased slightly over the years, from 2.7% in 1987–88 to 5.7% in 1999–2000. Among those who reported having a certificate in their primary teaching assignment, 1.8% of them, in both school years, had lower levels of certificates, which included the temporary certificate, emergency certificate, or waiver. Given the finding that the percentage of those having no certificate increased and the percentage of those who had lower levels of certificates remained the same, the study seems to point to an unpromising trend for the professionalization of teaching.

Second, when we view data from the perspective of school location, in comparison to suburban and rural schools, urban schools are at a disadvantaged position. The study found that in 1987–88, 1993–94, and 1999–2000, urban schools had not only a higher percentage of teachers who did not have any kind of certificate, but also a higher percentage of teachers who had lower levels of certificates in their primary teaching assignment. Given other research findings suggesting that teachers' level of certification is positively related to the level of students' achievement, the current study seems to point to an equity issue in staffing the classrooms in urban, suburban, and rural schools.

Third, where school level is concerned, we found that there was a slightly higher percentage of public school teachers who did not have a certificate in their primary teaching assignment at the secondary level than at the elementary level. Factors such as the shortage of teachers in certain subjects at the secondary level and the more specialized certificate might be related to this phenomenon.

Finally, the percentage of those who did not have any kind of certificate or had lower levels of certificate was much higher among new teachers than among all teachers for each of the three survey years. Furthermore, among the new teachers, the percentage of those who did not have any kind of certificates in their primary teaching assignment increased from 5.5% in 1987–88, to 7.4% in 1993–94, and to 14% in 1999–2000. Both the disparity between the recent entrants and all teachers in the teaching force and the trend among recent entrants are causes for concern. Given the finding that having no certification or having lower levels of certification are associated with teacher attrition, and that the level of teacher certification is positively related to the level of student achievement, the certification characteristics of the new teachers are a cause for concern in the context of teacher attrition, student learning, and the professionalization of the teaching force.

References

Ballou, D., & Podgursky, M. (1993). Teacher training and licensure: A Layman's guide. In M. Kanstroroom & C. Finn (Eds.), *Better teachers, better schools*. Washington, DC: Thomas Fordham Foundation.

Cochran-Smith, M., & Fries, M. K. (2001). Sticks, stones and ideology: The discourse of reform in teacher education. *Educational Researcher, 30* (8), 3–15.

Cornett, L. M. (1990). Alternative certification: State policies in the SREB states. *Peabody Journal of Education, 67* (3), 5–83.

Darling-Hammond, L. (1990). Teaching and knowledge: Policy issues posed by alternative certification for teachers. *Peabody Journal of Education, 67* (3), 123–154.

Darling-Hammond, L. (1994). Who will speak for the children? *Phi Delta Kappan, 76* (1), 21–34.

Darling-Hammond, L. (2000). Teacher quality and student achievement: A review of state policy evidence. *Education Policy Analysis Archives, 8* (1). Available at http://epaa.asu.edu/epaa/v8n1/.

Darling-Hammond, L. (2002). Research and rhetoric on teacher certification: A response to "Teacher certification reconsidered." *Education Policy Analysis Archives*, 10 (36). Available at http://epaa.asu.edu/epaa/v10n36.html.

Darling-Hammond, L., Berry, B., & Thoreson, A. (2001). Does teacher certification matter? Evaluating the evidence. *Educational Evaluation and Policy Analysis, 23* (1), 57–77.

Feiman-Nemser, S., & Buchman, M. (1987). When is student teaching teacher education? *Teaching and Teacher Education, 3* (4), 255–273.

Feistritzer, C. E. (2007). *Alternative teacher certification: A state-by-state analysis 2007*. Washington, DC: National Center for Alternative Certification.

Feistritzer, C. E., & Chester, D. T. (2000). *Alternative teacher certification: A state-by-state analysis 2000*. Washington, DC: National Center for Education Information.

Fetler, M. (1999). High school staff characteristics and mathematics test results, *Education Policy Analysis Archives, 7* (9). Available at http://epaa.asu.edu/epaa/v7n9.html.

Fuller, E. J. (1999). *Does teacher certification matter? A comparison of TAAS performance in 1997 between schools with low and high percentages of certified teachers.* Austin, TX: Charles A. Dana Center, University of Texas at Austin.

Glass, G. V. (2008). *Alternative certification of teachers.* Boulder and Tempe: Education and the Public Interest Center & Education Policy Unit. Retrieved February 22, 2009 from http://epicpolicy.org/publication/alternative-certification-of-teacher.

Goldhaber, D., & Brewer, D. (2000). Does teacher certification matter? High school certification status and student achievement. *Educational Evaluation and Policy Analysis, 22* (2), 129–145.

Grossman, P. L. (1989a). A study in contrast: Sources of pedagogical content knowledge for secondary English. *Journal of Teacher Education, 40,* 24–31.

Grossman, P. L. (1989b). Learning to teach without teacher education. *Teachers College Record, 91* (2), 191–208.

Kennedy, M. M. (1991). Some surprising findings on how teachers learn to teach. *Educational Leadership, 49* (3), 14–17.

Kirby, S. N., Darling-Hammond, L., & Hudson, L. (1989). Nontraditional recruits to mathematics and science teaching. *Educational Evaluation and Policy Analysis, 11* (3), 301–323.

Laczko-Kerr, I., & Berliner, D. C. (2002, September 6). The effectiveness of "Teach for America" and other under-certified teachers on student academic achievement: A case of harmful public policy. *Education Policy Analysis Archives, 10* (37). Retrieved February 22, 2009 from http://epaa.asu.edu/epaa/v10n37/.

Lasley II, T. J., Bainbridge, W. L., & Berry, B. (2002). Improving teacher quality: Ideological perspectives and policy prescriptions. *The Educational Forum, 67* (1), 14–25.

McDiarmid, G. W., & Wilson, S. M. (1991). An exploration of the subject matter knowledge of alternate route teachers: Can we assume they know their subjects? *Journal of Teacher Education, 42* (2), 93–103.

The National Commission on Teaching and America's Future. (1997). *Doing what matters most: Investing in quality teaching.* New York, NY: National Commission on Teaching and America's Future.

Natriello, G., & Zumwalt, K. (1993). New teachers for urban schools? *Education and Urban Society, 26* (1), 49–62.

Natriello, G., Hansen, A. Frisch, A., & Zumwalt, K. (1996). *Characteristics of entering teachers in New Jersey*. New York: Teachers College, Columbia University.

Shen, J. (1997a). Has the alternative certification policy materialized its promise? A comparison between traditionally and alternatively certified teachers in public schools. *Educational Evaluation and Policy Analysis, 19* (3), 276–283.

Shen, J. (1997b). Teacher retention and attrition in public schools: Evidence from SASS-91. *Journal of Educational Research, 91*(2), 81–88.

Shen, J. (1998). The impact of the alternative certification policy on the elementary and secondary teaching force in public schools. *Journal of Research and Development in Education, 32* (1), 9–16.

Shen, J. (2000). The impact of the alternative certification policy: Multiple perspectives. In J. D. McIntyre & D. M. Byrd (Eds.), *Research on effective models for teacher education: Teacher education year book VIII* (pp. 235–247). Thousand Oaks, CA: Corwin.

Shen, J., & Palmer, L. B. (2005). Attrition patterns of inadequately prepared teachers. In J. R. Dangel & E. M. Guyton (Eds.), *Research on alternative and non-traditional education* (Teacher education yearbook XIII) (pp. 143–157). Lanham, MD: Scarecrow.

Shulman, L. S. (1987). Knowledge and teaching: Foundations of the new reform. *Harvard Educational Review, 57* (1), 1–22.

Shulman, L. S. (2002). Truth and consequences: Inquiry and policy in research on teacher education. *Journal of Teacher Education, 53* (3), 248–253.

Stoddart, T. (1990). Los Angeles Unified School District Intern Program: Recruiting and preparing teachers for the urban context. *Peabody Journal of Education, 67*, (3) 84–122.

Stoddart, T. (1993). Who is prepared to teach in urban schools? *Education and Urban Society, 26* (1), 29–48.

Stoddart, T., & Floden, R. E. (1995). *Traditional and alternative routes to teacher certification: Issues, assumptions, and misconceptions*. East Lansing, MI: National Center for Research on Teacher Learning.

Zeichner, K. (1986). The practicum as an occasion for learning to teach. *South Pacific Journal of Teacher Education, 14* (2), 11–28.

CHAPTER THREE

Has the Public Teaching Force Become More Diversified?

National and Longitudinal Perspectives on Gender, Race, and Ethnicity

Jianping Shen, Gary L. Wegenke, and Van E. Cooley

Introduction

Racial, ethnic, and gender diversity is an important indicator of the characteristics of the public teaching force. Given the increasing diversity of the population in our nation in general and in our school-aged children in particular, we ask the question whether the public school teaching force has become more diversified between 1987–88 and 1999–2000. This argument for diversity is based on (a) a contrast between the racial, ethnic, and gender composition of the student and teacher populations both for now and for the projected future and (b) the idea that a diversified teaching force will provide more role models for students who are better equipped to engage in a culturally relevant approach to teaching our students (Miller, Strosnider, & Dooley, 2002).

Although whites have made up about 90% of the teaching force for nearly 30 years, the proportion of children who are of minority backgrounds has increased and is projected to continue to increase (Riley, 1998). The problem is complicated by the reality that minority children are less likely to be taught by competent teachers as many of the best teachers teach in low-poverty schools. This is also reflected by the fact that most teachers who earn National Board Certification teach in white middle class schools (Berry, 2008).

As Hodgkinson (2002) observed, "Student enrollments in the United States are becoming increasingly racially diverse (about 40%, although the state range is from 7% to 68%), the teaching force is actually becoming increasingly white" (pp. 102–105). The discrepancy between the racial/ethnic composition of the student body and that of the teaching force has been a concern to the general public as well as the education community. Past research indicates that minorities, especially Asian Americans, are less likely to enter teaching (Gordon, E. W., 1995; Gordon, J. A.; 2000;

Rong & Preissle, 1997). One compelling reason might be the racial composition of higher education faculty. Despite a 48% increase of students of color over the past 10 years, the racial composition of faculty remains unchanged. Teachers of color who serve as role models for preservice teachers are not being recruited for higher education positions (Harvey, 2002).

Related to the racial and diversity issue is the fact that teaching has been a feminized profession (Goodlad, 1990; Goodlad, Soder, & Sirotnik, 1990; Lortie, 1975). To attract more male teachers into teaching is also a challenge faced by the teaching profession. Chmelynski (2006) indicated that the number of male teachers is at the lowest point in 40 years, with less than 25% of all teachers being male. Only 9% of the elementary teachers are men. Black male teachers make up only 2.4% of K–12 teachers. The low socioeconomic status of teachers is one of the reasons why upwardly mobile blacks choose not to enter the teaching profession (Gordon, J. A., 2005).

Arguments for the Diversity of the Teaching Force

Sensitivity to Changes in the Student Body

At the same time school systems are becoming more racially diverse, students with traditionally middle class values are decreasing in numbers. These same students are being replaced by an increasing number of students who bring the culture of diversity with them to school each day. A diversified teaching faculty provides role models for students to seek out as their "in-school" adult support system. These racially and ethnically mixed adults are in a position to build trusting relationships with their students, by setting high but reasonable academic standards and creating strategies for coping with school related problems. In addition, the same adults as teacher role models can more easily motivate students to connect with resources not necessarily found in the student's home. These resources include printed materials, electronic technologies, and access to "advanced" programs that pave the way toward entrance into higher education or other career choices for individual students.

Roles and responsibilities of public school teachers are becoming more complex as teachers face a workplace agenda that places school reform and the diverse needs of students as the central focus for teaching and learning. As a result, the belief and value systems of many teachers in our school classrooms are being challenged. For example, daily lessons taught by teachers reflect a school's curriculum, which may not align with the culture and experiences students bring to the classroom. The art of teaching determines where the student's knowledge and understanding of a certain subject matter is before moving forward. A disconnect occurs between teacher and students when teachers assume all students come from similar family backgrounds and cultures. Finding a balance between the knowledge and experiences students bring to school and the desired school curriculum (what is taught) continues to challenge both teacher and students.

The Moral Imperative to Have a Diverse Teaching Staff

Another argument for diversifying the public teaching force is the moral need to continue a dialogue on race, ethnicity, and gender in America. The dialogue requires movement from what we say we value in our democratic society toward specific actions. Employing individuals from diversified backgrounds represents an action with a distinct message. The message is that issues of diversity in America are here to stay and not limited to polite and quiet dialogue. Sergiovanni (2001) emphasized that postmodernists advocated that diversity promoted cooperation and acceptance of differences and contributed to positive behaviors that resulted in building positive communities.

Relationships formed between school leaders (principal and teaching faculty), students, and parents are critical elements not only in addressing diversity issues in school, but also in concurrently serving as a model for addressing demographic changes taking place in many of our nation's communities. Public schools, supported by the community, remain places where students pursue their formal education, which includes opportunities to learn to respect individual differences. This is an important consideration for classroom teachers rethinking issues related to school restructuring and, through their students, building effective future communities. Students attending our nation's schools will be influenced through their interaction with the teachers and students and these interactions will likely impact their communities and, in turn, our democratic way of life. As our nation's schools become more diverse, we cannot expect students to leave their gender, race, ethnicity characteristics, as well as attitudes about cultural differences at the schoolhouse doors. It becomes a part of the teacher's responsibility to assist students to develop and nurture trusting relationships and demonstrate and model for students how to mediate differences they experience in their daily lives. Irvine (2003) stated that teachers of color often serve as translators and brokers of culture for culturally disadvantaged students. These teachers increase student

A Culturally Relevant Approach to Pedagogy

During the last 20 years, there has been a gradual emergence of a cultural approach to pedagogy. In conjunction with the theoretical inquiry, empirical studies were conducted to illustrate that "culturally appropriate"(Au & Jordan, 1981), "culturally congruent"(Cazden & Leggett, 1981), "culturally responsive" (Jordan, 1985), and "culturally compatible" (Vogt, Jordan, & Tharp, 1987) pedagogies are effective for minority students. These terms have essentially been used interchangeably by many authors.

Empirical studies have been conducted to investigate the effectiveness of the culturally relevant pedagogy. For example, Ladson-Billings (1995a, b; 1998) used a qualitative approach to study the pedagogical practice of eight exemplary teachers of African American students and concluded that these teachers' practices and reflections on their practices provide a way to define and recognize a culturally relevant pedagogy. She observed that culturally relevant pedagogy must meet the following three criteria: (1) the ability to develop students academically, (2) the willingness to nurture and support cultural competence, and (3) the development of a sociopolitical or critical consciousness. She also illustrated that culturally relevant pedagogy is distinguished by three broad propositions or conceptions regarding self and others, social relations, and knowledge. She concluded that the culturally relevant pedagogy broadens the notions of pedagogy beyond strictly psychological models. Finally, she predicted the increasing need for a culturally relevant theoretical perspective on the growing disparity between the racial, ethnic, and cultural characteristics of teachers and students along with the continued academic failure of African American, Native American, and Latino students.

Similarly, in an experimental study with 72 disadvantaged, African American fifth graders, Dill and Boykin (2000) randomly assigned the subjects into three learning contexts: (a) communal learning, (b) peer learning, and (c) individual learning. A 3 (learning contexts) X 2 (sexes) ANOVA revealed that students under the communal learning context recall significantly more text than students assigned to the peer and individual contexts, and that gender and interaction effects are not statistically significant. In another experimental study, Boykin and Cunningham (2001) found that African American students learn better in a context that permits high movement expression (HME). Boykin and Bailey (2000) argued that the culture of African American youth could be capitalized on to facilitate learning, and that the evidence of the impact of the cultural approach to pedagogy is accumulating.

Gender Diversification in the Teaching Force

In addition to race and ethnicity, gender is also an important factor related to the diversity of the teaching force. Students must be provided with both male and female role models throughout the educational process. Students need both male and female role models for socialization experience, perspective, and support. Gender diversification is even more important when the number of single-parent homes is considered. This in conjunction with the limited communication between parents and their children accentuates the importance of role models representing both genders. Societal factors that decrease parent-child communication have increased the importance of gender diversification.

From the Classroom to the Principal's Office

If we walk into a public school and look into the school's main office, chances are the principal is a white male. In the 1999–2000 school year, 22.9% of the secondary principals were female, 88.9% white, and only 9.1% African American (Shen, Wegenke, & Cooley, 2003). When we have a more diversified pool, it is more likely that we will have a more diversified principalship force. Female and minority teachers who contemplate becoming secondary principals face different challenges. However, their common problem is lacking access to the power structures that control systems (McGee-Banks, 2000). Further diversification of the teaching force will change the power structure and diversify the principalship as well.

The Focus and Data Source of the Study

In this chapter, using survey data collected from nationally representative samples of public school teachers in 1987–88, 1993–94, and 1999–2000, we inquire into whether the public teaching force has become more diversified over the years. We display data on the variation of diversity in different kinds of schools and across states. We also point out the areas that require our continuing efforts.

The National Center for Educational Statistics (NCES) has been conducting Schools and Staffing Survey (SASS) since 1987–88. SASS, the largest survey of K–12 education in the United States, was conducted in 1987–88, 1990–91, 1993–94, and 1999–2000. Among the components of the survey is a survey of public school teachers. The data for this chapter were extracted from SASS 1987–88, 1990–91, and 1999–2000.

Both the achieved and the weighted sample sizes for each of the three survey years are reported in Table 3.1. NCES developed a set of sampling weights for each survey so that we could more accurately estimate the population based on the sample. In other words, through the use of sampling weights, the results are applicable to the national and state levels. The return rates for all the surveys are around 90%, a rate that is indeed very high for this kind of survey.

Table 3.1 A Summary of the Achieved and the Weighted Sample Sizes for Public School Teachers

	1987–88	1993–94	1999–00
Achieved Sample Size	40,593	47,105	42,086
Weighted Sample Size	2,323,204	2,561,294	2,984,782

Results

The Overall Pattern of the Composition of the Public Teaching Force in Terms of Gender, Race, and Ethnicity from 1987–88 to 1999–2000

Table 3.2 illustrates the overall trend of the composition of the public teaching force in terms of gender, race, and ethnicity. Where gender is concerned, the data indicate that the percentage of female teachers increased slightly, from 70.5% in 1987–88, to 72.9% in 1993–94, and to 74.9 in 1999–2000. Therefore, it appears that despite the rhetoric of having more male teachers, the percentage of male teachers has actually been going down between 1987–88 and 1999–2000. Teaching is a feminized profession, and this is truer in 1999–2000 than in 1987–88.

Table 3.2. The Composition of Public School Teachers in Terms of Gender, Race, and Ethnicity between 1987–88 and 1999–2000

	1987–88	1993–94	1999–2000
Female	70.5	72.9	74.9
Male	29.5	27.1	25.1
American Indian or Alaska Native	1.1	.9	1.0
Asian or Pacific Islander	.9	1.2	1.8
African American	8.4	7.6	8.0
White	89.6	90.3	89.2
Hispanic	3.0	4.2	5.6
Non-Hispanic	97.0	95.8	94.4

Chapter Three

Where race is concerned, the percentage of minority teachers (including American Indian or Alaska Native, Asian or Pacific Islander, and African American) increased slightly from 10.4% in 1987–88 to 10.8% in 1999–2000. However, the increase is extremely small. When ethnicity is closely examined, the percentage of Hispanic teachers increased from 3.0% in 1987–88, to 4.2% in 1993–94, and to 5.6% in 1999–2000, with a 2.6 percentage-point increase over the 12-year period.

Overall the data indicated that as far as diversity is concerned, essentially the public teaching force did not make much progress between 1987–88 and 1999–2000. In fact, the percentage of male teachers decreased by 4.4 points; the percentage of minority teachers increased by an extremely small 0.4 points; and the percentage of Hispanic teachers reflected a 2.6-point increase. We have a tremendous task ahead of us in terms of diversifying the public teaching force.

The Composition of New Teachers in Terms of Gender, Race, and Ethnicity from 1987–88 to 1999–2000

Since retirement occurs over a long period of time, another angle to inquire into the composition of the teaching force is to study those who were hired recently because the characteristics of recent hires forecast the characteristics of the whole teaching force in the future. Table 3.3 shows the characteristics of new teachers in the 1987–88, 1993–94, and 1999–2000 school years. New teachers are defined as those who are in their first three years of teaching. Three consistent patterns emerged. First, the percentage of male teachers among the newly hired increased from 21.3% in 1987–88 to 25.1% in 1993–94, and to 26.0% in 1999–2000, a pattern that is encouraging. Second, the percentage of American Indian or Alaska Native, Asian or Pacific Islander, and African American teachers among the newly hired all increased over the years. Third, the percentage of Hispanic teachers among the newly hired increased from 4.0% in 1987–88, to 8.2% in 1993–94, and to 9.2% in 1999–2000.

Table 3.3. The Composition of the New Public School Teachers between 1987–88 and 1999–2000

	1987–88	1993–94	1999–2000
Female	78.7	74.9	74.0
Male	21.3	25.1	26.0
American Indian or Alaska Native	1.1	1.1	1.2
Asian or Pacific Islander	1.1	2.1	2.9
African American	6.8	6.0	9.6
White	91.0	90.8	86.4
Hispanic	4.0	8.2	9.2
Non-Hispanic	96.0	91.8	90.8

If we juxtapose the results in Table 3.2 and Table 3.3, it would appear that the increased percentages of minority teachers and Hispanic teachers among those newly hired have gradually translated into a higher percentage of minority teachers and Hispanic teachers in the entire teaching force between 1987–88 and 1999–2000. However, at face value, it seems inconsistent that the percentage of male teachers among the newly hired increased from 21.3% in 1987–88 to 26.0% in 1999–2000, but that the percentage of males among all teachers decreased from 29.5% in 1987–88 to 25.1% in 1999–2000. Among others, three factors might contribute to the declining percentage of males in the teaching force. First, in 1987–88, the percentage of males was 25.1% among all teachers and was 21.3% among the newly hired ones. Since the percentage was lower for new hires than for existing teachers, the percentage of males will likely decrease in the future. Second, several studies on teacher attrition found that male teachers are more likely to leave teaching than their female counterparts (Murnane, Singer, Willett, Kemple, & Olsen, 1991; Shen, 1997; Shen, 2002; Stinebrickner, 1998). Third, given the differentials in compensation between teaching and other professions that require the same level of education, the economic prosperity of the 1990s made males less likely to enter teaching, but more likely to leave.

The Current Status of the Composition of the Public School Teachers

Tables 3.4 and 3.5 display the most current data we have on the status of the composition of the public teaching force. In Table 3.4, we can see that female, Asian and Pacific Islander, African American, and Hispanic teachers are more likely to be found in urban schools than in rural schools. In the 1999–2000 school year, 75.5% of the urban public school teachers were female while the corresponding statistic for rural schools was 73.1%. The disparity in the distribution of African American teachers is even more significant. Among urban public school teachers, 16.0% were African American. The corresponding statistics were as low as 5.2% among the suburban counterparts and 4.6% among the rural counterparts. The disparity in the distribution of Hispanic teachers is also very significant. Among urban public school teachers, 10.2% were identified as Hispanic. The corresponding statistics for suburban and rural schools were 4.6% and 2.3%, respectively. Given the general population in urban, suburban, and rural areas, the finding that urban public school teachers are more diversified does not come as a surprise.

Table 3.4. The Composition (in percentages) of Public School Teachers by School Location in 1999–2000

	Overall	Location		
		Urban	Suburban	Rural
Female	74.9	75.5	75.4	73.1
Male	25.1	24.5	24.6	26.9
American Indian or Alaska Native	1.0	1.2	.7	1.4
Asian or Pacific Islander	1.8	3.2	1.7	.5
African American	8.0	16.0	5.2	4.6
White	89.2	79.6	92.4	93.5
Hispanic	5.6	10.2	4.6	2.3
Non-Hispanic	94.4	89.8	95.4	97.7

Data in Table 3.5 indicate that in 1999–2000 the public teaching force was more racially and ethnically diversified in schools where a high level of minority enrollment was found. For example, in schools where 50% or more students were minority, 26.9% of the teachers were minority, with Native American, Asian, and African American teachers constituting 1.5%, 4.5%, and 20.9% of the teaching force, respectively. In schools where 50% or more students were minority, Hispanic teachers comprised 13.7% of the teaching force. In contrast, in those schools where 0–4% of the students were minority, Native American, Asian, and African American teachers made up only 1.5% of the teaching force; Hispanic teachers were only 0.7% of the teaching force. The degree of racial and ethnic diversification found in the public teaching force is very uneven when we view the data from the perspective of the level of minority enrollment in schools. Where gender is concerned, there appears to be a higher percentage of male teachers in schools where minority enrollment was 19% or less than in those schools where minority enrollment was 20% or more.

Table 3.5. The Composition of Public School Teachers by Different Levels of Enrollment in Schools in 1999–2000

	Overall	Minority Enrollment in School			
		0–4%	5–19%	20–49%	>=50%
Female	74.9	72.7	74.0	76.7	75.8
Male	25.1	27.3	26.0	23.3	24.2
American Indian or Alaska Native	1.0	.8	.7	.8	1.5
Asian or Pacific Islander	1.8	.3	.6	1.3	4.5
African American	8.0	.5	1.2	6.2	20.9
White	89.2	98.5	97.5	91.7	73.1
Hispanic	5.6	.7	2.1	4.0	13.7
Non-Hispanic	94.4	99.3	97.9	96.0	86.3

In summary, since the level of minority enrollment and the location of the school are related, inquiry from these two perspectives yields similar results. There are higher levels of racial and ethnic diversity in urban schools and schools with a higher level of minority enrollment. However, there is less gender diversity in urban schools and schools with higher minority enrollment. In others words, there are lower percentages of male teachers in urban schools and schools with a higher level of minority enrollment.

Variation across the States

Figure 3.1 shows the percentage of male teachers in each state and the District of Columbia in 1999–2000. The data in Figure 3.1 illustrate a tremendous amount of variability across the states. In South Carolina, only 16.7% of the public teaching force was male, while the corresponding statistic was 33.6% in Wyoming. Male teachers constituted less than 20% of the public teaching force in South Carolina, Mississippi, Arkansas, Alabama, Louisiana, Georgia, Florida, North Carolina, and Tennessee. However, male teachers made up more than 30% of the teaching force in Wyoming, Alaska, Oregon, Washington, Montana, Massachusetts, Iowa, and Pennsylvania. The general pattern is that the percentage of male teachers in the public teaching force is lowest in the southeastern corner of the country and the highest in the northwestern states. Given the essentially equal distribution of males and females among the working population, the difference across the states is significant indeed.

Summary and Discussion

This chapter inquires into (a) how the composition of the public teaching force has evolved between 1987–88 and 1999–2000, a period of 12 years and (b) the variation of teacher diversity in 1999–2000. A few conclusions emerge from the data. First, we have not made much progress in diversifying the public teaching force between 1997–98 and 1999–2000. Where race and ethnicity are concerned, the profession has made a small progress. The percentage of non-white teachers increased slightly from 10.4% in 1987–88 to 10.8% in 1999–2000. The percentage of Hispanic teachers increased from 3.0% in 1987–88 to 5.6% in 1999–2000. As far as gender diversity is concerned, the profession actually regressed. The percentage of male teachers decreased slightly, from 29.5% in 1987–88 to 25.1% in 1999–2000. We have a challenge ahead of us in terms of diversifying the public teaching force.

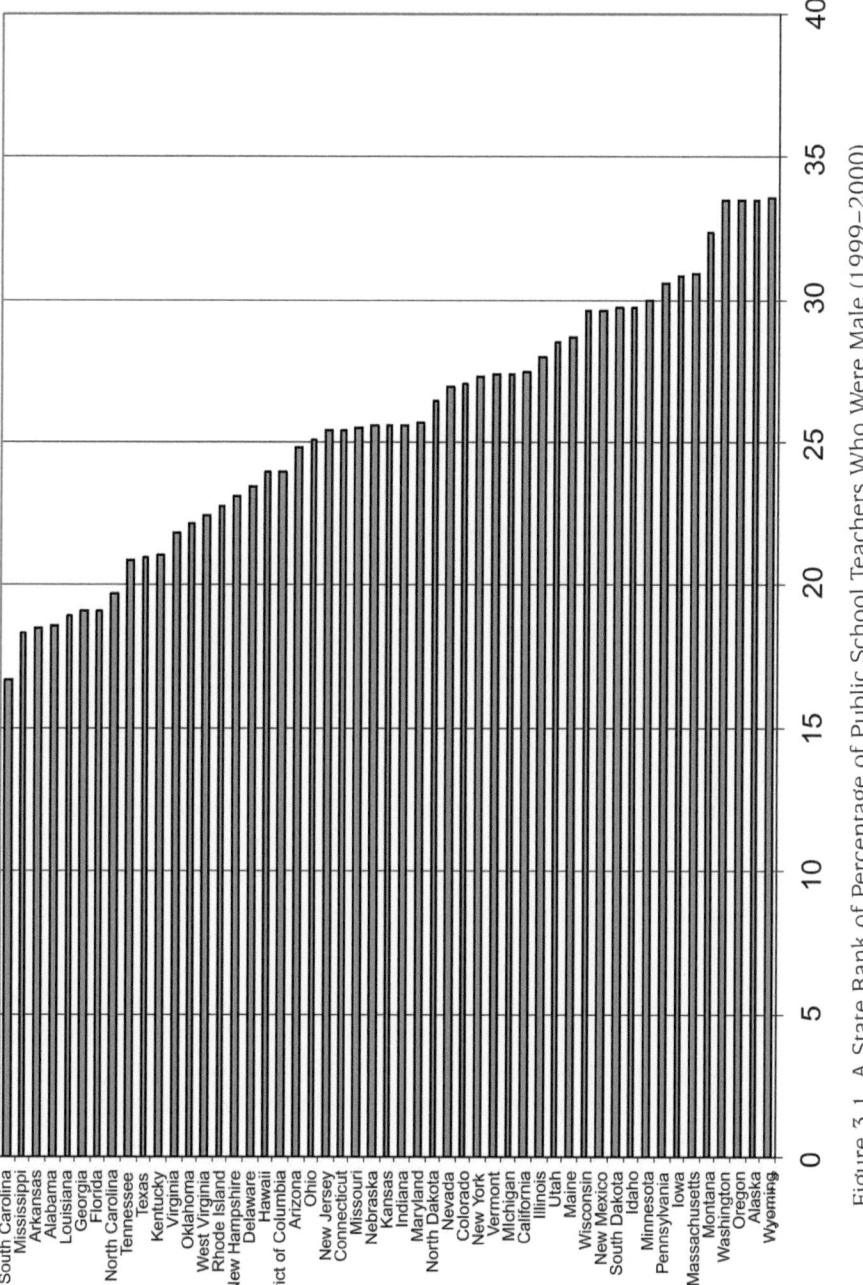

Figure 3.1. A State Rank of Percentage of Public School Teachers Who Were Male (1999–2000)

Second, although the teaching force as a whole has been only slightly diverse in terms of race and ethnicity and less so in terms of gender, the trends among newly hired teachers are more promising. The data revealed that among the newly hired teachers, there has been, between 1987-88 and 1999-2000, a consistently higher level of diversity in race, ethnicity, and gender. The crucial issue is that policies should be developed to retain the newly hired teachers in the teaching force so that over the years the characteristics of the newly hired ones will be translated into the characteristics of the whole teaching force. Previous studies indicate that about 20% of new teachers leave teaching within the first three years.

Finally, the study also found some variation in teacher diversity. Generally speaking, there is more racial and ethnic diversity in urban schools and schools with high levels of minority enrollment. The pattern for gender diversity is just the opposite. It is in rural schools and schools with low levels of minority enrollment where there is a high level of gender diversity. The study also identified a significant variation among the states, with the percentage of male teachers in Wyoming being more than twice of that in South Carolina.

In summary, we analyzed data collected from nationally representative samples of public school teachers between 1987-88 and 1999-2000 and found that there was a higher percentage of minority teachers but a lower percentage of males. As far as teacher diversification is concerned, there is a significant amount of variation across (a) urban, suburban, and rural schools, (b) schools with different levels of minority enrollment, and (c) the states. In the last 12 years, we made some progress in racial and ethnic diversification but regressed in gender diversification. We have a challenge ahead of us to further diversify the public teaching force.

References

Au, K., & Jordan, C. (1981). Teaching reading to Hawaiian children: Finding a culturally appropriate solution. In H. Trueba, G. Guthrie, & K. Au (eds.), *Culture and the bilingual classroom: Studies in classroom ethnography* (pp. 139-152). Rowley, MA: Newbury.

Berry, B. (2008). Staffing high needs schools: Insights from the nation's best teachers. *Phi Delta Kappan, 89*, 766-771.

Boykin, A. W., & Bailey, C. T. (2000). *The role of cultural factors in school relevant cognitive functioning: Description of home environmental factors, cultural orientations, and learning preference*. Washington, DC: Center for Research on the Education of Students Placed at Risk, Howard University.

Boykin, A. W., & Cunningham, R. T. (2001). The effects of movement expressiveness in story content and learning context on the analogical reasoning performance of African American children. *Journal of Negro Education, 70* (1-2): 72-83.

Cazden, C., & Leggett, E. (1981). Culturally responsive education: Recommendations for achieving low remedies II. In H. Trueba, G. Guthrie, & K. Au (eds.), *Culture and the bilingual classroom: Studies in classroom ethnography* (pp. 69-86). Rowley, MA: Newbury.

Chmelynski, C. (2006). Getting more men and blacks into teaching. *The Educational Digest, 71* (5), 40-42.

Dill, E. M., & Boykin, A. W. (2000). The comparative influence of individual, peer tutoring, and communal learning contexts on the text recall of African American children. *Journal of Black Psychology, 26* (1), 65-78.

Goodlad, J. I. (1990). *Teachers for our nations' schools.* San Francisco: Jossey-Bass.

Goodlad, J. I., Soder, R., & Sirotnit, K. (Eds.) (1990). *Places where teachers are taught.* San Francisco: Jossey-Bass.

Gordon, E. W. (1995). Culture and the sciences of pedagogy. *Teacher College Record, 97,* 32-46.

Gordon, J. A. (2000). Asian American resistance to selecting teaching as a career: The power of community and tradition. *Teachers College Record, 102,* 173-196.

Gordon, J. A. (2005). In search of educators of color. *Leadership 35* (2), 30-35.

Harvey, W. B. (2002). *Minorities in higher education 2001-2002: 19th annual status report.* Washington DC: American Council on Education.

Hodgkinson, H. (2002). Demographics and teacher education. *Journal of Teacher Education, 53* (2), 102-105.

Irvine, J. J. (2003). *Educating teacher for diversity: Seeing with a cultural eye.* New York: Teachers College Press.

Jordan, C. (1985). Translating culture: From ethnographic information to educational program. *Anthropology and Education Quarterly, 16,* 105-123.

Ladson-Billings, G. (1995a). Toward a theory of culturally relevant pedagogy. *American Educational Research Journal, 32,* 465-491.

Ladson-Billings, G. (1995b). But that's just good teaching? The case for culturally relevant pedagogy. *Theory into Practice, 34,* 159-165.

Ladson-Billings, G. (1998). Teaching in dangerous times: Culturally relevant approaches to teacher assessment. *The Journal of Negro Education, 67* (3), 255-267.

Lortie, D. C. (1975). *Schoolteacher: A sociological study.* Chicago: University of Chicago Press.

McGee-Banks, C. A. (2000). Gender and race as factors in educational leadership and administration. In Michael Fullan, *The Jossey-Bass Reader on Educational Leadership* (pp. 217-256). San Francisco: Jossey-Bass.

Miller, M., Strosnider, R. A., & Dooley, E. A. (2002). States' requirements for teachers' preparation for diversity. *Multicultural Education, 8* (2), 15-18.

Murnane, R. J., Singer, J. D., Willett, J. B., Kemple, J. J., & Olsen, R. J. (1991). *Who will teach? Policies that matter.* Cambridge, MA: Harvard University Press.

Riley, R. W. (1998). *The challenge for America: A high quality teacher in every classroom.* Speech to the National Press Club, September 15, 1998.

Rong, X. L., & Preissle, J. (1997). The continuing decline in Asian American teachers. *American Educational Research Journal, 34* (2), 267-293.

Sergiovanni, T. J. (2001). *The principalship: A reflective practice perspective.* Needham Heights, MA: Allyn & Bacon.

Shen, J. (1997). Teacher retention and attrition in public schools: Evidence from SASS91. *Journal of Educational Research, 91* (2), 81-88.

Shen, J. (2002). *New teachers' retention and attrition: A survival analysis using B&B: 93/97.* Kalamazoo, MI: Western Michigan University.

Shen, J., Wegenke, G. L., & Cooley, V. E. (2003). Has the public teaching force become more diversified? National and longitudinal perspectives on gender, race, and ethnicity. *Educational Horizons, 81* (3), 112-118.

Stinebrickner, T. R. (1998). An empirical investigation of teacher attrition. *Economics of Education Review, 17* (2), 127-136.

Vogt, L., Jordan, C., & Tharp, R. (1987). Explaining school failure, producing school success: Two cases. *Anthropology and Education Quarterly, 18,* 276-286.

SECTION 2

Inequitable Distribution of Public School Teachers

CHAPTER FOUR

Teacher Quality and Students Placed at Risk

Results from the Baccalaureate and Beyond Longitudinal Study 1993–97

Jianping Shen, Nancy B. Mansberger, and Huilan Yang

Introduction

The sweeping No Child Left Behind (NCLB) legislation seeks to impact U.S. education on a broad scale through provisions and mandates that target both resources and student outcomes. Among the more highly controversial elements of the act are those designed to hold districts accountable for raising the scores of all students, including traditionally underachieving populations such as minority, limited-English proficient (LEP) students, and students of low socioeconomic status.

One of the mandates of NCLB is that all students be taught by "highly qualified teachers." This mandate is based on growing evidence of the relationship between teacher qualifications and student achievement. Research has shown that differences in student achievement are significantly associated with teacher effects at the classroom level (Sanders, Wright, & Horn, 1997). These findings were expanded upon in a 1999 study that used data from a 50-state survey of policies, the 1993–94 Schools and Staffing Surveys (SASS), and the National Assessment of Educational Progress (NAEP), which found that teacher quality variables accounted for 67–87% of the total variance in student achievement (Darling-Hammond, 1999). Darling-Hammond determined that teacher quality characteristics such as certification status and degree in the subject taught are very significantly and positively correlated with student outcomes. Furthermore, these strong significant relationships with student achievement were evident even after controlling for student poverty and student language background. This chapter highlights the critical importance of highly qualified teachers.

Literature Review

What defines a "highly qualified teacher"? The definition used by the NCLB legislation is based on the preparation of teachers. Typically, research on teacher preparation has focused on the following characteristics of teacher quality: (1) The relationship between the general academic ability and scholastic background of teachers and the achievement of their students; (2) the impact of teacher preparation programs on the effectiveness of teachers; and (3) the outcomes observed in student achievement associated with the certification status of teachers.

Teachers' Academic Preparation

Teachers' knowledge in a subject area is found to be positively correlated with students' academic achievement. Darling-Hammond's (2002) recent review of literature in this area provides compelling evidence. For example, Druva and Anderson (1983) found that the amount of teachers' course work in the sciences had a positive correlation with students' science achievement, and that the positive correlation was greater when the researchers inquired into student achievement in higher-level science courses. Hawk, Coble, and Swanson (1985) came to similar conclusions. They studied middle school mathematics teachers and found that in comparison to those students taught by teachers not certified in math, students of fully certified math teachers made significantly more progress. Furthermore, Monk (1994) also found that there was a positive correlation between the amount of course work math and science teachers did and their students' achievement in these subjects.

More sophisticated statistical analyses also indicate the positive correlation between the quality of teachers' academic background and the level of student achievement. Darling-Hammond (2000) summarized studies by Ferguson (1991), Ferguson and Ladd (1996), and Armour-Thomas and colleagues (1989) and observed that multivariate studies using the school or district as the unit of analysis reveal positive correlation between the quality of teachers' academic characteristics and students' achievement, and that the positive correlation is even more prominent when student characteristics are controlled. For example, in the schools of New York City, the teachers' academic characteristics variable explains about 90% of the variance in schools' average achievement in reading and math.

Extent of Teacher Education, Preparation, or Training

In a 1993 study, Ferguson and Womack found that the amount of education course work was correlated to supervisor evaluations of teacher effectiveness. This finding was supported by a review of teacher preparation research in which a clear positive effect of teacher preparation experiences on teaching practices and student achievement was identified by researchers (Wilson, Floden, & Ferrini-Mundy, 2001). In particular, clinical experiences/internships were found by these researchers to be "perhaps the single most powerful element of teacher preparation" (Wilson, Floden, & Ferrini-Mundy, 2001, p. 2). These findings in turn validate an earlier 1985 study that determined that students enrolled in formal preservice preparation programs are more likely to be effective teachers than those who have not had such preparation (Evertson, Hawley, & Zlotnick, 1985).

Teachers' Certification

Between a looming national teacher shortage and the class size reduction reform, many (primarily urban) districts have been forced to employ "undercertified" teachers (*Dallas Morning News*, August 15, 2003; *Detroit Free Press*, August 17, 2003). Undercertified teachers are those who either lack regular teaching certification (teaching under emergency or provisional teaching certificates), have not participated in traditional university-based teacher preparation programs, or have not obtained academic majors in the subjects in which they teach. The use of undercertified teachers has been shown to have significant and substantial negative impact on student learning (Darling-Hammond, 1999; Fetler, 1999; Goe, 2002; Hawk, Coble, & Swanson, 1985; Navarette, 2003). According to researchers Laczko-Kerr and Berliner (2002),

> Teachers who have trained longer and harder to do the complex work of teaching do it better. The advantage of having a certified teacher is worth about two months on a grade-equivalent scale. . . the loss from having an undercertified teacher is 20 percent of an academic year, students pay a 20 percent penalty in academic growth for each year of placement with undercertified teachers. (p. 38)

However, there are indications that ensuring teacher quality might be an issue that disproportionately hits districts that serve a high proportion of children placed at risk. In a study conducted by the *Dallas Morning News*, more than 7,000 schools were rated on a scale that combined the percentages of how many of their teachers were certified, teaching in their specialty, and had at least two years' experience. Researchers found not only that the obtained "teacher preparation index" scores were strongly related with measures of student achievement, but also that schools with substantial numbers of poor and minority students, or large populations of limited English proficiency (LEP) students, were the *least likely* to have highly qualified, experienced teachers certified in the subject matter they are assigned to teach (Booth & Ramshaw, 2003). Similar findings have been documented by research on national teacher quality and distribution patterns (Ingersoll, 2002).

Given the overwhelming evidence on the relationship between teachers' qualifications and student learning, it is very important to inquire into the issue of equity—to find out whether students in poverty have gotten an equitable share of qualified new teachers. In this chapter, we present findings on the quality of the distribution of new teachers in relationship to the poverty level in schools.

The Data Source

The data for this chapter were extracted from the Baccalaureate and Beyond Longitudinal Study 1993–97 (B&B: 93/97). B&B: 93/97 was designed to examine the post-baccalaureate experiences of 1992–93 bachelor's degree recipients. Following a sample of approximately 11,200 men and women who received bachelor's degrees between July 1992 and June 1993, researchers collected data on this cohort via (a) interviews conducted when the students were seniors in college as part of the 1993 National Postsecondary Students Aid Study (NPSAS:93), (b) the B&B First Follow-up conducted in 1994 (B&B:93/94), and (c) the Second Follow-up in 1997 (B&B:93/97). Transcript data from the students' institution are also available for most of the cohort through the NPSAS. Among others, the B&B:93/97 study provides data to address issues related to patterns of preparation for, and engagement in, teaching .

The Characteristics of the Sample

The sample of the study consisted of those teachers who reported during the 1997 survey that their last teaching job was in a public school. Since some teachers could have entered and then left teaching, and others could have switched between public and private schools, their response to the question on "last teaching job sector" was the criterion used to classify public school teachers for this report. The last teaching job could mean "the last job" for those who entered and then left teaching, or the current job for those who were still in the teaching force.

The actual sample size was 1,144 and the weighted sample size was 112,118. The data reported in the study was relatively weighted. Through relative weights, we were able to not only approximate the population but also keep the achieved sample size. Among those in the sample, 73.3% were female, 85.5% were white (non-Hispanic); about 70% of them were still in the teaching force in 1997; and most of them had one (62.3%) or two (19.3%) regular teaching positions.

Findings

Academic Preparation before and during College

College Entrance Examination (Table 4.1)
Since most of the subjects took either or both ACT and SAT as their college entrance exam, we combined the two tests and examined the distribution of teachers with different quartiles of merged SAT/ACT scores. The quartile was based on all graduates in the B&B rather than the sample of the current report. Data in Table 4.1 suggests that schools with higher poverty levels had a higher percentage of new teachers whose SAT/ACT scores were in lower quartiles, and that the trend was statistically significant. For example, in schools where more than 50% of the students were in poverty, 34.0% of the new teachers had SAT/ACT scores in the first quartile and only 8.0% had scores in the fourth quartile. In contrast, in schools where only 0–4% of the students were in poverty, only 8.6% of the new teachers had SAT/ACT scores in the first quartile, but 22.9% had scores in the fourth quartile.

Table 4.1. Distribution of New Teachers with Various Merged SAT/ACT Quartiles across Schools with Different Levels of Students in Poverty

Percentage of Students in Poverty	Quartile			
	1st	2nd	3rd	4th
0–4	8.6	40.0	28.6	22.9
5–19	28.7	25.5	31.5	14.4
20–49	27.7	34.1	24.1	14.1
50 or more	34.0	28.7	29.3	8.0

Gamma = $-.13, p = .008$.

Taking Remedial Courses in Reading, Writing, and Math during College (Table 4.2)

There was a statistically significant relationship between the level of students in poverty and whether or not the new teacher took remedial courses in reading, writing, and math. Data in Table 4.2 indicates that about 11.2% of new teachers who worked in schools where 50% or more of the students were in poverty took remedial reading, writing, or math courses. The corresponding percentages for other kinds of schools were much lower, ranging from 0% to 7.0%.

Table 4.2. Distribution of New Teachers Who Did or Did Not Take Remedial Courses in Reading, Writing, and Math during Post-secondary Education across Schools with Different Levels of Students in Poverty

Percentage of Students in Poverty	Whether Took Remedial Courses	
	Did Not Take	Did Take
0–4	100.0	0.0
5–19	95.1	4.9
20–49	93.0	7.0
50 or more	88.8	11.2

$\chi^2(3) = 10.4, p = .02$, Cramer's $V = .12$.

Normalized College GPA Quartile (Table 4.3)

Data in Table 4.3 shows that there was no statistically significant relationship between percentage of students in poverty in school and the distribution of new teachers with various normalized college GPA quartiles (Gamma = –.06; $p = .15$).

Table 4.3. Distribution of New Teachers with Normalized College GPA Quartiles across Schools with Different Levels of Students in Poverty

Percentage of Students in Poverty	Normalized College GPA Quartile			
	1st	2nd	3rd	4th
0–4	16.7	28.6	23.8	31.0
5–19	20.6	27.7	27.3	24.5
20–49	22.8	21.1	29.8	26.3
50 or more	28.9	24.5	22.5	24.0

Gamma = –.06, $p = .15$.

The data related to academic preparation demonstrated that schools with higher poverty levels were more likely to have new teachers who had lower SAT/ACT scores and took remedial classes during college. However, there was no difference in college GPA for the teachers in schools with

Levels of Teacher Preparation and Certification

The Extent of Teacher Preparation (Table 4.4)

Demand due to teacher shortages has led to the creation of emergency or alternative certification. Hence, a number of teachers are hired annually who do not have regular teacher education and enter teaching without traditional preparation. Previous studies found that schools with higher percentages of students placed at risk are more likely to have teachers who are not fully prepared, a finding that our own data related to the level of teacher preparation and certification confirms. According to the definition for the B&B:93/97 data set, to be "fully prepared to teach" is to complete all the following: student teaching, certification, and participation in a teacher induction program, a standard that is very high indeed. Schools with higher levels of students in poverty were more likely to have new teachers who did not complete all the requirements for teacher preparation and the relationship was statistically significant. About 74.1% of the new teachers in schools where 50% or more students were in poverty did not complete all the requirements for teacher preparation and the corresponding percentages for other schools ranged from 61.8% to 65.3%.

Table 4.4. Distribution of New Teachers with Different Levels of Teacher Preparation across Schools with Various Levels of Students in Poverty

Percentage of Students in Poverty	Extent of Teacher Preparation	
	Did All	Did Not Do All
0–4	38.1	61.9
5–19	34.7	65.3
20–49	38.2	61.8
50 or more	25.9	74.1

$\chi^2(3) = 8.5, p = .04$, Cramer's $V = .11$

Whether or Not Currently Certified (Table 4.5)

The data suggest that there was a significant relationship between the level of students in poverty and the new teacher's certification status, and that schools with extremely high student poverty rate tend to have a higher percentage of new teachers who were not certified. In schools where 50% or more of the students were in poverty, 16.9% of the new teachers were uncertified. The corresponding percentages for schools with lower levels of students in poverty ranged from 8.5% to 14.6%.

Table 4.5. Distribution of Currently Certified or Uncertified New Teachers across Schools with Various Levels of Students in Poverty

Percentage of Students in Poverty	Certification Status	
	Not Certified	Certified
0–4	14.6	85.4
5–19	10.4	89.6
20–49	8.5	91.5
50 or more	16.9	83.1

$\chi^2(3) = 8.8, p = .03$, Cramer's $V = .11$.

Highest Certification (Table 4.6)

The data on highest certification indicated a statistically significant relationship between new teachers' highest certification and the level of poverty in the school (Table 4.6). The data clearly indicate that in schools where poverty levels were high, a very high percentage of new teachers had emergency, temporary, or other certificates. In schools where 50% or more students were in poverty, 9.9% of the new teachers had emergency, temporary, or other certificates. In schools where 20–49% of the students were in poverty, 3.0% of the new teachers had emergency, temporary, or other certificates. The corresponding percentages for schools with lower levels of students in poverty ranged from 0% to 0.9%.

Table 4.6. Distribution of New Teachers with Various Highest Certification across Schools with Different Levels of Students in Poverty

Percentage of Students in Poverty	Highest Certification			
	Advanced	Regular	Probationary	Emergency, Temporary, and Other
0–4	15.8	78.9	5.3	0.0
5–19	6.8	90.2	2.1	0.9
20–49	9.0	81.3	6.7	3.0
50 or more	6.8	78.6	4.7	9.9

$\chi^2(9) = 36.9, p < .001$, Cramer's $V = .13$.

The data in this section demonstrate that students in high poverty schools tend to have new teachers who are not fully prepared, do not have certification, and are more likely to have emergency, temporary, and other certificates. When we inquired into the highest levels of certification, the differences among schools with various levels of students in poverty were particularly substantial.

Discussion

Our research, as described in this chapter, has led us to two major findings. First, generally speaking, schools with higher levels of students in poverty tended to have less qualified new teachers. This was particularly true where the extent of teacher preparation and teachers' highest certification were concerned and, to a lesser extent, where teacher's precollegiate academic preparation was concerned. However, there was no statistically significant difference among various kinds of schools in terms of new teachers' college GPA quartiles.

Second, when we investigated whether or not new teachers currently had certification, there was a statistically significant, though somewhat variable, difference among schools with various levels of students in poverty. However, when we studied the extent of preparation and the highest certification that new teachers had, the schools placed at risk clearly had much less qualified new teachers. Therefore, the absence or ownership of a formal certificate to teach seems to capture only part of the essence of inequity. It is the quantity and quality of the preparation experience related to the certification status that revealed the disadvantages of schools with high levels of students in poverty.

In summary, the data indicated that, overall, schools placed at risk had less qualified new teachers. The less qualified teaching force would further exacerbate the inequity already existing in those schools placed at risk. We, as a profession and as a society, face a serious equity issue.

References

Armour-Thomas, E., Clay, C., Domanico, R., Bruno, K., & Allen, B. (1989). *An outlier study of elementary and middle schools in New York City: Final report*. New York: New York City Board of Education.

Booth, H., & Ramshaw, E. (2003) .Districts size up teachers. *Dallas Morning News*, August 15, 2003, 1N.

Darling-Hammond, L. (1999). *CTP research report: Teacher quality and student achievement: A review of state policy evidence*. Seattle, WA: Center for the Study of Teaching and Policy. Retrieved on September 26, 2003.
http://depts.washington.edu/ctpmail/publications/byauthor.shtml#Darling-Hammond,%20Linda.

Darling-Hammond, L. (2000). Teacher quality and student achievement: A review of state policy evidence. *Education Policy Analysis Archives, 8* (1). http://epaa.asu.edu/epaa/v8n1/.

Darling-Hammond, L. (2002). Research and rhetoric on teacher certification: A response to "Teacher Certification Reconsidered." *Education Policy Analysis Archives, 10* (36). Retrieved on September 10, 2002. http://epaa.asu.edu/epaa/v10n36.html.

Druva, C., & Anderson, R. (1983). Science teacher characteristics by teacher behavior and by student outcome: A meta-analysis of research. *Journal of Research in Science Teaching, 20* (5), 467–479.

Evertson, C., Hawley, W., & Zlotnick, M. (1985). Making a difference in educational quality through teacher education. *Journal of Teacher Education, 36* (3), 2–12.

Ferguson, P., & Womack, S. T. (1993). The impact of subject matter and education coursework on teaching performance. *Journal of Teacher Education, 44* (1), 55–63.

Ferguson, R. (1991). Paying for public education: New evidence on how and why money matters. *Harvard Journal of Legislation, 28* (2), 465–498.

Ferguson, R., & Ladd, H. (1996). How and why money matters: An analysis of Alabama schools. In Helen Ladd (Ed.), *Holding schools accountable*. Washington, DC: Brookings Institution.

Fetler, M. (1999). High school staff characteristics and mathematics test results. *Education Policy Analysis Archives, 7* (9). http://epaa.asu.edu/epaa/v7n9.html

Goe, L. (2002). Legislating equity: The distribution of emergency permit teachers in California. *Educational Policy Analysis Archives, 10* (42) .Retrieved on October 4, 2003. http://epaa.asu.edu/epaa/v10n42.

Hawk, P., Coble, C. R., & Swanson, M. (1985). Certification: Does it matter? *Journal of Teacher Education, 36* (3), 13–15.

Ingersoll, R. (2002). *CTP research report: Out-of-field teaching, educational inequality, and the organization of schools: An exploratory analysis.* Seattle, WA: Center for the Study of Teaching and Policy.

Laczko-Kerr, I., & Berliner, D. C. (2002). In harm's way: How undercertified teachers hurt their students. *Educational Leadership, 60* (4), 34–39.

Monk, D. H. (1994). Subject matter preparation of secondary mathematics and science teachers and student achievement. *Economics of Education Review, 13* (2), 125–145.

Navarette, R. (2003). Lack of teacher preparation hurts poor kids. *Detroit Free Press,* August 17, 2003, 15A.

Sanders, W. L., Wright, S. P., & Horn, S. P. (1997). Teacher and classroom context effects on student achievement: Implications for teacher evaluation. *Journal of Personnel Evaluation in Education, 11* (1), 57–67.

Wilson, S., Floden, R. & Ferrini-Mundy, J. (2001). *Teacher preparation research: Current knowledge, gaps, and recommendations* (R-01-3). Seattle, WA: Center for the Study of Teaching and Policy.

CHAPTER FIVE

The Distribution of the Quality of the Public Teaching Force
Results from Multiple Waves of Schools and Staffing Surveys

Jianping Shen

Introduction

The relationship between teacher qualification and student achievement has become a target for educational policies in the United States. Teacher qualifications are found to be one of the key factors associated with student performance (e.g., Darling-Hammond, 2000; Ferguson, 1991; Goldhaber & Brewer, 2000; Laczko-Kerr & Berliner, 2002; Monk, 1994; Sanders & Rivers, 1996). Yet, empirical data indicates that quality new teachers tend not to work in disadvantaged schools (Shen, Mansberger, & Yang, 2004) and that disadvantaged schools tend to have a lower percentage of quality teachers (Lu, Shen, & Poppink, 2007; Shen & Poppink, 2003). In this chapter, analyzing three waves of data from Schools and Staffing Survey conducted in 1987–88, 1993–94, and 1999–2000, we inquire into whether schools with high levels of minority enrollment have a fair share of quality teachers.

Literature Review: The Link between Teacher Qualification and Student Achievement

In recent years, researchers have conducted an increasing number of studies seeking to understand whether teachers with high qualifications can make a difference in students' learning (Chaney, 1995; Darling-Hammond, Berry, & Thoreson, 2001; Ferguson & Womack, 1993; Fuller, 1999; Hawk, Coble, & Swanson, 1985; Monk, 1994; Monk & King, 1994; Rowan, Chiang, & Miller, 1997). The research has firmly established the link between teacher qualification and student achievement. A high quality teacher does have a statistically significant impact on student achievement. For example, a review of teacher preparation research identifies a clear positive effect of teacher preparation experiences on student achievement, among others (Wilson, Floden, & Ferrini-Mundy, 2001). This finding, in turn, validates an earlier 1985 study that determined that prospective teachers enrolled in formal preservice preparation programs are more likely to be effective teachers than those who have not had such preparation (Evertson, Hawley, & Zlotnick, 1985).

Other studies also pinpoint the importance of teacher preparation. Monk's (1994) study of the relationship between teacher preparation and student achievement indicated that both subject content courses and subject-specific pedagogy courses in a teacher's preparation were positively related to student achievement. Subject-specific teacher preparation or teachers with a major in their subjects taught had a significantly positive impact on student achievement, particularly in mathematics and science (Chaney, 1995; Goldhaber & Brewer, 1998; Rowan, Chiang, & Miller, 1997; Weglinsky, 2000). Weglinsky (2000) found that, in math and science, students whose teachers majored or minored in the subject they taught outperformed peers whose teachers did not have a major or minor in their subject by 40% of a grade level.

Related to teacher preparation is teachers' certification status that is also found to be positively related to student achievement. Studies have shown that students taught by teachers certified in their subject performed better than those who were not (Goldhaber & Brewer, 2000; Hawk, Coble, & Swanson, 1985) and students taught by regularly certified teachers outperformed students taught by undercertified teachers (Laczko-Kerr & Berliner, 2002). Laczko-Kerr and Berliner (2002) found that students taught by regularly certified teachers made about 20% more academic growth per year than did students taught by undercertified teachers.

Some recent studies that focused their attention on the impact of teacher qualification on disadvantaged students' achievement revealed that disadvantaged students' achievement is especially sensitive to the qualification of their teachers (Nye et al., 2004; Sanders & Rivers, 1996). For example, Nye and colleagues (2004) found that teacher effects are much larger in low-Social Economic Status (SES) schools than in high-SES schools. Olson (2003) also found that having a highly qualified teacher for four or five years in a row could fundamentally close the gap in student achievement between students from low-income and high-income families. Sanders and Rivers (1996) found that disadvantaged students with the most effective teachers gained over 50 percentile points in their test scores while those with the least effective teachers gained 14 percentile points. These studies suggest that teachers with strong teacher qualifications can help disadvantaged students close the achievement gap.

As Ansell and McCabe (2003) pointed out, if we want to understand the root of the achievement gap, we should first understand the teacher gap that exists between the skill levels of teachers. Therefore, to end the achievement gap between minority and nonminority students and between those from rich and poor families, providing well-qualified teachers for those who need them most is a starting point for closing that gap. This study contributes to policy discussions on equity by studying whether schools with high-level of minority enrollment have a fair share of quality teachers.

Methods

The data presented in this chapter were extracted from the Schools and Staffing Survey (SASS). SASS, designed by the National Center for Education Statistics and implemented by the Bureau of Census, is the largest sample survey of the school systems in the United States. SASS is an integrated survey of school districts, schools, school principals, and school teachers. During SASS, researchers first sample schools. After the schools are decided, researchers select the chosen schools' local educational authorities (school districts) and principals, and teachers. Thus the data from the four components of SASS—(1) school districts, (2) schools, (3) school principals, and (4) school teachers—can be linked. This report utilized data on the level of minority enrollment (from the school survey) and teacher quality (from the teacher survey).

The main survey of SASS was implemented four times in 1987–88, 1990–91, 1993–94, and 1999–2000. In order to create a six-year interval, we used the data collected in 1987–88, 1993–94, and 1999–2000.

As will be discussed later in the chapter, the three waves of surveys, each of which had nationally representative samples of public school teachers, allow us to conduct not only a particular kind of longitudinal analysis called "trend study" but also a cross-sectional analysis using the most recent data available from the 1999–2000 survey.

The samples of the study consisted of those public school teachers who responded to the surveys. The actual sample size and the weighted sample size are displayed in Table 5.1. In each of the teacher surveys, more than 40,000 public school teachers took part and the weighted sample size was more than 2 million. The weighted sample size is the actual population size.

Table 5.1. Sample Size

	1987–88		1993–94		1999–2000	
	Actual	Weighted	Actual	Weighted	Actual	Weighted
All	40,593	2,323,204	47,105	2,561,294	42,086	2,984,782
Elementary	18,728	1,254,290	16,030	1,331,281	14,322	1,591,454
Secondary	21,865	1,068,914	31,075	1,230,013	27,764	1,393,328

The samples in the study have the following characteristics. First, through the process of weighting, the samples are nationally representative. Therefore, the findings reported in the following are nationally representative and applicable to the American public school teaching force and its subgroups such as the elementary or secondary public school teaching force. Second, there are three waves of nationally representative samples of public school teachers. Therefore, a particular kind of longitudinal study called "trend study" can be conducted. The trend study is very powerful at pinpointing whether the equity issue has exacerbated, remained the same, or lessened. The data offer us a rare opportunity to study whether schools with high levels of minority enrollment are more likely to have less qualified teachers.

The data reported in the study were relatively weighted. Through relative weights, we were able to not only approximate the population but also keep the achieved sample size. The teacher surveys provided weights to approximate the national populations. We calculated relative weights for all three waves of surveys. The relative weight was calculated by the following formula:

$$\text{relative weight} = \frac{\text{teacher final weight} \times \text{sample size}}{\text{sum of the teacher final weight}}$$

Findings

Teacher Certification Status and Minority Student Enrollment Level

The distribution of certified or uncertified teachers in their main teaching assignment across schools with various levels of minority enrollment: A cross-sectional perspective based on data collected in 1999–2000

In Tables 5.2, 5.3, and 5.4, we displayed cross-sectional data related to the distribution of certified or uncertified teachers in their main teaching assignment across schools with various levels of minority enrollment in 1999–2000. The data indicated that schools with more minority students had a higher percentage of teachers who did not have a certificate in their main teaching assignment. For example, the data in Table 5.2 revealed that in schools where 0–4% or 5–19% of the students were minority, 4.3% and 3.7% of the teachers, respectively, were not certified in their main teaching assignment. However, in schools where 50% or more of the students were minority, 8.3% of the teachers were not certified in their main teaching field. The difference was statistically significant. The same pattern could be found for both elementary and secondary teachers (Tables 5.3 and 5.4). Among secondary teachers who taught in schools where 50% or more of the students were minority, as high as 9.9% were not certified in their main teaching field.

Table 5.2. Distribution of All Certified or Uncertified Teachers in Their Main Teaching Assignment across Schools with Various Levels of Minority Enrollment in 1999–2000*

Having State Certification	Minority Enrollment Percentage			
	0–4	5–19	20–49	50 or more
Yes	95.7	96.3	94.4	91.7
No	4.3	3.7	5.6	8.3

*$\chi^2(3) = 265.1, p < .001$, Cramer's $V = .08$.

Table 5.3. Distribution of Certified or Uncertified Elementary Teachers in Their Main Teaching Assignment across Schools with Various Levels of Minority Enrollment in 1999–2000*

Having State Certification	Minority Enrollment Percentage			
	0–4	5–19	20–49	50 or more
Yes	96.8	97.3	96.3	92.8
No	3.2	2.7	3.7	7.2

*$\chi^2(3) = 184.7, p < .001$, Cramer's $V = .09$.

Table 5.4. Distribution of Certified or Uncertified Secondary Teachers in Their Main Teaching Assignment across Schools with Various Levels of Minority Enrollment in 1999–2000*

Having State Certification	Minority Enrollment Percentage			
	0–4	5–19	20–49	50 or more
Yes	94.6	95.2	92.3	90.1
No	5.4	4.8	7.7	9.9

*$\chi^2(3) = 129.2, p < .001$, Cramer's $V = .08$.

Chapter Five

The distribution of certified or uncertified teachers in their main teaching assignment across schools with various levels of minority enrollment: A longitudinal perspective based on data collected in 1987–88, 1993–94, and 1999–2000

Charts 5.1, 5.2, and 5.3 display statistics related to the trend of the percentage of certified or uncertified teachers in their main teaching assignment for schools with various levels of minority enrollment. The data in Chart 5.1 indicates two patterns of uncertified teachers when all teachers were considered. First, the phenomenon of teachers uncertified in their main teaching field became worse over the years. When all teachers were considered, the percentage of teachers who were uncertified in their main teaching assignment increased from 2.7% in 1987–88, to 3.5% in 1993–94, and to 5.6% in 1999–2000. Second, over the years, schools where more than 50% of the students were minorities had consistently higher percentages of teachers who were uncertified than did schools with lower levels of minority enrollment. In schools where more than 50% of the students were minority, the percentages of teachers who were uncertified in their main teaching field increased from 5.0% in 1997, to 5.9% in 1993–94, and to 8.3% in 1999–2000. Essentially, the same patterns existed when we disaggregated data for elementary and secondary teachers (Charts 5.2 and 5.3).

Chart 5.1. The Trend in the Percentage of *All Teachers* Who Were Uncertified in Their Main Teaching Assignment in Schools with Various Levels of Minority Enrollment

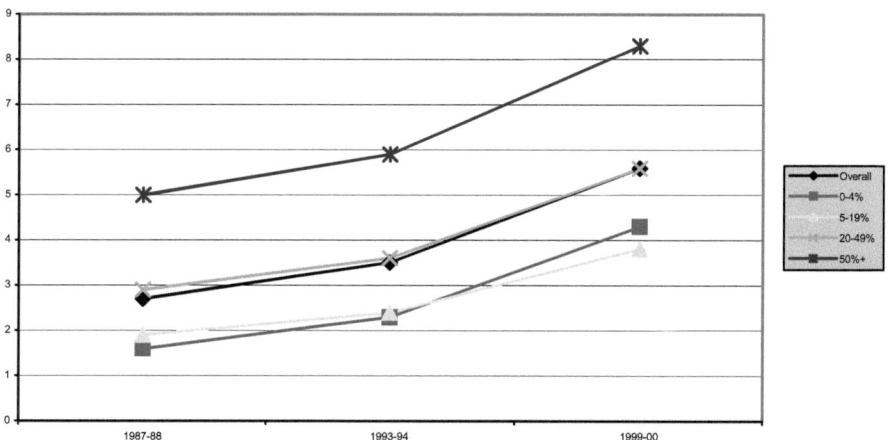

Chart 5.2. The Trend in the Percentage of *Elementary Teachers* Who Were Uncertified in Their Main Teaching Assignment in Schools with Various Levels of Minority Enrollment

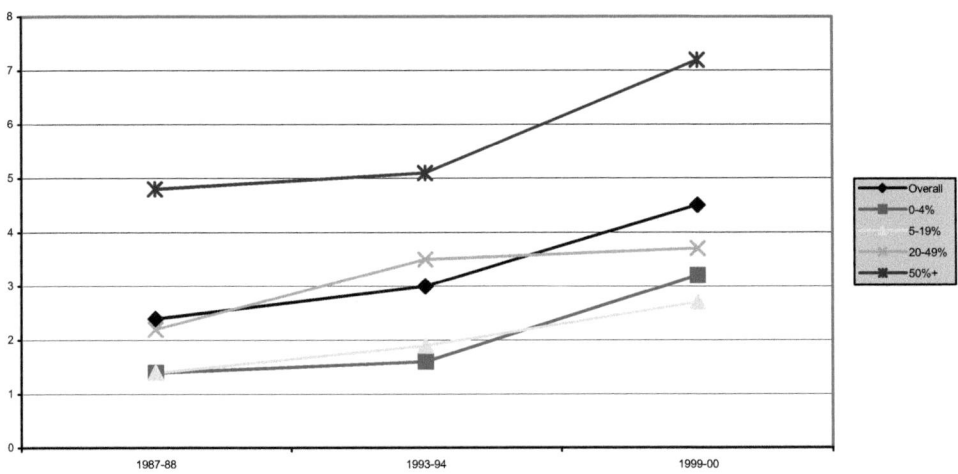

Chart 5.3. The Trend in the Percentage of *Secondary Teachers* Who Were Uncertified in Their Main Teaching Assignment in Schools with Various Levels of Minority Enrollment

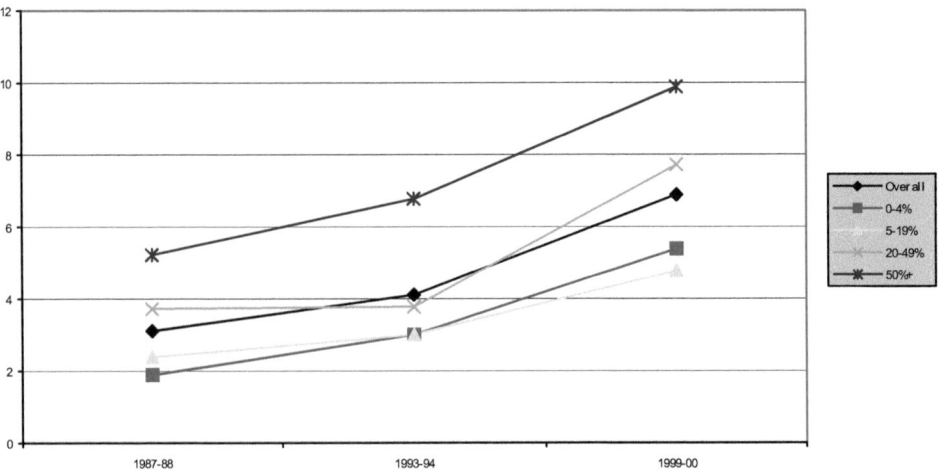

Teachers' Level of Certification and Schools' Minority Student Enrollment Level

In the foregoing section, we inquired into the relationship between whether teachers were certified and the type of schools where they taught. Whether or not a teacher was certified in the main teaching field is important. However, the level of certification a teacher has is perhaps more important because the levels of certification could include (a) advanced, regular, standard; (b) probationary; (c) provisional; (d) temporary; and (e) emergency. Obviously, the quality of an advanced certificate is certainly different from that of an emergency one. In this section, we inquire into the relation between teachers' level of certification and schools' minority student enrollment level.

The distribution of teachers with different levels of certification in their main teaching assignments across schools with various levels of minority enrollment: A cross-sectional perspective based on data collected in 1999–2000

The data are presented in Tables 5.5, 5.6, and 5.7. The data seem to reveal an inequitable distribution of teacher quality across schools with various levels of minority enrollment. In comparison to other schools, schools where 50% or more of the students were minorities had the highest percentage of teachers who had temporary or emergency certificates (3.4%) and had a lower percentage of teachers who have advanced, regular, or standard certificates (90.2%) (Table 5.5). Essentially, the same pattern held when we disaggregated data for elementary and secondary teachers, with the pattern being more prominent at the elementary level than at the secondary level (Tables 5.6 and 5.7).

Table 5.5. Distribution of All Teachers with Various Types of Certification in Their Main Teaching Assignment across Schools with Various Levels of Minority Enrollment in 1999–2000*

Type of certification	Minority Enrollment Percentage			
	0–4	5–19	20–49	50 or more
Advanced, regular, or standard	91.8	92.7	93.3	90.2
Probationary	2.9	3.2	2.8	2.7
Provisional	4.4	3.2	2.2	3.7
Temporary	0.7	0.7	1.3	1.6
Emergency	0.1	0.2	0.4	1.8

*$\chi^2(12) = 430.0, p < .001$, Cramer's $V = .07$.

Table 5.6. Distribution of Elementary Teachers with Various Types of Certification in Their Main Teaching Assignment across Schools with Various Levels of Minority Enrollment in 1999–2000*

Type of certification	Minority Enrollment Percentage			
	0–4	5–19	20–49	50 or more
Advanced, regular, or standard	92.9	93.7	93.6	89.4
Probationary	2.1	2.7	3.0	2.8
Provisional	4.5	3.1	2.1	4.2
Temporary	0.4	0.6	1.1	1.7
Emergency	0.1	0.0	0.3	1.9

*$\chi^2(12) = 344.0, p < .001$, Cramer's $V = .07$.

Table 5.7. Distribution of Secondary Teachers with Various Types of Certification in Their Main Teaching Assignment across Schools with Various Levels of Minority Enrollment in 1999–2000*

Type of certification	Minority Enrollment Percentage			
	0–4	5–19	20–49	50 or more
Advanced, regular, or standard	90.7	91.7	93.0	91.2
Probationary	3.8	3.7	2.6	2.7
Provisional	4.4	3.3	2.3	3.0
Temporary	1.0	0.9	1.6	1.5
Emergency	0.2	0.3	0.5	1.6

*$\chi^2(12) = 140.2, p < .001$, Cramer's $V = .05$.

The distribution of teachers with different levels of certification in their main teaching assignments across schools with various levels of minority enrollment: A longitudinal perspective based on data collected in 1987–88 and 1999–2000

The data were displayed in Charts 5.4, 5.5, and 5.6. Before discussing the patterns, a note should be made regarding the typology of certificate in the 1987–88, 1993–94, and 1999–2000 teacher surveys. The three surveys used the following typologies for teaching certificate:

1987–88	1993–94	1999–2000
Regular or standard state certification	Advanced professional certificate	Regular or standard state certificate or advanced professional certificate
Probationary certification	Regular or standard state certificate	Probationary certificate
Temporary, provisional, or emergency certification	The certificate offered in your state to persons who *have completed* what the state calls an "alternative certification program"	Provisional or other type given to persons who are still participating in what the state calls an "alternative certificate program"
	Provisional or other type given to persons who are still participating in what the state calls an "alternative certification program"	Temporary certificate
	Probationary certificate	Emergency certificate or waiver
	Temporary certificate	
	Emergency or waiver	

It is clear that the typology in 1993–94 was slightly different from those in 1987–88 and 1999–2000. However, the ones in 1987–88 and 1999–2000 were similar although the typology of 1999–2000 appeared to have more categories. Since those having advanced professional certificates must have regular or standard certificates and since the last three categories in the 1999–2000 typology could be combined into the third category in the 1987–88 typology, it is reasonable to assume the validity of comparison between 1987–88 and 1999–2000 when we used the following three categories: (1) advanced, regular, or standard; (2) probationary; and (3) temporary, provisional, emergency, and waiver.

The data in Chart 5.4 (where the category was all teachers) reveals the following patterns. First, in both 1987–88 and 1999–2000 school years, in comparison to other schools, schools where minority enrollment constituted more than 50% of the student enrollment had the highest percentages of teachers who were at the lower end of the certification typologies such as "temporary, provisional, emergency, or waiver." During 1987–88, in schools where minority enrollment was 50% or higher, as high as 5.8% of the teachers had "temporary, provisional, emergency, or waiver" certificates. The corresponding percentage was 7.1% in 1999–2000.

Second, when we compared the data collected in 1987–88 and 1999–2000, it appeared that the quality of teachers, as indicated by the type of certification teachers had, worsened in schools where 50% or more of the students were minority. Between 1987–88 and 1999–2000, in schools where minority students were the majority, the percentages of teachers who had "advanced, regular, or standard" certificates decreased from 91.4% to 90.2% and that for those who had "temporary, provisional, emergency, or waiver" certificates increased from 5.8% to 7.1%. In contrast, in other types of schools, the situation essentially remained the same or even improved slightly.

When we disaggregated the data for elementary and secondary teachers, the following two patterns were also true (Charts 5.5 and 5.6). Moreover, the patterns were clearer at the elementary level than at the secondary one.

Chart 5.4. The Trend in the Percentage of *All Teachers* Who Had Temporary, Provisional, Emergency, and Waiver Certification in Their Main Teaching Assignments in Schools with Various Levels of Minority Enrollment

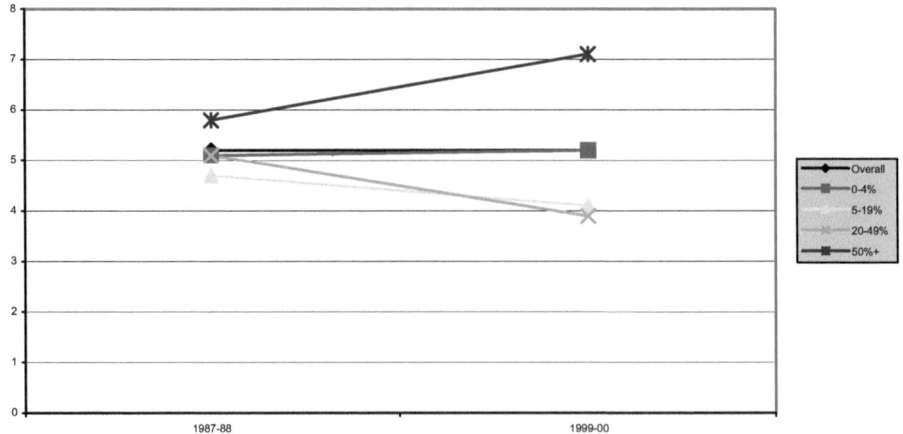

Chart 5.5. The Trend in the Percentage of *Elementary Teachers* Who Had Temporary, Provisional, Emergency, and Waiver Certification in Their Main Teaching Assignments in Schools with Various Levels of Minority Enrollment

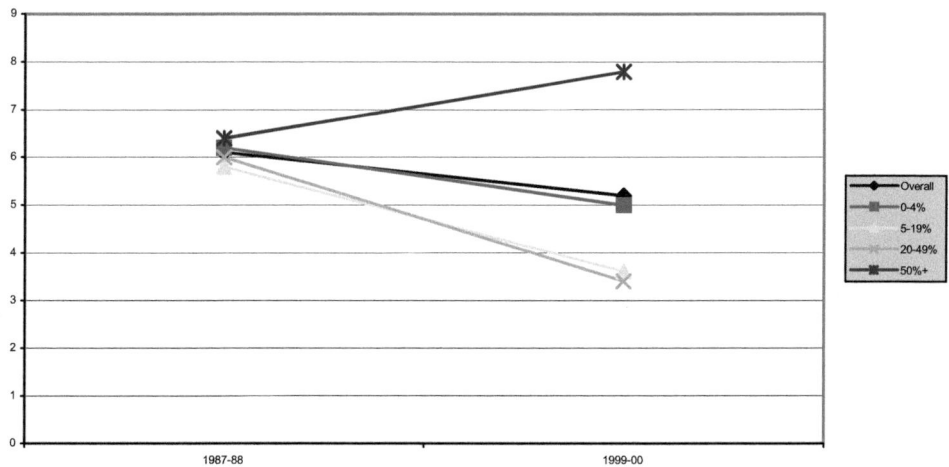

Chart 5.6. The Trend in the Percentage of *Secondary Teachers* Who Had Temporary, Provisional, Emergency, and Waiver Certification in Their Main Teaching Assignments in Schools with Various Levels of Minority Enrollment

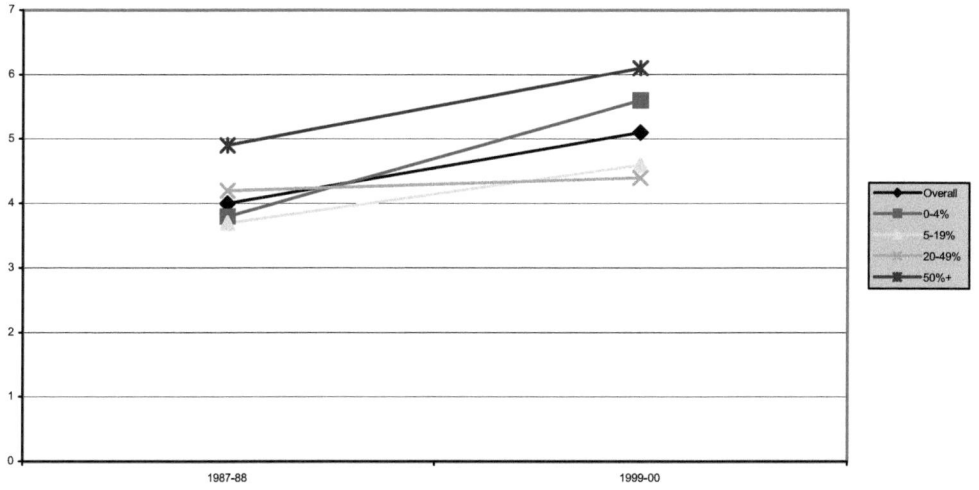

Summary

Using the nationally representative data collected during SASS over a 12-year period, we inquired into the relationship between level of minority enrollment and teacher qualification. We were interested in knowing whether schools with a high level of minority enrollment had an equitable share of quality teachers.

We operationalized teacher quality from two perspectives—(1) whether a teacher had a certificate in the primary teaching assignment, and (2) the type of certification that a teacher had in her/his primary teaching assignment. We analyzed data from both cross-sectional and longitudinal perspectives. The major finding was that in comparison to other schools, schools with the highest level of minority enrollment, that is, those where 50% or more of the enrollment were minority, were and continued to be disadvantaged in terms of having a fair share of quality teachers.

Cross-sectionally, when we analyzed the most recent data collected in 1999–2000, schools where 50% or more of the enrollment were minority had (a) the highest rate of teachers who were not certified in their primary teaching fields, and (b) the highest rate of teachers who had low levels of certification (i.e., temporary and emergency). The following is a summary of the statistics.

Table 5.8. A Summary of Statistics on Teacher Quality

Dimensions of Teacher Quality	Minority Enrollment Percentage			
	0–4	5–19	20–49	50 or more
Percentage of uncertified teachers in the primary teaching field	4.3	3.7	5.6	8.3
Percentage of teachers having temporary or emergency certificates	0.8	0.9	1.7	3.4

Longitudinally, when we analyzed data collected in 1987–89, 1993–95, and 1999–2000, schools where 50% or more of the enrollment were minority had the lowest teacher quality as variously shown in this report. For example, among all teachers, the percentage of teachers who were uncertified in their primary teaching assignment increased from 2.7% in 1987–88, to 3.5% in 1993–94, and to 5.6% in 1999–2000. The situation was much worse in schools where 50% or more of the enrollment were minority. The percentages increased from 5.0% in 1987–88, to 5.9% in 1993–94, and to 8.3% in 1999–2000 (Chart 5.1).

Furthermore, the inequity among schools with various levels of minority enrollment had become worse when some measures were considered. For example, where percentage of teachers who had temporary, provisional, emergency, and waiver certificates in their primary teaching field was concerned, among all teachers, the percentage remained at 5.2% in 1987–88 and in 1999–2000. However, the corresponding statistics for those in schools where 50% or more of the students were minority increased from 5.8% in 1987–88 to 7.1% in 1999–2000 (Chart 5.4).

The data clearly indicated that schools with higher levels of minority enrollment were and continued to be disadvantaged in terms of having quality teachers. Many minority students have already been disadvantaged due to family circumstances. Characteristics related to the teaching force in these schools continue to put the children in a more disadvantaged position. An equitable distribution of quality teachers is indeed a serious policy challenge.

References

Ansell, S. E., & McCabe, M. (2003, January 9). Off target. *Education Week*, Retrieved May 20, 2005, from http://counts.edweek.org/sreports/qc03/templates/article.cfm?slug=17target.h22.

Chaney, B. (1995, May). *Student outcomes and the professional preparation of eighth-grade teachers in science and mathematics.* Unpublished manuscript. Prepared for NSF Grant RED-9255255. Rockville, MD: Westat.

Darling-Hammond, L. (2000). Teacher quality and student achievement: A review of state policy evidence. *Educational Policy Analysis Archives, 8* (1). Retrieved January 30, 2004, from http://epaa.asu.edu/epaa/v8n1.

Darling-Hammond, L., Berry, B., & Thoreson, A. (2001). Does teacher certification matter? Evaluating the evidence. *Educational Evaluation and Policy Analysis, 23* (1), 57–77.

Evertson, C., Hawley, W., & Zlotnick, M. (1985). Making a difference in educational quality through teacher education. *Journal of Teacher Education, 36* (3), 2–12.

Ferguson, P., & Womack, S. T. (1993). The impact of subject matter and education coursework on teaching performance. *Journal of Teacher Education, 44* (1), 55–63.

Ferguson, R. F. (1991). Paying for public education: New evidence on how and why money matters. *Harvard Journal on Legislation, 28* (2), 465–498.

Fuller, E. J. (1999). *Does teacher certification matter? A comparison of TAAS performance in 1997 between schools with low and high percentages of certified teachers.* Austin: Charles A. Dana Center, University of Texas at Austin.

Goldhaber, D., & Brewer, D. (1998). When should we reward degrees for teachers? *Phi Delta Kappan, 80* (2), 134–138.

Goldhaber, D., & Brewer, D. (2000). Does teacher certification matter? High school certification status and student achievement. *Educational Evaluation and Policy Analysis, 22*(2), 129–145.

Hawk, P. P., Coble, C. R., & Swanson, M. (1985). Certification: It does matter. *Journal of Teacher Education, 36*(3), 13–15.

Laczko-Kerr, I., & Berliner, D. C. (2002, September 6). The effectiveness of "Teach for America" and other under-certified teachers on student academic achievement: A case of harmful public policy. *Education Policy Analysis Achieves, 10* (37). Retrieved February 13, 2004 from http://epaa.asu.edu/epaa/v10n37/.

Lu, X., Shen, J., & Poppink, S. (2007). Are teachers qualified? A national study of secondary public school teachers using SASS 1999–2000. *School Leadership and Policy, 6* (2), 129–152.

Monk, D. H. (1994). Subject area preparation and secondary mathematics and science teachers and student achievement. *Economics of Education Review, 13* (2), 125–45.

Monk, D. H., & King, J. A. (1994). Multilevel teacher resource effects on pupil performance in secondary mathematics and science: The case of teacher subject matter preparation. In E. G. Ehrenberg (Ed.), *Choices and consequences: Contemporary policy issues in education* (pp. 29–58). Ithaca, NY: ILR Press.

Nye, B., Konstantopoulos, S., & Hedges, L. V. (2004). How large are teacher effects? *Educational Evaluation and Policy Analysis, 26* (3), 237–257.

Olson, L. (2003). Quality counts reveals national "teacher gap". *Education Week 22* (16), 10.

Rowan, B., Chiang, F., & Miller, R. J. (1997). Using research on employees' performance to study the effects of teachers on students' achievement. *Sociology of Education, 70* (4), 256–284.

Sanders, W., & Rivers, J. (1996). *Cumulative and residual effects of teachers on future student academic achievement.* Knoxville: University of Tennessee, Value-Added Research and Assessment Center.

Shen, J., & Poppink, S. (2003). The certification characteristics of the public school teaching force: National, longitudinal and comparative perspectives. *Educational Horizons, 81*(3), 130–137.

Shen, J., Mansberger, N., & Yang, H. (2004). Teacher quality and students placed at risks: Results from the Baccalaureate and Beyond longitudinal study 1993–97. *Educational Horizons, 82* (3), 226–235.

Weglinsky, H. (2000). *How teaching matters. Bringing the classroom back into discussions of teacher quality. A policy information center report.* Princeton, NJ: Milken Family Foundation and Educational Testing Service.

Wilson, S. M., Floden, R. E., Ferrini-Mundy, J. (2001). *Teacher preparation research: Current knowledge, gaps, and recommendations.* Seattle, WA: University of Washington, Center for the Study of Teaching and Policy.

SECTION 3

Alternative Certification

CHAPTER SIX

Has the Alternative Certification Policy Materialized Its Promise?
A Comparison between Traditionally and Alternatively Certified Teachers in Public Schools[1]

Jianping Shen

The number of states allowing alternative certification increased from 18 in 1986 to 50 in 2008. It is estimated that in 2005–06 alone, 59,000 certificates were issued via the alternative routes to teaching (Feistritzer, 1993; Feistritzer & Chester, 1996, 2008). However, there has been a continuing debate on this alternative to traditional university-based teacher education. Proponents argue that the alternative route to teaching will improve the teaching force by reducing teacher shortage, raising teacher quality, and diversifying the teaching force, while opponents maintain that the alternative certification policy degrades the professional status of teaching and ultimately hinders student learning. This chapter, by comparing the characteristics of traditionally certified (TC) and alternatively certified (AC) teachers in public schools, inquires into whether the alternative certification policy has fulfilled its promise.

Literature Review

The arguments for AC are multifaceted. First, as summarized by Stoddart and Floden (1995), there has been a shortage of qualified teachers in urban schools and in subject areas such as mathematics and science; therefore, AC should be employed to alleviate the shortage. Second, it has been argued that good teaching is based primarily on subject matter knowledge and an enthusiasm for teaching. Hence, opportunities should be provided to those people who are competent in subject matter knowledge and interested in teaching but would not otherwise have the opportunity to go into teaching (Kearns, 1990; Kerr, 1983; Kramer, 1991). Third, it has been argued that AC teachers are older, more likely to come from minority groups, and more likely to have worked in other jobs than the traditional teacher education population. Therefore, the teaching force can be diversified through AC policy (Cornett, 1990; Kirby, Darling-Hammond, & Hudson, 1989; Stoddard, 1990). This is particularly true for urban schools (Stoddart, 1993; Natriello & Zumwalt, 1993). Finally, it has been argued that the traditional university-based teacher education has monopolized preparation of teachers, and AC introduces competition into this area (Bliss, 1990; Cornett, 1990; Fenstermacher, 1990).

The arguments against AC are also multifaceted. First, it has been argued that AC lowers the cost of entering teaching and degrades the professional status of teaching (Darling-Hammond, 1990; Kirby, Darling-Hammond, & Hudson, 1989). Ultimately, students—particularly those disadvantaged students in inner-city schools where teacher shortage occurs more frequently—are hurt by AC policy (Darling-Hammond, 1990, 1994). Second, the assumption that AC teachers know the subject matter and can learn to teach by working on the job has been questioned (Feiman-Nemser & Buchman, 1987; Kennedy, 1991; Zeichner, 1986). Research suggests that pedagogical content knowledge plays a very important role in teaching, and that teachers without teacher education or certified alternatively have more difficulties learning to teach than those certified traditionally (Darling-Hammond, 1990; Grossman, 1989a, b; McDiarmid & Wilson, 1991; Shulman, 1987; Wilson, Shulman, & Richert, 1987). Third, it has been argued that AC policy fails to deliver on the promise of bringing into teaching those who have higher academic qualifications (Natriello et al., 1990).

There are limitations in the existing studies on AC policy. First, data sources have been limited to a school district (Stoddart, 1990), a state (Bliss, 1990; Hutton, Lutz, & Williamson, 1990; Lutz & Hutton, 1989; Natriello & Zumwalt, 1993), several states (Cornett, 1990), several programs (Kirby, Darling-Hammond, & Hudson, 1989), or a combination of several school districts and states (Zumwalt, 1991). Therefore, it has not been possible to generalize findings to the national scene. Second, most empirical studies of AC policy collected data in the mid-1980s. Given the history of AC policy, these studies were not able to explore the impact of AC policy on the public teaching force. Finally, previous studies were preoccupied with curricular characteristics of AC programs; sociological aspects of AC policy, such as the differences between AC and TC teachers, were largely ignored. The current study was conducted to overcome some of these limitations and to contribute to the knowledge of AC policy.

Chapter Six

The Focus of This Chapter

The current chapter inquires into whether AC policy has fulfilled its promise by comparing the characteristics of TC and AC teachers in public schools. Data for the chapter were collected during the Schools and Staffing Survey 1993–94 (SASS93), a national survey of school teachers, among others, conducted by the National Center for Education Statistics in the 1993–94 academic year.

Consistent with the purpose of the current chapter, the following questions were posed: What percentage of the public teaching force were AC teachers? Did TC and AC teachers differ in demographics, work experience, academic qualification, career pattern, and what and where they taught? Because of the comprehensiveness of the data of SASS93, TC and AC teachers were compared along the following dimensions: gender, race, and ethnicity; age; main activity the year before entering teaching; degree earned; subject specialization for bachelor's degree; what and where they taught; intention to become teachers if starting over again; and plans to remain in teaching. By inquiring into a wide range of issues, the chapter is able to comprehensively examine policy implications of TC and AC practices.

Methods

Sample

SASS93 had a nationally representative sample, and the achieved sample size was 47,105 (weighted $N = 2,561,294$). Because AC policy has been in place on a large scale primarily for the last decade, the chapter focuses only on those teachers who were certified in the last ten years. Otherwise, the sample would be overrepresented by TC teachers, hindering the detection of AC policy effect.

TC teachers in the study were those who indicated in the survey that they had the advanced professional certificate or the regular/standard state certificate, while AC teachers were those who had the certificate through, as it was phrased in the questionnaire, "what the state calls an 'alternative certificate program.'" As a result of constructing a subsample from SASS93, the relative weighted sample for the study was 14,721, including 13,602 TC teachers and 1,119 AC teachers (weighted $N = 800,412$).

Weighting

Because the sample design of SASS93 involved stratification, disproportionate sampling of certain strata, and clustered probability sampling, the resultant SASS93 sample was not a random sample. Therefore, a relative sample weight, which was based on SASS93 teachers' final weight, was used not only to approximate the population but also to adjust it down to the actual sample size of the study. Thus, the findings of the study are generalizable to public school teachers who were certified in the last ten years.

Analysis Methods

The purpose of the chapter is to inquire into a wide range of issues related to TC and AC teachers and then to draw policy implications. Therefore, this chapter is more policy- than theory-oriented. In the analyses of the study, descriptive statistics were extensively used.

Results

Demographics

Gender
Among 13,602 TC teachers, 23.7% were male and 76.3% female. As to 1,119 AC teachers, 25.7% were male and 74.3% female. There was little difference[2] between TC and AC teachers in their gender composition: $\chi^2 (1) = 2.18, p = .13$.

Race and ethnicity
There was a difference between TC and AC teachers in their race and ethnicity background. Among TC teachers, 87.2% were white and 12.8% non-white, a category that included American Indian/Alaska Native, Asian or Pacific Islander, Black, and Hispanic. However, among AC teachers, 79.3% were white and 20.7% non-white. There was a higher percentage of non-white teachers among AC teachers than among TC teachers: $\chi^2 (1) = 55.02, p < .001$. The data indicated that AC policy did allow recruitment of a higher percentage of minority teachers into the public teaching force.

Age
The distribution of TC and AC teachers across four age ranges is displayed in Table 6.1. There was a higher percentage of those less than 30 years of age among AC teachers than among TC teachers, while the percentage of teachers 50 or older was higher for TC teachers than for AC teachers. It

seems that a higher percentage of young teachers were certified through AC than through TC, and AC policy did not bring more older people into the public teaching force.

Table 6.1. Distribution of TC and AC Teachers in Relation to Respondents' Age

Age	TC Teacher (%)	AC Teacher (%)
Less than 30 years	28.1	33.4
30–39	35.7	34.7
40–49	27.5	27.4
50 or more	8.7	4.5
Total	100	100

Note: $\chi^2(3) = 32.48, p < .001$.

Work Experience and Professional Preparation

Main activities before entering teaching

Table 6.2 displays data on "What was your main activity the year before you began teaching at the elementary or secondary level?" A higher percentage of TC teachers (68.7%) than AC teachers (51.0%) were studying at college. However, the percentage of those holding teaching- or education-related positions (23.8%) and outside-of-education jobs (22.2%) was higher among AC teachers than among TC teachers (16.5% and 11.2%, respectively). Given the definitions of TC and AC, these findings were not unanticipated because it was expected that AC teachers would include a higher percentage of people holding positions in fields other than education. However, the surprise was that among AC teachers, 51.0% came right out of college, another 23.8% already held teaching- or education-related positions, and only 22.2% came from occupations other than education. This suggests that AC policy brought some experienced people into teaching but at the same time allowed many fresh college graduates to circumvent the TC process.

Table 6.2. Distribution of TC and AC Teachers in Relation to Main Activities the Year Before Entering Teaching

Main Activity	TC Teacher (%)	AC Teacher (%)
Student at a college or university	68.7	51.0
Teaching- or education-related positions	16.5	23.8
Positions outside of education	11.2	22.2
Caring for family members, unemployed, or retired	3.6	3.0
Total	100	100

Note: $\chi^2(3) = 185.89, p < .001$.

Degrees earned
The percentage of those who had a bachelor's degree was higher among TC teachers (99.0%) than among AC teachers (96.7%): $\chi^2(1) = 46.29$, $p < .001$. It appears that as far as possessing bachelor's degree was concerned, AC teachers had lower academic qualifications. Another way to compare the educational attainment by TC and AC teachers was to examine the highest degree that they earned. The data in Table 6.3 demonstrate that as far as earned highest degrees were concerned, TC teachers had higher educational attainment than did AC teachers. The percentage of those who had a master's degree was lower among AC teachers (22.2%) than among TC teachers (31.8%). However, the fact that AC teachers were younger might be a factor here. It is particularly disturbing to note that 2.4% of AC teachers had no degrees at all. The data on both bachelor's degree and highest degree suggested that AC failed to attract personnel with higher academic qualifications.

Table 6.3. Distribution of TC and AC Teachers in Relation to Highest Degree Earned

Highest Degree Earned	TC Teacher (%)	AC Teacher (%)
No degree earned	0.06	2.4
Associate or bachelor's degree	63.8	71.3
Master's degree	31.8	22.2
Doctorate	3.9	4.1
Total	100	100

Note: $\chi^2(3) = 84.67, p < .001$.

Subject specialization
As illustrated in the literature review, one of the objectives of AC was to overcome the shortage of mathematics and science teachers. This seems to be supported by the data on subject specialization of the respondents' bachelor's degrees. There was a higher percentage of teachers with a bachelor's degree in mathematics, science, or engineering among AC teachers (6.5%) than among TC teachers (5.4%): $\chi^2(1) = 9.15, p < .005$.

Where and What TC and AC Teachers Taught

School level
Among TC teachers, 54.6% were in elementary schools and 45.4% in secondary schools, whereas 47.9% of AC teachers were in elementary schools and 52.1% in secondary schools: $\chi^2(1) = 18.81, p < .001$. There was a higher percentage of AC teachers in secondary schools.

Locale

The distribution of AC and TC teachers in relation to locale is displayed in Table 6.4. A higher percentage of AC teachers (20.9%) than TC teachers (10.6%) worked in large central cities where teacher shortage was severe and teacher attrition rates high.

Table 6.4. Distribution of AC and TC Teachers in Relation to Locale

Locale	TC Teacher (%)	AC Teacher (%)
Large central city	10.6	20.9
Midsize central city	17.1	15.9
Large city urban fringe	16.5	12.6
Midsize city urban fringe	11.1	9.0
Large town	2.8	1.0
Small town	21.6	21.9
Rural	20.3	18.7
Total	100	100

Note: $\chi^2(6) = 126.80, p < .001$.

Schools where AC and TC teachers taught

Since there is a higher percentage of minority students in large central cities, given the findings in the previous paragraph, it can be hypothesized that a higher percentage of AC teachers work in schools where there is a high percentage of minority students. This hypothesis was supported by the data of the study (Table 6.5). A higher percentage of AC teachers (37.8%) than TC teachers (26.8%) worked in schools where 50–100% of the students were minority.

Table 6.5. Distribution of TC and AC Teachers in Relation to Schools with Different Percentages of Minority Students

Minority Students in Schools (%)	TC Teacher (%)	AC Teacher (%)
0–4	24.0	23.2
5–19	25.3	24.0
20–49	23.9	15.0
50–100	26.8	37.8
Total	100	100

Note: $\chi^2(3) = 75.20, p < .001$.

Subjects taught

The percentage of those who taught mathematics or science in elementary and secondary schools was higher among AC teachers (19.2%) than among TC teachers (13.5%): $\chi^2(1) = 28.49, p < .001$. AC policy seems to channel more mathematics and science teachers into the public teaching force.

Career Pattern

Becoming a teacher again

The respondents were asked "If you could go back to your college days and start over again, would you become a teacher or not?", and they indicated their answers by using a scale ranging from 1 (certainly would become a teacher) to 5 (certainly would not become a teacher). The means for TC and AC teachers were 2.057 and 2.062, respectively, $t(14718) = 0.14, p = .89$. Therefore, there was no difference between AC and TC teachers when they rethought their plans to become teachers in retrospect. But, as will be illustrated in the next paragraph, this was not the case with their plan to remain in teaching.

How long they planned to remain in teaching

As shown in Table 6.6, there was a difference between TC and AC teachers in their plan to remain in teaching. The differences between TC and AC teachers occurred primarily in the categories of "until I am eligible for retirement" and "undecided at this time." A lower percentage of AC teachers (19.7%) than of TC teachers (22.7%) chose "until I am eligible for retirement," but a higher percentage of AC teachers (26.0%) than of TC teachers (22.3%) responded "undecided at this time." These findings question AC teachers' intention to treat teaching as a lifelong career.

Table 6.6. Distribution of TC and AC Teachers in Relation to Their Plan to Remain in Teaching

Plan to Remain in Teaching (%)	TC Teacher (%)	AC Teacher (%)
As long as I am able	37.6	37.3
Until I am eligible for retirement	22.7	19.7
Will probably continue unless something better comes	13.7	13.6
Definitely plan to leave teaching as soon as I can	3.7	3.4
Undecided at this time	22.3	26.0
Total	100	100

Note: $\chi^2(4) = 10.98, p < .05$.

Discussion

The data indicate that among public school teachers who were certified in the last ten years and were teaching in the 1993–94 school year, 7.5% were AC teachers. However, AC teachers were unevenly distributed across regions. For example, AC teachers constituted 14.0% of the public teaching force in the Northeast, 9.4% in the Midwest, and much lower in the South and the West. The data indicate that AC policy had a greater impact on the public teaching force in the Northeast and Midwest than in the South and West.

Some of the claims by proponents of AC policy are supported by the data. First, in comparison to TC teachers, a higher percentage of AC teachers had a bachelor's degree in mathematics, science, or engineering, and a higher percentage of AC teachers actually taught mathematics or science in public schools. AC policy appears to recruit more mathematics and science teachers into the public teaching force. Second, there was a higher percentage of minority teachers among AC teachers than among TC teachers. Thus, AC policy seems to contribute to diversity in the teaching force. Finally, in comparison to TC teachers, there was a higher percentage of AC teachers who worked in central large cities and in schools where minority students composed more than 50% of the student body. AC policy seems to contribute to alleviating the severity of the problem of teacher shortage in urban schools. However, as will be discussed later, alleviating the problem of teacher shortage through AC has its associated and inherent shortcomings.

Some findings of the study are inconsistent with AC proponents' arguments and raise some concerns regarding the impact of AC policy. First, although a high percentage of both AC and TC teachers had a bachelor's degree, AC teachers appeared to have lower academic qualifications than did TC teachers, a finding that is consistent with that of Natriello and his colleagues (1990). Among AC teachers in the study sample, 2.4% had no degrees at all.

Second, although AC policy attracted a higher percentage of people with experience in occupations other than teaching or education, 51% of AC teachers came directly from college and another 23.8% already held teaching- or education-related positions. This not only questions the degree to which AC policy has delivered on its promise to recruit experienced personnel from other occupations but also raises the concern of whether some fresh college graduates took advantage of AC policy to circumvent the traditional teacher education program.

Third, the percentage of those who treated teaching as a lifelong career was lower among AC teachers than among TC teachers. This was manifested in the comparison of AC to TC teachers, wherein it became clear that a lower percentage of AC teachers planned to teach until retirement while a higher percentage of them were undecided regarding their plan to remain in teaching. This finding is consistent with the human capital theory, as applied by Kirby and Grissmer (1993), which posits that individuals make a systematic assessment of benefits and costs of entering and staying in a profession. There are two types of human capital—general and specific. The greater the accumulation of specific human capital, the lower the probability of attrition. Since specific human capital tends to be a small amount when a person enters teaching through AC, AC teachers are more likely to leave teaching. Given the findings that there has already been a high teacher attrition rate in schools, particularly in urban schools (Corcoran, Walker, & White, 1988; Haberman, 1987; Shen, 1997), AC policy is likely to exacerbate teacher attrition. In the long run, the argument to alleviate teacher shortage through AC appears to be self-defeating.

Finally, given the findings that AC teachers had lower academic qualifications and that a lower percentage of AC teachers treated teaching as a lifelong career, AC policy might not be conducive to improving the conditions in inner-city schools where AC teachers concentrated. As Darling-Hammond (1990, p. 149) argued persuasively, "There are important issues of educational equity associated with the use of alternative certification as a policy response to teacher shortages in economically disadvantaged school districts. States may be avoiding costlier solutions at the expense of students who are already underserved."

Studies usually lead to questions for further inquiries. This study was not without its limitations that suggest a need for further research. The first limitation was largely due to the fact that the data were cross-sectional rather than longitudinal. Therefore, this study was not able to pinpoint the career pattern of AC and TC teachers over time; the possibly different career patterns of these teachers might have influenced the composition of the sample from which data for this study were derived. The second limitation was that alternative certification is a complex phenomenon, and the approach of the study was to compare AC and TC teachers without differentiating alternative certification programs, which vary from state to state and in many cases even within a state (Hawley, 1990; Stoddart & Floden, 1995; Zumwalt, 1991). Therefore, some alternative certification programs might be more effective than others. Finally, we must inquire into the teaching quality of AC and TC teachers, an aspect that the data of the study cannot address. Interpretation of the findings of this study should take these limitations into account. However, the limitations do not negate the findings. Rather, they point to directions for further study.

Who should be certified to teach this nation's children is a very important issue for the future of the teaching profession and ultimately for school quality and student learning. The findings of this study, based on a large, nationally representative sample of public school teachers, confirmed some of the arguments for AC policy but also raised some concerns.

Notes

1. The author is aware of Goodlad's (1989) argument that there should be distinctions between accreditation (for a program), certification (for successfully finishing the program), and licensing (for the privilege to join a profession). According to his definitions, *licensing* should replace *certification* in this chapter. However, in order to be consistent with the existing literature, the latter is used.
2. Since the sample size of the study was large, there was an issue of statistical significance versus practical significance. Therefore, the term "statistically significant" was not used and the test statistics were presented as heuristics (Sirotnik, 1982; Stevens, 1992).

References

Bliss, T. (1990). Alternate certification in Connecticut: Reshaping the profession. *Peabody Journal of Education, 67* (3), 35–54.

Corcoran, T. B., Walker, L. J., & White, J. L. (1988). *Working in urban schools.* Washington, DC: Institute for Educational Leadership.

Cornett, L. M. (1990). Alternate certification: State policies in the SREB states. *Peabody Journal of Education, 67* (3), 55–83.

Darling-Hammond, L. (1990). Teaching and knowledge: Policy issues posed by alternate certification for teachers. *Peabody Journal of Education, 67* (3), 123–154.

Darling-Hammond, L. (1994). Who will speak for the children? How "Teach for America" hurts urban schools and students. *Phi Delta Kappan, 76* (1), 21–34.

Feiman-Nemser, S., & Buchman, M. (1987). When is student teaching teacher education? *Teaching and Teacher Education, 3* (4), 255–273.

Feistritzer, C. E. (1993). National overview of alternative teacher certification. *Education and Urban Society, 26* (1), 18–28.

Feistritzer, C. E., & Chester, D. T. (1996). *Alternative teacher certification: A state-by-state analysis 1996*. Washington, DC: National Center for Education Information.

Feistritzer, C. E., & Chester, D. T. (2008). *Alternative teacher certification: A state-by-state analysis 2008*. Washington, DC: National Center for Education Information.

Fenstermacher, G.D. (1990). The place of alternate certificate in the education of teachers. *Peabody Journal of Education, 67* (3), 3–34.

Goodlad, J. I. (1989, October–November). Has the National Board got it right? *AACTE Briefs*, pp. 2, 8.

Grossman, P. L. (1989a). A study in contrast: Sources of pedagogical content knowledge for secondary English. *Journal of Teacher Education, 40* (5), 24–31.

Grossman, P. L. (1989b). Learning to teach without teacher education. *Teachers College Record, 91* (2), 191–208.

Haberman, M. (1987). *Recruiting and selecting teachers for urban schools*. New York: ERIC Clearing House on Urban Education (ERIC Document Reproduction Service No. ED 292 942).

Hawley, W. D. (1990). The theory and practice of alternative certification: Implications for the improvement of teaching. *Peabody Journal of Education, 67* (3), 3–34.

Hutton, J. B., Lutz, F. W., & Williamson, J. L. (1990). Characteristics, attitudes, and performance of alternative certification interns. *Educational Research Quarterly, 14* (1), 38–48.

Kearns, D. (1990, February 28). Do teachers really need licenses? *Wall Street Journal*, p. 14.

Kennedy, M. M. (1991). Some surprising findings on how teachers learn to teach. *Educational Leadership, 49* (3), 14–17.

Kerr, D. H. (1983). Teaching competency and teacher education in the United States. *Teachers College Record, 81* (3), 525–552.

Kirby, S. N., Darling-Hammond, L., & Hudson, L. (1989). Nontraditional recruits to mathematics and science teaching. *Educational Evaluation and Policy Analysis, 11* (3), 301–323.

Kirby, S. N., & Grissmer, D. W. (1993). *Teacher attrition: Theory, evidence, and suggested policy options*. Santa Monica, CA: Rand.

Kramer, R. (1991). *Ed school follies: The miseducation of America's teachers*. New York: Free Press.

Lutz, F. W., & Hutton, J. B. (1989). Alternative teacher certification: Its policy implications for classroom and personnel practice. *Educational Evaluation and Policy Analysis, 11* (3), 237–254.

McDiarmid, G. W., & Wilson, S. M. (1991). An exploration of the subject matter knowledge of alternate route teachers: Can we assume they know their subjects. *Journal of Teacher Education, 42* (2), 93–103.

Natriello, G., Hansen, A., Frisch, A., & Zumwalt, K. (1990). *Characteristics of entering teachers in New Jersey.* Unpublished manuscript. New York: Teachers College, Columbia University.

Natriello, G., & Zumwalt, K. (1993). New Teachers for urban schools? *Education and Urban Society, 26* (1), 49–62.

Shen, J. (1997). Teacher retention and attrition in public schools. *Journal of Educational Research 91* (2), 81–88.

Shulman, L. S. (1987). Knowledge and teaching: Foundations of the new reform. *Harvard Educational Review, 57* (1), 1–22.

Sirotnik, K. A. (1982). The contextual correlates of the relative expenditures of classroom time on instruction and behavior: An exploratory study of secondary schools and classes. *American Educational Research Journal, 19* (2), 275–292.

Stevens, J. (1992). *Applied multivariate statistics for the social sciences.* Hillsdale, NJ: L. Erlbaum Associates.

Stoddart, T. (1990). Los Angeles Unified School District Intern Program: Recruiting and preparing teachers for the urban context. *Peabody Journal of Education, 67* (3), 84–122.

Stoddart, T. (1993). Who is prepared to teach in urban schools? *Education and Urban Society, 26* (1), 29–48.

Stoddart, T., & Floden, R. E. (1995). *Traditional and alternative routes to teacher certification: Issues, assumptions, and misconceptions.* East Lansing, MI: National Center for Research on Teacher Learning.

Wilson, S. M., Shulman, L. S., & Richert, A. E. (1987). "150 different ways" of knowing: Representations of knowledge in teaching. In J. Calderhead (Ed.), *Exploring teachers' thinking* (pp. 104–124). Eastbourne, UK: Cassell.

Zeichner, K. (1986). The practicum as an occasion for learning to teach. *South Pacific Journal of Teacher Education, 14* (2), 11–28.

Zumwalt, K. (1991). Alternate routes to teaching: Three alternative approaches. *Journal of Teacher Education, 42* (2), 83–92.

CHAPTER SEVEN

Alternative Certification, Minority Teachers, and Urban Education

Jianping Shen

Introduction

Alternative certification has had a dramatic growth in the last 20 years. According to Feistritzer's (2008) survey, between 1986 and 2007 the number of states allowing alternative certification increased from 18 to 50. The number of teaching certificates issued via alternative routes increased from 275 in 1985–86 to 6,932 in 1995–96 and to 59,000 in 2005–06. The trajectory of the development of alternative certification programs continues to be steeply upward.

From the very beginning there has been a debate on the merit of alternative certification. Proponents of alternative certification argue that it will improve the teaching force by diversifying the workforce—attracting more male, minority, and mature people into teaching (e.g., Chesley, Wood, & Zepeda, 1997; Cornett, 1990; Edelfelt, 1994; Stoddart, 1990). Opponents suggest that alternative certification lowers the professional standard of entry into teaching and ultimately hinders student learning (e.g., Darling-Hammond, 1990, 1994; Kirby, Darling-Hammond, & Hudson, 1989). The body of literature on the impact of alternative certification continues to grow (e.g., Dill, 1996; Shen, 1997a). In terms of the issues of minority teacher and urban education, the empirical research on alternative certification suggests that by recruiting more minority teachers through alternative certification, the teaching force is being diversified—a phenomenon that is particularly obvious in urban schools (e.g., Stoddart, 1993; Natriello & Zumwalt, 1993). Thus alternative certification appears to reduce the teacher shortage in urban schools.

As far as the empirical research on alternative certification is concerned, one of the shortcomings of the current literature is that the scope of its data source is limited, and we do not know how alternative certification, minority teacher, and urban education are related at the national level. We know even less about the characteristics of minority teachers who are alternatively certified. By analyzing data collected during the

Schools and Staffing Survey 1993-94 (SASS93), this study first inquires into the link between alternative certification, minority teachers, and urban education and then compares the characteristics of alternatively certified (AC, also for alternative certification) minority teachers and those of traditionally certified (TC, also for traditional certification) and AC white teachers.

Methods

The data for the study are extracted from the Public School Teacher Questionnaire of SASS93, which is a large, national survey designed by the National Center for Education Statistics and carried out by the U.S. Bureau of the Census. SASS93 provides the first nationally representative sample to investigate the impact of AC policies on the public teaching force.

Because AC policies have been in place on a large scale primarily for the last decade, this study focuses only on those teachers who were certified in the ten years prior to the 1993-94 survey. TC teachers in this study are those who had the advanced professional certificate or the regular/standard state certificate, while AC teachers are those who had the certificate through, as it is phrased in the questionnaire, "what the state calls an 'alternative certificate program.'" Because the sample design of SASS93 involves clustered probability sampling, stratification, and disproportionate sampling of certain strata, the resultant SASS93 sample is not a random one. Therefore, a relative sample weight, based on SASS93 teachers' final weight, is used to approximate the population but is adjusted down to the actual sample size of the study. As a result, the relative weighted sample for this study includes 14,719 respondents—13,601 TC teachers and 1,118 AC teachers, with the weighted N being 800,412. Thus, the sample is nationally representative of public school teachers certified in the ten years prior to the 1993-94 survey, and the following findings are generalizable to the national scene.

The Link between AC, Minority Teacher, and Urban Education

In the sample of this study, among TC teachers 87% are white and 13% are minority.[1] In contrast, among AC teachers 79% are white and as many as 21% are minority. Therefore, AC recruits a significantly higher percentage[2] of minority teachers than does TC: $\chi^2(1) = 55, p < .001$. Table 7.1 (p.110) displays data on the distribution of four groups of teachers in relation to the type of community where they teach. It is interesting to note that a very high percentage of minority teachers, particularly AC minority, work in urban schools: 67% of TC minority teachers and 87% of AC minority teachers work in urban schools while the corresponding percentage for white teachers is about 40%. By the same token, TC minority teachers, particularly AC minority, are much less likely to work in suburban and rural areas than their white counterparts.

Since there is a higher percentage of minority students in urban schools, another angle from which to investigate the link among AC, minority teachers, and urban education is to inquire into the distribution of teachers in relation to the type of schools with a different percentage of minority students (Table 7.2, p. 110): 67% of TC minority teachers and 89% of AC minority teachers work in schools where minority students constitute 50–100% of the student body. In contrast, only 21% and 25% of the TC and AC white teachers, respectively, work in schools where 50–100% of the student body is minority. Thus, AC recruits a significantly higher percentage of minority teachers into schools where minority students are the majority.

The aforementioned results indicate a link among AC, minority teachers, and urban education at the national level. In comparison to TC, AC recruits a significantly higher percentage of minority teachers into urban schools where minority students constitute more than 50% of the student body. Then, the following questions arise: What is the impact of this link on urban education? Has urban education benefited from AC? The following addresses these questions by comparing the characteristics of four groups of teachers—TC white, TC minority, AC white, and AC minority.

Comparative Characteristics of the Four Groups of Teachers

Demographic Characteristics

Gender
The data in Table 7.3 (p.111) suggest that there is a higher percentage of females among AC minority teachers than among all three other groups. As many as 80% of those in the AC minority group are female. AC does not appear to recruit a higher percentage of minority males into teaching, but it does attract a higher percentage of white males.

Age
The distribution of the four groups of teachers in relation to age is displayed in Table 7.4 (p.111). AC policies appear to recruit a group of teach-

ers different from TC teachers. However, the effect of AC policies is differential for white and minority AC teachers. In comparison to TC, AC attracts a high percentage of white teachers who are less than 30 (36%), but a high percentage of minority teachers who are between 40 and 49 (35%). As far as the AC policy of attracting older candidates is concerned, it has worked with AC minority teachers but not with AC white teachers.

Main activity before entering teaching
Related to the variable of age is the issue of the main activity before a teacher's entry into teaching, through which we can study whether AC policies attract more teachers who have work experience in professions other than teaching and education. The data in Table 7.5 (p. 111) seem to suggest that AC policies do recruit a higher percentage of those who have work experience outside of teaching and education, and this is particularly true for AC minority teachers. The percentages of those who have experience in business or military service is 10%, 16%, 21%, and 28% for TC white, TC minority, AC white, and AC minority teachers, respectively. AC also recruits a higher percentage of those who have experience in teaching or education than does TC. However, it should be pointed out that 53% of AC white teachers and 44% of AC minority teachers are fresh college graduates. It appears that many college graduates circumvent TC and enter teaching through AC.

Educational Attainment

Three percent of both AC white and AC minority teachers do not possess a bachelor's degree while the corresponding figure for TC white and TC minority teachers is 1%: $\chi^2(3) = 50$, $p < .001$. Therefore, as far as possessing a bachelor's degree is concerned, AC teachers—both white and minority—appear to have a lower qualification. However, an inquiry into the highest degree possessed reveals some new information (Table 7.6, p. 111): 10% of AC minority teachers have educational attainment higher than the master's degree, the highest among all four groups. Among the four groups, AC white teachers have the highest percentage of those possessing the associate or bachelor's degree as the highest qualification. Therefore, on the one hand, AC attracts a higher percentage of those with no degrees into teaching, on the other hand, it has a differential impact on AC white and minority teachers—AC recruits a much higher percentage of AC minority teachers (than of AC white teachers) who have a master's or higher degree. As the data indicate, the percentage of those having a degree higher than a master's is the highest among AC minority teachers—

and AC Educational attainment is only one of the quality indicators; we should compare the groups on other quality indicators, particularly pedagogical skills, in future studies.

Teaching Math and Science

One of the arguments for AC is that it will attract more math and science teachers, who are often in short supply. The data in Table 7.7 (p. 112) indicate that the percentage of those who teach math and science among AC white (15%) and AC minority teachers (14%) is higher than that among TC white (11%) and TC minority teachers (9%). Therefore, AC recruits more math and science teachers. Then, what about the qualification of those AC math and science teachers? Do a higher percentage of AC white and minority teachers specialize in math, science, and engineering than do TC white and minority teachers? The data in Table 7.8 (p. 112) suggest an affirmative answer. Furthermore, when it comes to recruiting candidates with a bachelor's degree in math, science, or engineering, AC policies attract a higher percentage of AC white teachers (9%) than AC minority teachers (7%). Again AC policies seem to have a differential impact on AC white and AC minority teachers. Another interesting pattern to note is that the percentage of AC white (15%) and minority teachers (14%) who teach math and science is much higher than the percentage of AC white (9%) and AC minority (7%) teachers who possess a bachelor's degree in math, science, or engineering. Apparently, many AC teachers who teach math and science do not have the necessary qualifications.

Other Professional Characteristics

School level
An inquiry into the school level at which AC teachers work reveals again the differential impact of AC policies on AC white and minority teachers. The data in Table 7.9 (p. 112) indicate that a higher percentage of AC minority teachers (60%) than AC white teachers (45%) teach at the elementary level. However, the percentage of AC minority teachers who work at the secondary level is the lowest among the four groups.

Plan to remain in teaching
To recruit minority teachers into teaching is one issue, to retain them in teaching is another. The statistics in Table 7.10 (p. 112) raise the issue of AC teachers' and particularly AC minority teachers' intention to treat teaching as a lifelong career. The percentages of AC minority teachers choosing the option "continue until something better comes along," "defi-

nitely plan to leave teaching as soon as possible," and "undecided at this time" are highest among the groups. The percentage of AC minority teachers choosing "until I am eligible for retirement" is the lowest among the groups. Given the fact that teacher retention is a serious issue for teaching and that teachers with higher educational qualifications tend to leave earlier (Murnane, Singer, & Willett, 1989; Murnane, Singer, Willett, Kemple, & Olsen, 1991; Schlechty & Vance, 1981; Shen, 1997b), it is imperative that we develop policy incentives to retain quality AC minority teachers.

Discussion

The data of the current study suggest a link among AC, minority teachers, and urban education. In comparison to the other three groups of teachers, a higher percentage of minority teachers enter teaching via AC and teach in urban schools where minority students make up more than 50% of the student body. Given the research findings that, generally speaking, minority candidates are less likely to enter teaching (Gordon, 1994) and that the number of certain groups of minority teachers continues to shrink in comparison to the increasingly represented minorities in the study population (Rong & Preissle, 1997), AC appears to be constructive in recruiting more minority teachers. AC policies appear to have more impact on minority teachers than on white teachers, and more on urban education than on suburban and rural education.

When we compare AC minority teachers with TC teachers, we see that some of the objectives for AC policies are met. AC recruits into teaching a higher percentage of older minority candidates who have more experience in business and military service. It also attracts a higher percentage of teachers who teach math and science and have a bachelor's degree in math, science, or engineering. However, some of the objectives for AC are not fulfilled. AC fails to attract a higher percentage of male minority teachers who work at the secondary level. Also, a higher percentage of AC minority teachers do not treat teaching as a lifelong career. Where educational attainment is concerned, the impact of AC is mixed. Although AC attracts a higher percentage of minority teachers who have educational attainment higher than the master's degree, it also lets into teaching many minority teachers who do not have any degrees.

When we compare AC minority with AC white teachers, AC policies appear to have a differential impact on the two groups. AC policies are more successful in getting older minority teachers than in attracting AC white teachers when it comes to recruiting those who have higher educational qualification and more experience in business and military service. However, AC minority teachers, in comparison to AC white teachers, have a higher percentage of female teachers, have a greater tendency to work at the elementary level, are less willing to treat teaching as a lifelong career, and are less likely to have a bachelor's degree in math, science, or engineering.

In summary, when we compare AC minority teachers with both TC teachers and AC white teachers, we find mixed results in terms of the impact of AC policies on minority teachers and urban education. It is encouraging to see a high percentage of AC minority teachers who have high education qualifications and much work experience teaching math and science in urban schools where minority students are concentrated. These AC minority teachers act as role models for students in urban schools. As the foregoing data indicate, AC attracts more minority teachers, who are mostly women working at the elementary level. Therefore, AC is able to diversify the teacher community from the perspective of race and ethnicity, but not from that of gender and school level. One of the most serious issues with AC is that it attracts a high percentage of minority teachers who do not have any degrees. Therefore, AC appears to be a double-edged sword in diversifying and improving the teaching force in general and minority teaching force in particular. AC will remain a controversial issue in the years ahead.

Table 7.1. Distribution (in percentage) of Four Groups of Teachers in Relation to the Type of Community Where They Teach

Type of Community	TC White	TC Minority	AC White	AC Minority
Urban	41	67	40	87
Suburban	14	11	12	3
Rural and Small Town	45	22	49	10

Test statistics: $\chi^2(6) = 629, p < .001$

Table 7.2. Distribution (in percentage) of Four Groups of Teachers in Relation to Percentage of Minority Students in the School

Percentage of Minority Students in School	TC White	TC Minority	AC White	AC Minority
0–4	27	3	29	1
5–19	28	10	29	3
20–49	25	20	17	7
50–100	21	67	25	89

Test statistics: $\chi^2(9) = 2003, p < .001$

Chapter Seven

Table 7.3. Distribution (in percentage) of Four Groups of Respondents in Relation to Gender

Gender	TC White	TC Minority	AC White	AC Minority
Male	24	25	27	20
Female	76	76	73	80

Test statistics: $\chi^2(3) = 8.5, p < .05$

Table 7.4. Distribution (in percentage) of Four Groups of Teachers in Relation to Age

Age	TC White	TC Minority	AC White	AC Minority
Less than 30	29	24	36	24
30–39	35	40	34	36
40–49	28	27	26	35
50 or more	9	10	4	5

Test statistics: $\chi^2(9) = 72, p < .001$

Table 7.5. Distribution (in percentage) of Four Groups of Teachers in Relation to Main Activity before Entering Teaching

Main Activity before Entering Teaching	TC White	TC Minority	AC White	AC Minority
Studying in college	70	61	53	44
Teaching-or education-related position	16	19	24	24
Business or military service	10	16	21	28
Unemployed, caring for family member, or retired	4	4	3	3

Test statistics: $\chi^2(9) = 260, p < .001$

Table 7.6. Distribution (in percentage) of Four Groups of Teachers in Relation to Highest Degrees Possessed

Highest Degree Possessed	TC White	TC Minority	AC White	AC Minority
No degree obtained	0	0	3	3
Associate or Bachelor's	64	65	74	60
Master's	32	29	21	28
Above master's	4	6	3	10

Test statistics: $\chi^2(9) = 147, p < .001$

Table 7.7. Distribution (in percentage) of Four Groups of Teachers in Relation to the Subject Taught

Subject Taught	TC White	TC Minority	AC White	AC Minority
Mathematics and science	11	9	15	14
Other	89	91	85	86

Test statistics: $\chi^2(3) = 23, p < .001$

Table 7.8. Distribution (in percentage) of Four Groups of Teachers in Relation to Subject Specialization for Bachelor's Degree

Subject Specialization	TC White	TC Minority	AC White	AC Minority
Mathematics, science, or engineering	6	6	9	7
Other	94	94	91	93

Test statistics: $\chi^2(3) = 20, p < .001$

Table 7.9. Distribution (in percentage) of Four Groups of Teachers in Relation to the Level of School They Teach

School Level	TC White	TC Minority	AC White	AC Minority
Elementary	54	58	45	60
Secondary	46	42	55	40

Test statistics: $\chi^2(3) = 43, p < .001$

Table 7.10. Distribution (in percentage) of Four Groups of Teachers in Relation to Their Plan to Remain in Teaching

Plan to Remain in Teaching	TC White	TC Minority	AC White	AC Minority
As long as I am able	38	37	37	37
Until I am eligible for retirement	23	19	21	14
Continue until something better comes along	13	16	13	16
Definitely plan to leave teaching as soon as possible	4	3	5	
Undecided at this time	22	23	26	28

Test statistics: $\chi^2(12) = 47, p < .001$

Notes

1. The concept "minority" includes "American Indian or Alaska Indian Native," "Asian or Pacific Islander," "Black, Not Hispanic," and "Hispanic." The percentages reported in the following might not add up to 100 due to rounding.
2. Since the result of statistical testing depends, in part, on the sample size, the null hypothesis could be easily rejected because of the large sample of the study. The chi-square and p values are reported as heuristics, and more attention should be paid to the difference in percentages.

References

Chesley, L. S., Wood, F. H., & Zepeda, S. J. (1997). Meeting the needs of alternatively certified teachers. *Journal of Staff Development, 18* (1), 28–32.

Cornett, L. M. (1990). Alternate certification: State policies in the SREB states. *Peabody Journal of Education, 67* (3), 55–83.

Darling-Hammond, L. (1994). Who will speak for the children? How "Teach for America" hurts urban schools and students. *Phi Delta Kappan, 76* (1), 21–34.

Darling-Hammond, L. (1990). Teaching and knowledge: Policy issues posed by alternate certification for teachers. *Peabody Journal of Education, 67* (3), 123–154.

Dill, V. S. (1996). Alternative teacher certification. In J. Sikula, T. J. Buttery, & E. Guyton (Eds.), *Handbook of research on teacher education* (2nd ed.) (pp. 932–960). New York: Macmillan.

Edelfelt, R. A. (1994). Final thoughts on alternative certification. *The Educational Forum, 58* (2), 220–223.

Feistritzer, C. E. (2008). *Alternative teacher certification: A state-by-state analysis 2008.* Washington, DC: National Center for Education Information.

Gordon, J. A. (1994). Why students of color not entering teaching: Reflections from minority teachers. *Journal of Teacher Education, 45* (5), 346–353.

Kirby, S. N., Darling-Hammond, L., & Hudson, L. (1989). Nontraditional recruits to mathematics and science teaching. *Educational Evaluation and Policy Analysis, 11* (3), 301–323.

Murnane, R. J., Singer, J. D., & Willett, J. B. (1989). The influences of salaries and "opportunity costs" on teachers' career choices: Evidence from North Carolina. *Harvard Educational Review, 59* (3), 325–346.

Murnane, R. J., Singer, J. D., Willett, J. B., Kemple, J. J., & Olsen, R. J. (1991). *Who will teach? Policies that matter.* Cambridge, MA: Harvard University.

Natriello, G., & Zumwalt, K. (1993). New teachers for urban schools? *Education and Urban Society, 26* (1), 49–62.

Rong, X. L., & Preissle, J. (1997). The continuing decline in Asian American teacher. *American Educational Research Journal, 34* (2), 267–293.

Schlechty, P. C., & Vance, V. S. (1981). Do academically able teachers leave education? The North Carolina case. *Phi Delta Kappan, 63* (2), 106–112.

Shen, J. (1997a). Has the alternative certification policy materialized its promise? *Educational Evaluation and Policy Analysis, 19* (3), 276–283.

Shen, J. (1997b). Teacher retention and attrition in public schools: Evidence from SASS91. *Journal of Educational Research, 91* (2), 81–88.

Stoddart, T. (1990). Los Angeles Unified School District Intern Program: Recruiting and preparing teachers for the urban context. *Peabody Journal of Education, 67* (3), 84–122.

Stoddart, T. (1993). Who is prepared to teach in urban schools? *Education and Urban Society, 26* (1), 29–48.

CHAPTER EIGHT

Alternative Certification and Math and Science Teachers

Jianping Shen

Introduction

The last decade has witnessed a tremendous development of alternative certification in this country. The number of states allowing alternative certification increased from 18 in 1986 to 41 in 1997. Four other states are considering or have already proposed the policy. It is estimated that about 50,000 people had been licensed through state-run alternative programs by 1996 (Feistritzer, 1993; 1997; Feistritzer & Chester, 1996; Stoddart & Floden, 1995).

The major arguments for alternative certification include the following: (a) to diversify the teaching force by recruiting more minority teachers (Bradshaw & Hawk, 1996; United States Department of Education, 1991; Zumwalt, 1991), (b) to reduce teacher shortages in the fields of math and science as well as in rural and urban areas (Natriello & Zumwalt, 1993; Norton & Andersen, 1997; Stoddart, 1990, 1993), (c) to provide opportunities for bringing bright college graduates into teaching without going through the traditional teacher education program (Fenstermacher, 1990; Kerr, 1983), and (d) to recruit those people who have already had a broad range of experiences so as to meet the escalating demands created by an increasing population of school-aged learners (Edelfelt, 1994; Darling-Hammond, 1990).

Given the fact that alternative certification continues to gain momentum, it is imperative to evaluate its impact. This chapter investigates whether the objectives of alternative certification have been met in the practice, with a particular focus on math and science (M&S) teachers in public schools. The chapter first inquires into whether alternative certification reduces the shortage of M&S teachers and then compares the characteristics of traditionally certified (TC) and alternatively certified (AC) M&S teachers. To be more specific, the following questions are asked:

Do AC policies reduce the shortage of M&S teachers?
Do AC policies diversify the teaching force by recruiting more male and minority people into the public teaching force?

Do AC policies reduce teacher shortages in urban and rural school districts?
Do AC policies improve the quality of the teaching force by recruiting persons who are older and more devoted to teaching?
Do AC policies improve the quality of the public teaching force by recruiting persons who have higher educational qualifications and a broader range of experiences outside of teaching than the average TC teachers?

Data Source

The data for the study were extracted from, among others, the Schools and Staffing Survey 1993-94 (SASS93)—which is a large, national survey conducted by the National Center for Education Statistics—and from the responses obtained using the Public School Teacher Questionnaire. SASS93 provided the first nationally representative sample to investigate the impact of AC policies.

Because AC policies have been in place on a large scale primarily since 1998, this study focused only on those teachers who were certified in the ten years prior to the 1993-94 survey. TC teachers in this study were those who had the advanced professional certificate or the regular/standard state certificate, while AC teachers were those who had the certificate through, as phrased in the questionnaire, "what the state calls an 'alternative certificate program.'" The extracted sample from SASS93 was weighted to ensure national representativeness. As a result, the relative weighted sample for this study included 14,719 subjects—13,601 TC teachers and 1,118 AC teachers (weighted $N = 800{,}412$). Thus, the sample was nationally representative of teachers certified in the ten years prior to the 1993-94 survey, and the following findings were generalizable to the national scene.

Results

Do AC Policies Reduce the Shortage of M&S Teachers?

Among TC teachers in the sample, 13.4% were M&S teachers. The corresponding percentage for AC teachers was 19.2%. Statistically, there was a significantly higher percentage of M&S teachers among AC than TC teachers ($\chi^2 = 28.7$, $p < .001$). Therefore, AC policies appeared to reduce the teacher shortage in math and science. There was also a statistically significantly higher percentage of math and science majors among AC teachers (7.6%) than among TC teachers (5.4%) ($\chi^2 = 9.0$, $p < .001$). Therefore,

AC policies seemed to be effective in recruiting M&S teachers—Compared to TC teachers, AC teachers had a higher percentage of not only those who were actually teaching math and science but also of those who had a major in the two subjects.

Do AC Policies Diversify the Teaching Force by Recruiting More Male and Minority People into the Public Teaching Force?

Gender

Among those TC M&S teachers certified between 1984–85 and 1993–94, 42.1% of them were male and 57.9% were female. The corresponding percentages for AC M&S teachers were 39.3% and 60.7%, respectively. The results suggested that there was no statistically significant difference between AC and TC M&S teachers in their gender composition ($\chi^2 = .64$, $p = .42$). In other words, AC policies did not recruit a statistically significantly higher percentage of male M&S teachers into the public teaching force than did TC policies.

Minority

Among TC M&S teachers in the sample, 88% of them were white and 12% minority. The corresponding percentages for AC teachers were 84.7% and 15.3%, respectively. Although the percentage of minority teachers was slightly higher among AC M&S teachers than among TC M&S teachers, there was no statistically significant difference between TC and AC M&S teachers in racial and ethnic composition ($\chi^2 = 2.04, p = .15$).

Do AC Policies Reduce Teacher Shortages in Urban and Rural School Districts?

The data on where TC and AC teachers taught are displayed in Table 8.1. Although the percentage of those who worked in large or midsize central cities was higher among AC M&S teachers than among TC M&S teachers, there was no statistically significant difference between TC and AC M&S teachers in terms of location.

Table 8.1. Distribution of TC and AC M&S Teachers in Relation to Locale

Locale	TC Teacher (%)	AC Teacher (%)
Large or midsize central city	27.9	28.7
Urban fringe of large or midsize central city	27.5	20.4
Small town/rural area	44.6	50.9

Test statistics: $\chi^2(2) = 5.42, p = .07$

However, when we inquired into the distribution of TC and AC M&S teachers in relation to the percentage of minority students in the school (Table 8.2), it was clear that a much higher percentage of AC than TC M&S teachers taught in those schools where minority students constituted more than 50% of the student population. AC M&S teachers appeared to be concentrated in inner-city schools.

Table 8.2. Distribution of TC and AC M&S Teachers in Relation to Percentage of Minority Students in School

Percentage of Minority Students in School	TC Teacher (%)	AC Teacher (%)
0–4	22.7	24.8
5–19	25.3	27.2
20–49	26.3	13.6
50–100	25.7	34.0

Test statistics $\chi^2(3) = 17.5, p = .001$

Do AC Policies Improve the Quality of the Teaching Force by Recruiting Persons who are Older and More Devoted to Teaching?

The mean age of TC M&S teachers in the sample was 35.36, while the corresponding statistic for AC M&S teachers was 35.41. Therefore, AC policies did not appear to recruit older people into teaching. The respondents were also asked the following: "if you could go back to your college days and start over again, would you become a teacher or not?" The respondents rated their answers on a 5-point scale, ranging from 1 (certainly would become a teacher) to 5 (certainly would not become a teacher). The means for TC and AC M&S teachers were 2.28 and 2.20, respectively. Therefore, there was essentially no difference between TC and AC M&S teachers in their devotion to teaching.

Do AC Policies Improve the Quality of the Public Teaching Force by Recruiting Persons Who Have Higher Educational Qualifications and a Broader Range of Experiences Outside of Teaching Than the Average TC Teachers?

Educational attainment
All AC M&S teachers in the sample had a bachelor's degree while 0.4% of their TC counterparts did not have a bachelor's degree. Where the highest degree was concerned, there was a statistically significant difference between TC and AC M&S teachers (Table 8.3). Generally speaking, AC M&S

teachers had a higher educational attainment than did their TC counterparts. It was encouraging to see that 7.9% of the AC M&S teachers belonged to the category of "above master's degree."

Table 8.3. Distribution of TC and AC M&S Teachers in Relation to the Highest Degree Earned

Degree	TC Teacher (%)	AC Teacher (%)
No degree	3	0
Associate or bachelor's degree	62.5	73.5
Master's degree	33.3	18.6
Above master's degree	3.9	7.9

Test statistics: $\chi^2(3) = 24.4, p < .001$

Experience before entering teaching

TC and AC M&S teachers' main activity the year before entering teaching is reported in Table 8.4, which suggests that the two groups were statistically significantly different in this regard. The percentages of those who held education-related positions and of those who worked in business or military service were higher among AC M&S teachers (24.3% and 25.6%, respectively) than among TC M&S teachers (12.1% and 16.1%, respectively). All these statistics supported the argument that AC policies recruited a higher percentage of teachers who have already had a broad range of work experiences. However, 45.3% of AC M&S teachers came right out of college. Given the fact that about half of AC M&S teachers were fresh college graduates and that AC did recruit a high percentage of those who had a broad range of work experiences, AC policies appear to be a double-edged sword.

Table 8.4. Distribution of TC and AC M&S Teachers in Relation to Main Activity before Entering Teaching

Main Activity before Entering Teaching	TC Teacher (%)	AC Teacher (%)
Studying in college	68.5	45.3
Teaching- or education-related position	12.1	24.3
Business or military service	16.1	25.2
Unemployed, caring for family member, or retired	3.3	5.1

Test statistics: $\chi^2(3) = 47.9, p < .001$

Discussion

As the foregoing analyses indicate, as far as M&S teachers are concerned, some of the arguments for AC are supported by the national data: (a) AC recruits a higher percentage of M&S teachers into the public teaching force than does TC; (b) a higher percentage of AC than that of TC M&S teachers work in those schools where minority students are concentrated; (c) a higher percentage of AC than that of TC M&S teachers have experiences in business or military service; and (d) AC M&S teachers have higher educational attainment than their TC counterparts.

However, the following arguments for AC are not supported by the national data. In comparison to TC, AC does not seem to diversify the public teaching force by recruiting more male and minority M&S teachers and fails to recruit older and more devoted M&S teachers. Nonetheless, even in areas where the arguments for AC are not supported by the data, AC does not appear to be less effective than TC. Therefore, as far as M&S teachers are concerned, AC appears to be successful.

There are two areas where AC policies need to be improved. First, 45.3% of AC M&S teachers are fresh college graduates. This raises the issue of whether a large number of fresh college graduates circumvent the traditional teacher education program. Second, there was no difference between TC and AC M&S teachers in terms of race and ethnic composition, but a higher percentage of AC than TC M&S teachers work in inner-city schools where more than 50% of the students are minority. Therefore, one the one hand, many of the M&S classrooms are staffed because of AC, on the other hand, minority students in inner-city schools are less likely to have minority role models in their M&S classrooms.

Conclusion

The teaching force is one of the most important resources in the educational process (Darling-Hammond, 1994; Darling-Hammond, Berry, & Thoreson, 2001; Darling-Hammond, Holtzman, Gatlin, & Heilig, 2005; Grossman, 1989; Guyton & Farokhi, 1987). With the release of research results of the Third International Mathematics and Science Study, the quality of M&S teachers of our public schools becomes a more crucial issue (Peak, 1996; Schmidt, 1997a, b). This study finds that as far as TC and AC M&S teachers' demographic and professional characteristics are concerned, AC policies appear to be successful in recruiting M&S teachers for our public schools. However, there are also a few issues that deserve our attention.

References

Bradshaw, L. K., & Hawk, P. P. (1996). *Teacher certification: Does it really make a difference in student achievement?* Greenville, NC: Eastern North Carolina Consortium for Assistance and Research in Education.

Darling-Hammond, L. (1990). Teaching and knowledge: Policy issues posed by alternate certification for teachers. *Peabody Journal of Education, 67(3)*, 123–154.

Darling-Hammond, L. (1994). Who will speak for our children? How "Teach for America" hurts urban schools and students. *Phi Delta Kappan, 76(1)*, 21–34.

Darling-Hammond, L., Berry, B., & Thoreson, A. (2001). Does teacher certification matter? Evaluating the evidence. *Educational Evaluation and Policy Analysis, 23* (1), 57–77.

Darling-Hammond, L., Holtzman, D. J., Gatlin, S. J., & Heilig, J. V. (2005). Does teacher preparation matter? Evidence about teacher certification, Teach for America, and teacher effectiveness. *Educational Policy Analysis Archives, 13* (42). Retrieved January 10, 2009 from http://epaa.asu.edu/epaa/v13n42.

Edelfelt, R. A. (1994). Final thoughts on alternative certification. *Educational Forum, 58*, 220–223.

Feistritzer, C. E. (1993). National overview of alternative teacher certification. *Education and Urban Society 26(1)*, 18–28.

Feistritzer, C. E. (1997). *Alternative teacher certification: A state-by-state analysis 1997.* Washington, DC: National Center for Education Information.

Feistritzer, C. E., & Chester, D. T. (1996). *Alternative teacher certification: A state-by-state analysis 1996.* Washington, DC: National Center for Education Information.

Fenstermacher, G. D. (1990). The place of alternative certification in the education of teachers. *Peabody Journal of Education, 67(3)*, 155–185.

Grossman, P. L. (1989). Learning to teach without teacher education. *Teachers College Record, 91(2)*, 191–208.

Guyton, E., & Farokhi, E. (1987). Relationships among academic performance, basic skills, subject matter knowledge, and teaching skills of teacher education graduates. *Journal of Teacher Education, 38(5)*, 37–42.

Kerr, D. H. (1983). Teaching competency and teacher education in the United States. *Teachers College Record, 84(3)*, 525–552.

Natriello, G., & Zumwalt, K. (1993). New teachers for urban schools? *Education and Urban Society 26(1)*, 49–62.

Norton, M. S., & Andersen, M. (1997). Alternative teacher certification: A study of first-year personnel in eleven western states. *Planning and Changing, 28(4)*, 240–245.

Peak, L. (1996). *Pursuing excellence: A study of U.S. eighth-grade mathematics and science teaching, learning, curriculum, and achievement in international context.* Washington, DC: National Center for Education Statistics.

Schmidt, W. H. (1997a). *Many visions, many missions: A cross-national investigation of curricular intentions in school mathematics.* Boston: Kluwer Academic Press.

Schmidt, W. H. (1997b). *Many visions, many missions: A cross-national investigation of curricular intentions in school science.* Boston: Kluwer Academic Press.

Stoddart, T. (1990). Los Angeles Unified School District Intern Program: Recruiting and preparing teachers for the urban context. *Peabody Journal of Education, 67(3)*, 84–122.

Stoddart, T. (1993). Who is prepared to teach in urban schools? *Education and Urban Society, 26(1)*, 29–48.

Stoddart, T., & Floden, R. E. (1995). *Traditional and alternative routes to teacher certification: Issues, assumptions, and misconceptions.* East Lansing, MI: National Center for Research on Teacher Learning.

United States Department of Education (1991). *Alternative certification for teachers.* Washington, DC: Author.

Zumwalt, K. (1991). Alternate routes to teaching: Three alternative approaches. *Journal of Teacher Education, 42(2)*, 83–92.

SECTION 4

Teacher Attrition

CHAPTER NINE

Inadequate Preparation Does Impact Teacher Attrition

Jianping Shen and Louann Bierlein Palmer

Introduction

The retention of elementary and secondary teachers has been an issue of continuing concern in education. In addition to the issue of quality, high rates of teacher attrition disrupt program continuity and planning, hinder student learning, and increase school districts' expenditures on recruiting and hiring. In this study we inquire into one segment of the new teacher population, those who enter the classroom without adequate preparation and/or those without full certification. This survival analysis was completed using data collected during the Baccalaureate and Beyond Longitudinal Study 1993-97 (i.e., B&B:93/97), which is a national longitudinal survey of recent college graduates.

The number of states allowing some type of alternative certification program increased from just 8 in 1983 to all 50 (plus the District of Columbia having some sort of alternative route to teacher certification) in 2007 (Feistritzer, 2007). Indeed, Feistritzer notes that about one-third of all new teachers across the nation are coming through alternative teacher certification programs. Yet, empirical studies indicate that the impact of such alternative certification policies has been mixed. This study examines the attrition patterns of those who begin teaching without participating in all aspects of what some deem adequate preparation (i.e., student teaching and an induction program), as well as full certification, compared to those following the more traditional preparation and certification routes.

We begin by reviewing the literature on various kinds of entries into teaching, and teacher attrition. We then discuss the methodology of the study, including data source, sample, and data analysis method. Finally, we present the results and discuss the implications of the findings.

Literature Review

Alternative Preparation Programs

Recent years have witnessed the continuing debate on alternative teacher certification programs and their impact on the teaching force (Duffrin, 2004; Wright, 2001). The arguments for high-quality alternative certification are offered from various perspectives. First, there has been a shortage of qualified teachers in urban schools and in subject areas such as math and science; therefore, alternative certification is often employed to alleviate such shortages (Peske & Haycock, 2006; Stoddart & Floden, 1995). Second, it has been argued that good teaching is based primarily on subject matter knowledge and an enthusiasm for teaching (Hess, 2001). Hence, opportunities should be provided to people who are competent in subject matter knowledge but who would not otherwise have the opportunity to go into teaching. Third, it has been argued that alternatively certified teachers are older, more likely to come from minority groups, and more likely to have worked in other jobs than the traditional teacher education population. Therefore, the teaching force can be diversified through alternative certification, which is particularly true for urban schools (Roach & Cohen, 2002). Finally, it has long been argued that university-based teacher education has monopolized preparation of teachers, and alternative certification introduces competition into this area (Kramer, 1991; Goldhaber, 2002).

The arguments against alternative certification are also varied. First, it has been argued that alternative certification lowers the cost of entering teaching and degrades the professional status of teaching (Kirby, Darling-Hammond, & Hudson, 1989). Second, some claim that ultimately students—particularly those disadvantaged students in inner-city schools where teacher shortages occur more frequently—are hurt by this policy (Darling-Hammond, 1994), and that underprepared teachers can actually hinder student learning (Darling-Hammond, 2002; Laczko-Kerr & Berliner, 2002). Third, the assumption that teachers certified alternatively know the subject matter and can learn to teach by working on the job has been questioned (Kennedy, 1991). Some research suggests that pedagogical content knowledge plays a very important role in teaching, and that teachers without teacher education or certified alternatively have more difficulties learning to teach than do those certified traditionally (Grossman, 1989a, b; McDiarmid & Wilson, 1991). Finally, it has been argued that alternative certification fails to fulfill the promise that it will recruit those who have higher academic qualifications (Natriello, Hansen, Frisch, & Zumwalt, 1990).

Recent empirical studies indicate that teachers' certification or licensing status is related to students' learning. A review of 92 studies on teacher preparation by the Education Commission of the States suggests that research provides limited support for the conclusion that alternative-route programs can produce teachers who become as effective as traditionally trained teachers (Allen, 2003). As some examples, Goldhaber and Brewer (2000) found that except for mathematics and science teachers with emergency certificates, fully certified teachers have a statistically significant positive impact on student test scores relative to teachers who are not certified in their subject area. Later on, using the same data source, Darling-Hammond, Berry, and Thoreson (2001) argued that even for math and science, those teachers who have more teacher education training appear to do better in producing student achievement. Furthermore, as cited by Darling-Hammond (2000), Fuller's study (1999) indicated that when school districts have higher percentages of licensed teachers, their pass rates on the Texas state achievement tests are significantly higher, after holding constant some characteristics related to student family background, school, and teacher. Fetler's research (1999) also found that when the percentage of teachers on emergency certificates is higher, average student score is significantly lower, after controlling for student poverty. Furthermore, Grossman's (1989a, b) in-depth qualitative studies of first-year English teachers indicated the difficulties experienced by those who entered teaching without teacher education. Finally, using national data collected in 1993–94 and 1994–95, researchers found that alternative certification policies have not fulfilled all their promises (e.g., Shen, 1997a, 1997b, 1998, 2000).

On the other hand, Boyd, Goldhaber, Lankford, and Wyckoff (2007) found that "highly selective alternative route programs can produce effective teachers who perform about the same as teachers from traditional routes after two years" (p. 45). In a similar vein, a comprehensive study of teachers participating in Teach for America found that the students of such teachers, compared with the students of control teachers, demonstrated progress equivalent to that achieved in one month of additional math instruction (Decker, Mayer, & Glazerman, 2004). Yet it is important to note that the control teachers in that study had substantially lower rates of certification and formal education training when compared to a nationally representative sample of teachers, helping to make the case for the importance of adequate preparation.

Teacher Attrition

Teacher attrition is a key factor that impacts the characteristics of the teaching force. National surveys conducted by the U.S. Department of Education indicated that about 20% of new teachers leave teaching within the first three years of entering teaching (Whitener et al., 1997). Overall, the teacher attrition pattern is found to follow a U-shaped curve over a life cycle. Attrition rate is high for young teachers during the early stage of their professional lives, low for middle-aged teachers, and high again for senior teachers as they approach retirement (Grissmer & Kirby, 1987; Murnane, Singer, & Willett, 1989; Singer, 1993).

Darling-Hammond (2003) notes that there is mounting evidence linking inadequate teacher preparation and higher attrition rates. She cites several state-based studies depicting higher attrition rates among teachers coming from alternative certification programs (e.g., Raymond, Fletcher, & Luque, 2001).

From a national perspective, Henke, Chen, and Geis (2000) found attrition rates to be significantly lower among those teachers who received more adequate preparation. These researchers analyzed data from the Baccalaureate and Beyond Longitudinal Study 1993-97 (B&B:93/97) and found that 15% of those who had participated in a student teaching experience prior to entering the classroom left the profession within five years, compared to 29% of those who had not completed student teaching. Of those involved in a first-year teacher induction program, 15% left, compared to 26% of those who had not participated in a teacher induction program. And, 14% of those with certification left, compared to 49% of those without certification. These national data, along with a growing number of state-specific research studies, all point to a strong linkage between adequate teacher preparation and better attrition rates.

Conceptualization and Research Question

So why are analyses derived from the B&B:93/97 national data set (such as the one reported in this chapter, and that done by Henke, Chen, and Geis, 2000) of such value, and what more can be learned from this data set?

First, the longitudinal national data available through the B&B:93/97 gives such studies methodological rigor. Many previous studies on teacher attrition are based on retrospective data. One of the shortcomings associated with retrospective data is that there is a time gap, and thus there is a possible reconstruction process based on the experience after leaving teaching or continuing to teach for a period of time. Another shortcoming with other national data sets is that researchers must investigate the phenomenon of teacher attrition using a short time span. For example, studies have been conducted to inquire into teacher attrition by analyzing the data from Schools and Staffing Survey (SASS) 1990-91 and Teacher Follow-up Survey (TFS) 1991-92 (e.g., Shen, 1997a, 1997b), and SASS 1993-94 and TFS 1994-95 (e.g., Boe, Bobbitt, Cook, & Barkanic, 1998; Boe, Bobbitt, Cook, Barkanic, & Maislin, 1998). For both data sets, the time gap is only one year between the main survey and the subsequent follow-up survey. The study reported here (using B&B:93/97) has month-to-month data on new teachers' employment status during a five-year period.

Second, related to the longitudinal data over a longer period of time is the analysis approach that this current study takes. As will be discussed in detail in the methodological section, this study uses survival analysis methods to fully utilize the information in the data. Previous studies on teacher attrition often divided teachers into two groups: those who leave and those who continue. This dichotomized variable loses a lot of information because it does not indicate when a teacher leaves. The outcome measure of this reported study—months of teaching before attrition happens or does not happen—is much richer than just a dichotomous variable.

Method

The Data Source

The data of the study are extracted from the Baccalaureate and Beyond Longitudinal Study 1993-97 (i.e., B&B:93/97). B&B:93/97 was designed to examine the post-baccalaureate experiences of 1992-93 bachelor's degree recipients. Based on a sample of approximately 11,200 men and women who received bachelor's degrees between July 1992 and June 1993, the available data on this cohort include interviews conducted as part of the 1993 National Postsecondary Student Aid Study (NPSAS:93) when the students were seniors in college, the Baccalaureate and Beyond First Follow-up conducted in 1994 (B&B:93/94), and the Second Follow-up in 1997 (B&B:93/97). Transcript data from the NPSAS institutions are also available for most of the cohort. Therefore, the data allow researchers to study the connections between college graduates' careers as undergraduates and their post-baccalaureate experiences as students and employees. The B&B:93/97 study provides data to address, among others, issues related to patterns of preparation for, and engagement in, teaching.

The Sample

The B&B cohort comprised of 11,192 individuals who were evaluated to be eligible for follow-up in 1997. A full 83% of the sample responded to all three rounds; these 9,274 respondents (weighted N = 1,181,376) are classified as the B&B panel. Among the B&B panel, 1,702 respondents (weighted N = 181,313) went into teaching and they constituted the sample of the study.

Data Analysis Approach

A Cox regression model is used to examine teacher attrition in the B&B:93/97 subsample specified previously. This data analysis approach is a form of survival or event history method. Survival analysis enables researchers to use various factors—for example, gender—to predict teacher attrition over a period of time. Methodologically, survival analysis is an excellent approach to modeling the length of time it takes for an event to take place, even when some of those in the sample have not experienced the event. We can model when an event is likely to occur by using survival analysis methods.

Studies on teacher attrition usually dichotomize the event, that is, they create a dichotomous variable that divides the teachers into two categories—those who leave and those who continue. The dichotomous variable is then used as an outcome measure to be predicted by various variables such as gender and race/ethnicity. The problem with the approach to dichotomizing the outcome measure is that a large amount of information is lost. For example, if a researcher chooses to use the dichotomous approach to study teacher attrition over a period of ten years, through the dichotomy those who left teaching during the first year are classified the same as those who left during the tenth year. Since we have data on teachers' month-to-month employment status, we are able to use the Cox model, one that is designed for continuous data.

Results

Overall Attrition Pattern

Figure 9.1 shows the cumulative survival pattern of new teachers. Among 1,702 college graduates who entered teaching at different points of time after graduation, 579 left teaching within the 40-month (five-academic-year) period since graduation from college, with an attrition rate of 34.0%. Based on the panel sampling weights, the attrition rate is slightly higher at

34.2%. The attrition occurred steadily over the time with a noticeable precipitation during the first month and at the end of each academic year, a pattern that is consistent with the usual attrition rate at the end of an academic year. The cumulative survival rates, as estimated in the life table, are 81.1% at the end of the first academic year, 72.0% at the end of the second, 63.3% at the end of the third, 58.7% at the end of the fourth, and 54.6% at the end of the fifth academic year. The estimated attrition rates in this study are higher than those calculated in another national study based on the Teacher Follow-up Survey 1993–94, where it was found that about 20% of the new teachers leave teaching within the first three years of entering the profession (Whitener et al., 1997). The current study's data analysis approach, taking into account different time points for entry, as well as its sampling frame might be factors in leading to a different estimate.

Figure 9.1. Estimated Survival Function for College Graduates Who Entered Teaching

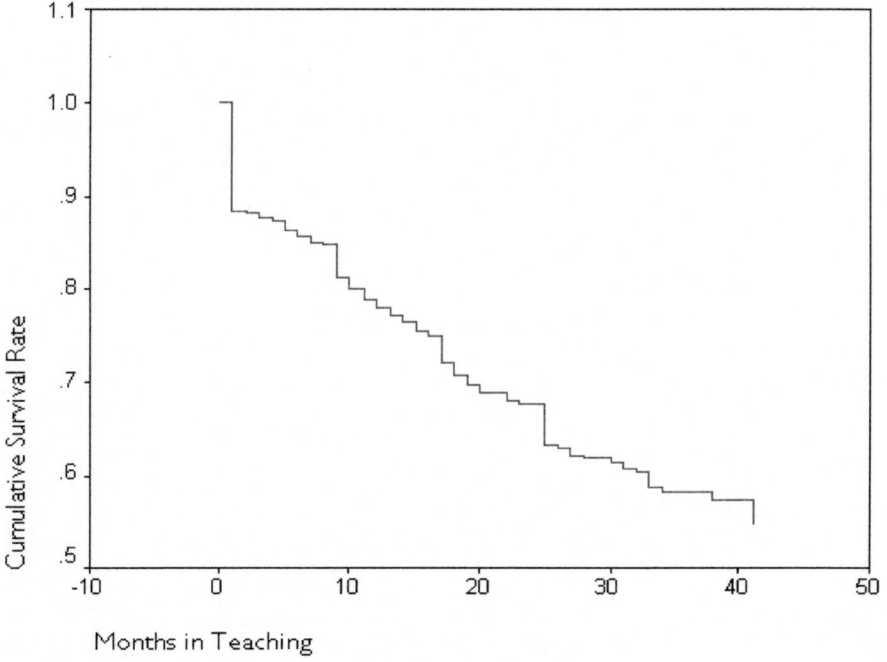

Various Types of Entry into Teaching

In addition to examining the overall attrition pattern for new teachers, this study examines attrition rates as they relate to "various kinds of entry into teaching" as viewed from five perspectives: (1) how a teacher first entered teaching, (2) extent of teacher preparation, (3) whether ever certified to teach when the follow-up surveys were conducted in 1994 and 1997, (4) whether certified when the 1997 follow-up survey was conducted, and (5) highest certification between 1994 and 1997.

How a teacher first entered teaching

There is a statistically significant difference in hazard rates between those who "prepared, taught" and those who "taught, no training" when they first entered teaching (Figure 9.2) (Wald = 117.1, df = 1, p < .001). From the "taught, no training" group to the "prepared, taught" group, there is a statistically significant 355% increase in hazard rates. The data unequivocally demonstrate that those who "prepared, taught" are much more likely to stay in teaching than those who "taught, no training."

Figure 9.2. Estimated Survival Functions for Two Groups That Entered Teaching Differently

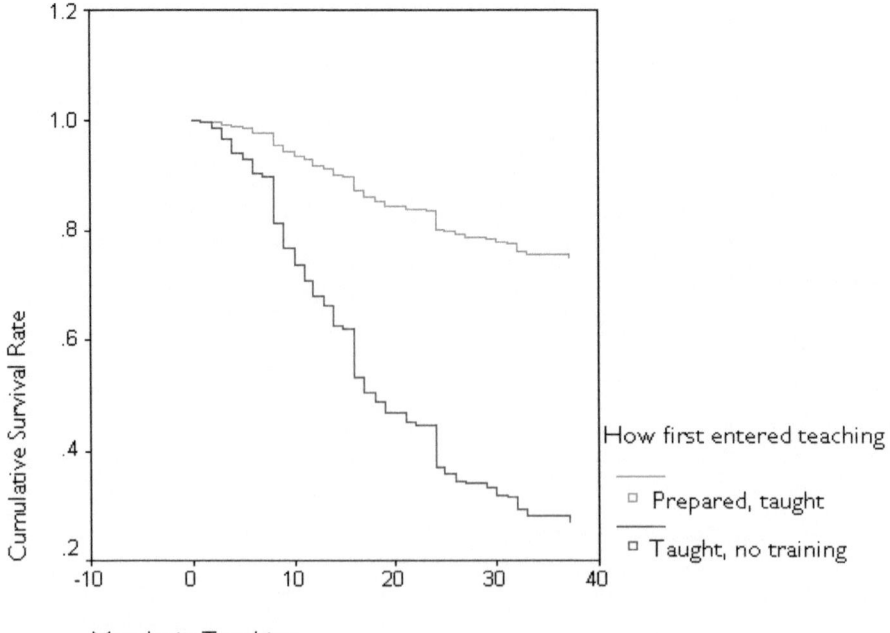

Fully prepared to teach

Figure 9.3 shows the survival pattern of two groups of teachers: those who are fully prepared to teach and those who are not. According to the definition used by the National Center for Education Statistics for the B&B:93/97 data set, "fully prepared to teach" includes "the completion of all the following: student teaching, getting certified and participating in a teacher induction program." The hazard rate for those teachers who are not fully prepared is 111% more than that for those who are fully prepared to teach. Statistically, those who are fully prepared are significantly more likely to stay in teaching (Wald = 26.6, $df = 1$, $p < .001$).

Figure 9.3. Estimated Survival Functions for Two Groups of Teachers with Different Levels of Teacher Preparation

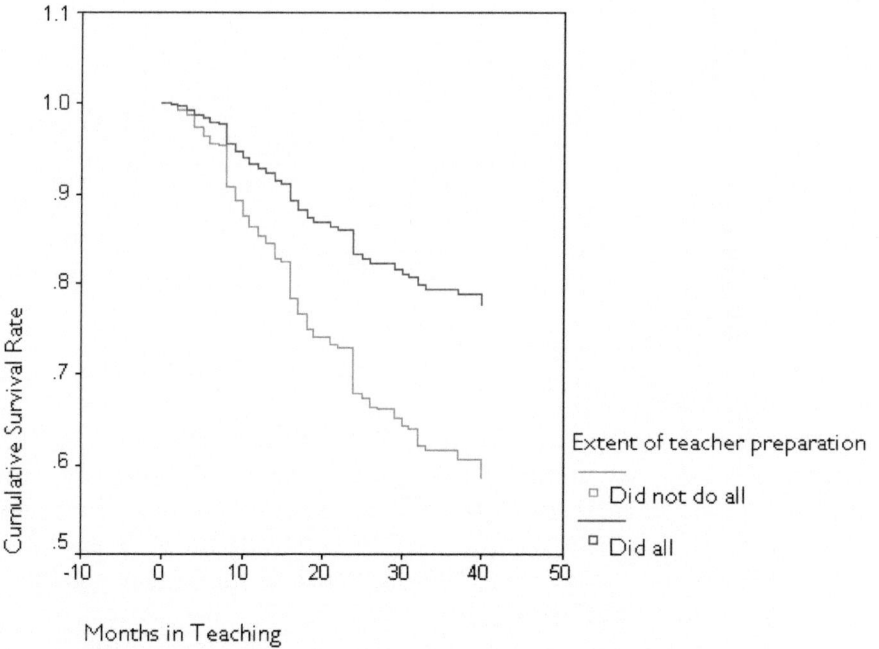

Ever certified to teach

The data in Figure 9.4 indicate that those ever certified to teach are much more likely to stay in teaching than those not ever certified. The hazard rate for those ever certified was only about 17% of that for those not ever certified, a difference that is statistically significant (Wald = 208.3, $df = 1$, $p < .001$).

Figure 9.4. Estimated Survival Functions for Teachers Who Were Certified to Teach and Those Who Were Not Ever

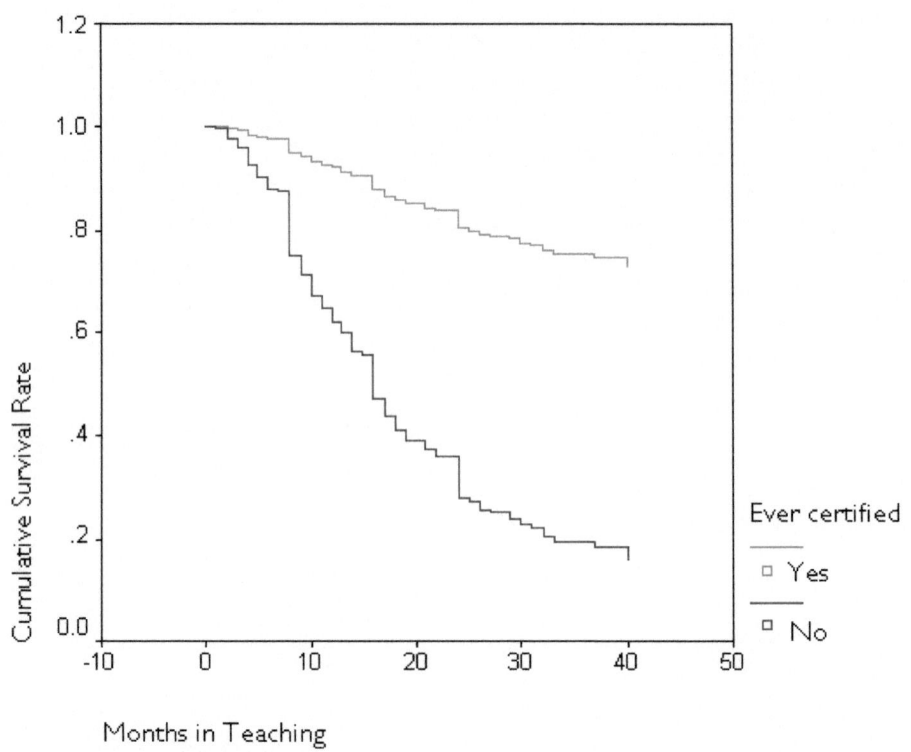

Current certification status in 1997
Using data from "whether currently certified to teach" when the 1997 survey was conducted, we compare the survival pattern of those who were currently certified to teach in 1997 with those who were not. The hazard rate for those who were certified to teach was only about 33% of that for those who were not certified, and the difference is statistically significant (Figure 9.5) (Wald = 46.7, $df = 1$, $p < .001$).

Figure 9.5. Estimated Survival Functions for Teachers Who Were Currently Certified to Teach in 1997 and Those Who Were Not

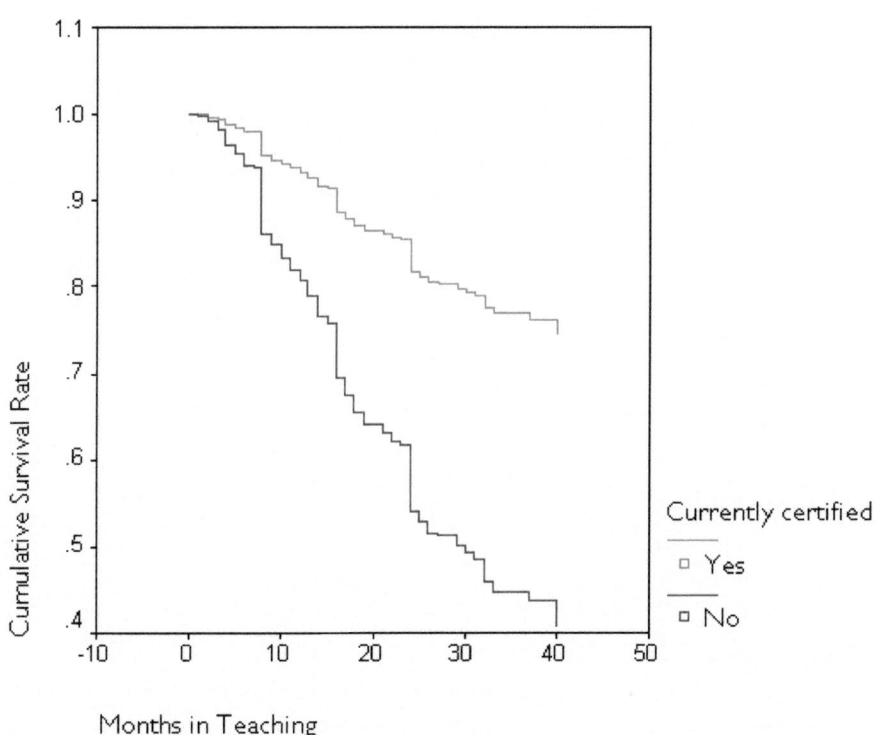

Highest certification between 1994 and 1997
The data in this paragraph provide a perspective on those who are certified, that is, how the type of certification is related to teacher attrition. The data in Figure 9.6 suggest that there is a statistically significant difference in attrition patterns among those who have various types of certification (Wald = 9.7, $df = 1$, $p < .05$). In comparison to the group with "advanced" certification, the hazard rates for those with "emergency and other" or "probationary" certification increase by 213% and 111%, respectively; the increases are statistically or marginally significant (Wald = 5.3, $df = 1$, $p = .021$; Wald = 3.6, $df = 1$, $p = .057$, respectively). In comparison with the "advanced" certification group, the hazard rates for attrition increase by 18% for the "regular" certificate group and by 28% for the "temporary" certification group, but the increases are not statistically significant.

Figure 9.6. Estimated Survival Function for Teachers with Different Levels of Highest Certification Between 1994 and 1997

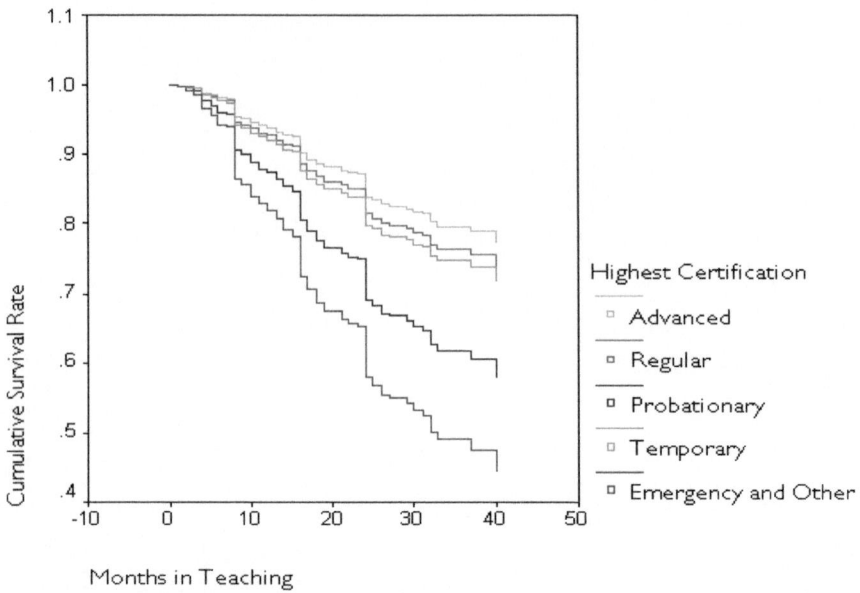

Summary and Discussion

The results in the foregoing analyses reveal a relationship between teacher attrition, on the one hand, and adequate preparation and full certification, on the other. Using this national sample, the evidence is unequivocally clear that (a) those who enter teaching fully prepared are more likely to stay in teaching than those who are not; (b) those who are certified are more likely to stay in teaching than those who are not; and (c) those who have "emergency and other" certificates are more likely to leave teaching than those who have advanced and regular certification. Ideally, if we had a time-varying variable on certification status, we would arrive at a definitive relationship between certification and attrition. However, when we operationalized entry into teaching in five different perspectives, the results all pointed in the same direction—those who enter teaching without full preparation, uncertified, or with "emergency and other" certificates are much more likely to leave teaching. The results clearly indicate that it is more difficult to survive in the teaching profession for those who lack adequate preparation and certification.

The findings of the study spotlight several policy concerns. First, the overall attrition rate for new teachers is higher than previously found in other national studies. Data indicate that about 34% of those who enter teaching at some point in the 5-year period after obtaining a bachelor's degree leave teaching by the end of the fifth academic year. The estimated cumulative survival rates are 81.1% by the end of the first academic year, 63.3% by the end of the third academic year, and 54.6% by the end of the fifth academic year. Even among those who enter teaching fully prepared (which is defined as completing student teaching, getting certified, and participating in a teacher induction program), the attrition rate is still as high as 26.4% by the end of the 5-year period. Teacher attrition disrupts program continuity and planning, hinders student learning, and increases school districts' expenditures on recruiting and hiring. As Ingersoll (2005, 2007) argues, teacher attrition is one of the most important factors contributing to teacher shortage.

The other key policy issue focuses on those entering teaching through various alternative routes, which may not include all aspects of being fully prepared. The findings support what other studies (e.g., Darling-Hammond; 2003; Grossman, 1989a, 1989b, 1990, 1994) have concluded, that those who are more fully prepared and have full certification (usually aspects of traditional preparation program and high-quality alternative certification programs) are more likely to stay in teaching. Generally speaking, those who enter teaching via emergency certificates or those with less stringent kinds of alternative certification do not continue to teach as long as those who enter teaching via the traditional route of teacher education.

Given the increasing teacher shortage and the proliferation of nontraditional entries into teaching, these findings have serious implications for the professional community as well as for society as a whole to reflect upon how to attract and retain quality teachers for our nation's children. The revolving door for teachers is simply not constructive for student learning and the professionalization of our teaching force.

References

Allen, M (2003). *Eight questions on teacher preparation: What does the research say?* Denver, CO: Education Commission of the States.

Boe, E., Bobbitt, S. A., Cook, L. H., & Barkanic, G. (1998). *National trends in teacher supply and turnover for special and general education.* Philadelphia: University of Pennsylvania.

Boe, E., Bobbitt, S. A., Cook, L. H., Barkanic, G., & Maislin, G., (1998). *Teacher turnover in eight cognate areas: National trends and predictors.* Philadelphia: University of Pennsylvania.

Boyd, D., Goldhaber, D., Lankford, H., & Wyckoff, J. (2007). The effect of certification and preparation on teacher quality. *The Future of Children, 17*(1). 45–68.

Darling-Hammond, L. (1994). Who will speak for the children? *Phi Delta Kappan, 76*(1), 21–34

Darling-Hammond, L. (2000). Teacher quality and student achievement: A review of state policy evidence. *Education Policy Analysis Archives, 8*(1). Retrieved February 23, 2001, from http://epaa.asu.edu/epaa/v8n1/.

Darling-Hammond, L. (2002). Research and rhetoric on teacher certification: A response to "teacher certification reconsidered," *Education Policy Analysis Archives, 10*(36). Retrieved January 19, 2009 from: http://epaa.asu.edu/epaa/v10n36.html.

Darling-Hammond, L. (2003). Keeping good teachers: What leaders can do. *Educational Leadership, 60*(8), 6–13.

Darling-Hammond, L., Berry, B., & Thoreson, A. (2001). Does teacher certification matter? Evaluating the evidence. *Educational Evaluation and Policy Analysis, 23*(1), 57–77.

Decker, P. T., Mayer, D. P., & Glazerman, S. (2004). *The effects of Teach for America on students: Findings from a national evaluation.* Princeton, NJ: Mathematica Policy Research.

Duffrin, E. (2004, September). Alternative certification: No consensus on pros, cons. *Catalyst.* Retrieved January 15, 2009, from http://www.catalyst-chicago.org/arch/09-04/0904altresearch.htm.

Feistritzer, C. E. (2007). *Alternative teacher certification: A state-by-state analysis 2007.* Washington, DC: National Center for Alternative Certification.

Fetler, M. (1999). High school staff characteristics and mathematics test results. *Education Policy Analysis Archives, 7*(9) [Entire issue]. Retrieved November 9, 199, from http://epaa.asu.edu/epaa/v7n9.html

Fuller, E. J. (1999). *Does teacher certification matter? A comparison of TAAS performance in 1997 between schools with low and high percentages of certified teachers.* Austin, TX: Charles A. Dana Center, University of Texas at Austin.

Goldhaber, D. (2002). The mystery of good teaching. *Education Next, 2*(1), 50–55.

Goldhaber, D., & Brewer, D. (2000). Does teacher certification matter? High school certification status and student achievement. *Educational Evaluation and Policy Analysis, 22*(2), 129–145.

Grissmer, D. W., & Kirby, S. N. (1987). *Teacher attrition: The uphill climb to staff the nation's schools.* Santa Monica, CA: Rand Corporation.

Grossman, P. L. (1989a). Learning to teach without teacher education. *Teachers College Record, 91,* 191–208.

Grossman, P. L. (1989b). A study in contrast: Sources of pedagogical content knowledge for secondary English. *Journal of Teacher Education, 40*(5), 24–31.

Grossman, P. L. (1990). *The making of a teacher: Teacher knowledge and teacher education.* New York: Teachers College Press.

Grossman, P. L. (1994). *Preparing teachers of substance: Prospects for joint work* (Occasional Paper No. 20). Seattle, WA: Center for Educational Renewal, College of Education, University of Washington.

Henke, R., Chen, X., & Geis, S. (2000). *Progress through the teacher pipeline: 1992–93 college graduates and elementary/secondary school teaching as of 1997.* Washington, DC: National Center for Education Statistics, U.S. Department of Education.

Hess, F. (2001). *Tear down this wall: The case for a radical overhaul of teacher certification.* Washington, DC: Progressive Policy Institute.

Ingersoll, R. M. (2005). The problems of underqualified teachers: A sociological perspective. *Sociology of Education, 78*(2), 175–178.

Ingersoll, R. M. (2007). *Misdiagnosing the teacher quality problem.* Philadelphia: Consortium for Policy Research Policy Brief, University of Pennsylvania.

Kennedy, M. M. (1991). Some surprising findings on how teachers learn to teach. *Educational Leadership, 49*(3), 14–17.

Kirby, S. N., Darling-Hammond, L., & Hudson, L. (1989). Nontraditional recruits to mathematics and science teaching. *Educational Evaluation and Policy Analysis, 11*(3), 301–323.

Kramer, R. (1991). *Ed school follies: The miseducation of America's teachers.* New York: Free Press.

Laczko-Kerr, I., & Berliner, D. C. (2002). The effectiveness of "Teach for America" and other under-certified teachers on student academic achievement: A case of harmful public policy. *Education Policy Analysis Archives, 10*(37). Retrieved on January 19, 2009 from: http://epaa.asu.edu/epaa/v10n37/.

McDiarmid, G. W., & Wilson, S. M. (1991). An exploration of the subject matter knowledge of alternate route teachers: Can we assume they know their subjects. *Journal of Teacher Education, 42*(2), 93–103.

Murnane, R. J., Singer, J. D., & Willett, J. B. (1989). The influences of salaries and "opportunity costs" on teachers' career choices: Evidence from North Carolina. *Harvard Educational Review, 59,* 325–346.

Natriello, G., Hansen, A., Frisch, A., & Zumwalt, K. (1990). *Characteristics of entering teachers in New Jersey.* Unpublished manuscript. Teachers College, Columbia University, New York.

Peske, H., & Haycock, K. (2006). *Teaching inequity: How poor and minority students are shortchanged on teacher quality.* Washington, DC: Education Trust.

Raymond, M., Fletcher, S., & Luque, J. (2001). *Teach for America: An evaluation of teacher differences and student outcomes in Houston, Texas.* Stanford, CA: Center for Research on Educational Outcomes, The Hoover Institution, Stanford University.

Roach, V., & Cohen, B. A. (2002). *Moving past the politics: How alternative certification can promote comprehensive teacher development reforms.* Alexandra, VA: National Association of State Boards of Education.

Shen, J. (1997a). Has the alternative certification policy materialized its promise? A comparison between traditionally and alternatively certified teachers in public schools. *Educational Evaluation and Policy Analysis, 19*(3), 276–283.

Shen, J. (1997b). Teacher retention and attrition in public schools: Evidence from SASS91. *Journal of Educational Research, 91*(2), 81–88.

Shen, J. (1998). The impact of the alternative certification policy on the elementary and secondary teaching force in public schools. *Journal of Research and Development in Education, 32,* 9–16.

Shen, J. (2000). The impact of the alternative certification policy: Multiple perspectives. In J. D. McIntyre & D. M. Byrd (Eds.), *Research on effective models for teacher education: Teacher education year book VIII* (pp. 235–247). Thousand Oaks, CA: Corwin.

Singer, J. D. (1993). Are special educators' career paths special? Results from a 13-year longitudinal study. *Exceptional Children, 59,* 262–279.

Stoddart, T., & Floden, R. E. (1995). *Traditional and alternative routes to teacher certification: Issues, assumptions, and misconceptions.* East Lansing, MI: National Center for Research on Teacher Learning.

Whitener, S. D., Gruber, K. J., Lynch, H., Tingos, K., Perona, M., & Fondelier, S. (1997). *Characteristics of stayers, movers, and leavers: Results from the teacher followup survey: 1994–95.* Washington, DC: U.S. Department of Education.

Wright, S. (2001). The alternative route to certification. *Techniques, 76*(5), 24–27.

CHAPTER TEN

Teacher Retention and Attrition in Public Schools
Evidence from the 1990–91 Schools and Staffing Survey

Jianping Shen

Introduction

The retention of public school teachers has been an issue of continuing concern in education. Some studies reveal that bright college graduates are less likely to enter the teaching profession, and that even if they do, they leave in a short period of time (Kelly, 2004; Murnane et al., 1991; Schlechty & Vance, 1981). This phenomenon is a cause for concern about the quality of the teaching force. In addition to the issue of quality, high rates of teacher attrition disrupt program continuity and planning, hinder student learning, and increase school districts' expenditures on recruiting and hiring. The study intends to inquire into teacher retention and attrition by conducting discriminant function analyses on data gathered in the 1990–91 Schools and Staffing Survey (SASS91) and the 1991–92 Teacher Followup Survey (TFS92) and draw some policy implications for teacher retention in public schools. As will be discussed in the following, SASS91 and TFS92, conducted by the National Center for Education Statistics, are large, national surveys that include questionnaires for, among others, schools, administrators, and teachers.

Literature Review

There are essentially two approaches to studying teacher retention and attrition. The first is the multivariate or theoretical approach that inquires into a set of variables simultaneously to test theories explaining why teachers choose to stay in or leave the teaching profession, such as the human capital theory (Kirby & Grissmer, 1993), the social learning theory (Chapman, 1984; Chapman & Green, 1986), and the theory of teachers as economically rational decision-makers (Theobald, 1990). The second is the bivariate approach that inquires into the relation between retention/attrition and another variable. For example, Murnane and colleagues

(1991) studied the individual roles of salary, gender, ethnicity, and subject specialization in teacher retention. The following briefly reviews the main findings of the two approaches.

The human capital theory of occupational choice, as applied by Kirby and Grissmer (1993), posits that individuals make a systematic assessment of benefits and costs of entering and staying in a profession. There are two types of human capital—general and specific. The greater the accumulation of specific human capital, the lower the probability of attrition. Therefore, younger teachers are more likely to leave, and attrition is more likely to occur early in the career. As a matter of fact, Lortie's (1975) explication on easy and casual entry into teaching is a special case of the human capital theory because the specific human capital tends to be of a small amount if entry into an occupation is easy and casual. Chapman (1984) and Chapman and Green (1986) studied four groups of University of Michigan graduates with teaching certificates—(a) taught continuously, (b) taught intermittently, (c) left teaching, and (d) never taught. They found that the groups differed in personal characteristics, educational experience/initial commitment, professional integration into teaching, external influences, and career satisfaction. They then concluded that teacher retention/attrition was a result of social learning process. Theobald (1990) studied teachers in the state of Washington in the 1984–85 and 1986–87 school years and found, among others, that a decision to continue teaching in the same school district the following year was negatively related to property wealth of the community and positively related to salary. Teachers seemed to be economically rational decision-makers.

The bivariate approach is more prevalent in the literature. One of the most recent and comprehensive studies was conducted by Murnane and colleagues (Murnane et al., 1991). Analyzing data from North Carolina and Michigan, Murnane and colleagues found, among others, the following: teacher attrition is high during the initial years of work; mature women stay, younger women leave; elementary school teachers stay the longest, chemistry and physics teachers the shortest; teachers with high test scores are more likely to leave earlier; teachers who are paid more stay longer; regardless of race, teachers who work in large urban districts tend to have shorter teaching careers than do teachers working in smaller suburban districts; after controlling for district differences, it was found that black teachers are less likely to leave teaching than are white teachers.

Generally speaking, Murnane and colleagues' study confirms some conventional wisdom and many research findings such as brighter teachers are more likely to leave teaching (Schlechty & Vance, 1981). However, there are some contradictions as well. For example, Bobbitt and colleagues (1991, 1994) surveyed teachers in the 1988–89 and 1991–92 school years and found that the rate at which public school teachers of general education subjects leave the profession vary little by field. Science and math teachers, in particular, are no more likely to leave the teaching profession than teachers of other general education subjects such as English, reading, and social studies. The difference in findings between Murnane's and Bobbitt's studies might be due to the time frame (the former study used data collected in the years from the late 1960s to mid-1980s while the latter study collected data during the 1988–89 and 1991–92 school years) and/or due to the geographic representation (the former study focused on data from North Carolina and Michigan while the latter study had a nationally representative sample).

Also contrary to Murnane and colleagues' conclusion on the impact of school district is Heyns's (1988) inquiry into teacher attrition that used data presented in the 1972 National Longitudinal Study. Her analysis suggested that teachers are more likely to leave relatively good schools, in favorable locations, rather than problem schools. Later, Theobald (1990) found that teachers in wealthy, highly assessed valuation districts are more likely to leave their jobs than comparable teachers elsewhere, when other factors are held constant. He speculated that one of the explanations for the above phenomenon is the sociological principle of relative deprivation. In other words, the social and financial position of teachers in wealthy districts tends to be lower than their counterparts' in poor and economically depressed districts.

In addition to gender, subject area, and academic ability, other personal variables that were studied include age, race, family factors (e.g., marital status and whether having children), and initial teaching experience. Teacher attrition pattern is found to follow a U-shaped curve over a life cycle. Attrition rate is high for young teachers during the early stages of their professional life, low for middle-aged teachers, and high again for old teachers as they approach retirement (Grissmer & Kirby, 1987; Hanushek, Kain, & Rivkin, 2004; Ingersoll, 2001; Murnane, Singer, & Willett, 1989; Singer, 1993). Race is found to be unrelated to teacher attrition (Chapman & Hutcheson, 1982; Heyns, 1988; Ingersoll, 2002; Singer, 1993; Smith & Ingersoll, 2004; Theobald, 1990). However, other studies found that majority teachers in urban areas are more likely to leave than are minority teachers (Dworkin, 1980), and that African American teachers are less likely to leave teaching than are whites (Bloland & Selby, 1980; Kelly, 2004). As to family factors, women with children are more likely to stay in teaching or reenter teaching than those who are not married and have no children (Heyns, 1988), and teachers from higher social classes are more likely to leave teaching (Dworkin, 1985). Another important factor in teacher retention is teachers' initial field experience. A positive experience is found to be positively correlated with teacher retention (Chapman & Green, 1986; Metzke, 1988).

In addition to salary, other school-related factors studied include teacher/student ratio, teachers' involvement in decision making, administrative support, teaching level, student characteristics, and school location. Teacher retention is found to be positively correlated with a larger teacher/student ratio (Theobald, 1990), more involvement in decision making by teachers (Bacharach, 1990; Darling-Hammond & Wise, 1983; Liu & Meyer, 2005), and having more support from the administration (Bobbitt, Faupel, & Burns, 1991; Metzke, 1988; Smith & Ingersoll, 2004). It is found that teachers leave the profession sooner at the secondary level than at the elementary level (Heyns, 1988; Keith, Warren, & Dilts, 1983; Murnane, Singer, & Willett, 1989) and that there is a higher attrition rate in urban schools (Corcoran, Walker, & White, 1988; Haberman, 1987) where new teachers feel it is difficult to completely learn how to work effectively with urban students (Grant, 1989).

Although both the multivariate and bivariate approaches have contributed to our knowledge of teacher retention and attrition, they have their pitfalls. Empirical data tend to support the aforementioned theories, but each theory explains teacher retention and attrition only from a certain perspective. In other words, other theories might explain teacher retention and attrition equally well. Furthermore, the multivariate approach tends to narrow the scope of variables included in a study because of the particular focus on supporting a theory. This narrowness of focus is alleviated by the bivariate approach because many issues can be studied by repeating inquiry into retention/attrition and another variable. Nonetheless, the bivariate approach does not take into consideration the relationship between and among those variables related to retention/attrition. The study combines the strengths of these two approaches by capitalizing on the richness and uniqueness of the SASS91 and TFS92 data.

Conceptualization and Research Question

On the basis of literature review, the study assumes that teacher retention and attrition are a function of, among others, individual factors, school-related factors, and the interaction between these two groups of factors as reflected in individuals' perceptions of school- and profession-related issues. This provides a general framework for selecting variables for the study. The study inquires specifically into whether the following three groups—(1) teachers who stayed in the same school, (2) teachers who voluntarily moved to another school, and (3) teachers who left teaching of their own accord between the 1990-91 and 1991-92 school years—differ on personal characteristics, school characteristics, and their perceptions of school- and profession-related issues; if so, how do they differ.

In comparison to the existing literature, the study has the following strengths. First, as will be discussed in the method section, the study inquires into the issue of teacher retention and attrition in public schools by using a nationally representative sample. Billingsley's (1993) comprehensive review of literature on teacher retention and attrition indicates that in this particular research area, most of the studies used data from a school district, a state, or several states. A nationally representative sample is very difficult and expensive to study this issue.

Second, the link between SASS91 and TFS92 gives the study some methodological strengths. Most of the studies on teacher retention are based on retrospective data. One of the shortcomings associated with retrospective data is that there is a time gap, and thus there is a possible reconstruction process based on the experience had after leaving teaching or continuing to teach for a period of time. The approach of the study is analogous to the "thinking aloud technique" in psychological studies. 56,051 teachers were first surveyed in SASS91 regarding their demographics, work load, school policy, and perceptions on various issues; 5,075 of the SASS91 participants—including teachers who stayed in the same school, moved to another school, or left teaching—were surveyed again in TFS92. Therefore, the SASS91 survey data are instances of teachers' "thinking aloud" or "acting out" that serve as predictors of their status in the following school year.

Third, as will be shown in the following, the study takes into account many variables in relation to teachers' and schools' characteristics. One of the shortcomings of the existing research approach is that many studies are narrowly focused on selecting variables, which is justifiable in terms of supporting a theory or a position on some variables' role in teacher retention. However, at this stage it is more constructive to stand on the shoulders of previous studies and broaden the selection of variables. Furthermore, an inquiry into variables of different nature will have policy implications for various aspects of the retention issue. For instance, those unchangeable personal characteristics have more ramifications for recruitment and hiring than for retention. SASS91 surveyed teachers, administrators, schools, and school districts. Therefore, a wide range of meaningful variables can be selected from the SASS91 data.

Finally, the coding of reasons for leaving teaching or schools enables us to distinguish between those who leave teaching or change schools voluntarily and those who do so involuntarily, two distinctly different groups (Kirby & Grissmer, 1993). In almost all previous studies, voluntary and involuntary leavers and movers were not distinguished.

TFS92 (Bobbitt et al., 1994, p. 39) defined teachers who stay in the same school, leave school, and leave teaching in the following:

> Stayers: Teachers who stayed in the same school between school years 1990–91 and 1991–92
> Movers: Teachers who moved to a different school between school years 1990–91 and 1991–92
> Leavers: Teachers who left the teaching profession between school years 1990–91 and 1991–92

As indicated in the foregoing and will be discussed in detail in sample description, the study includes only stayers and voluntary movers and leavers. In other words, this study does not include involuntary leavers who left teaching because of retirement, health, caring for family members, or school staffing action. Neither does the study include those involuntary movers who moved to another school due to school staffing action. By focusing on voluntary movers and leavers, the study is able to better capture the nature of teachers' attrition. Besides, the implications of studying involuntary leavers and movers are limited in comparison to inquiring into voluntary leavers and movers. For the purpose of simplicity, the terms "movers" and "leavers" rather than "voluntary movers" and "voluntary leavers" will be used in the following.

In summary, taking advantage of the strength of the SASS91 and TFS92 data, the study inquires into whether stayers, movers, and leavers differ on personal characteristics, school characteristics, and the interaction between personal and school characteristics as reflected in teachers' perceptions of school- and profession-related issues; if they do differ, the study will continue to inquire into the dimension(s) along which they differ.

Method

Sample

The achieved sample size of public school teacher is 4,761 in TFS92. According to the original coding by National Center for Education Statistics, among the 4,761 (weighted N = 2,553,474) who returned survey questionnaires, 2,233 were stayers, 1,069 were movers, and 1,459 were leavers. Among the 1,069 movers, 374 were involuntary movers due to school staffing action. Among the 1,459 leavers, 775 were involuntary leavers due to retirement, health, and school staffing action. In sum, the sample of the study includes 2,233 stayers, 695 voluntary movers, and 684 voluntary leavers, with a total of 3,612 (weighted N = 2,404,592). Because the sample design of TFS92 involved stratification, disproportionate sampling of certain strata, and clustered probability sampling, the resultant TFS92 sample was not a random sample. Therefore, a modified TFS92 sample weight, which is based on TFS92 teachers' final weight, was used to approximate the population but was adjusted down to the actual sample size of the study. For detailed information regarding TFS92 sampling and weighting, please refer to Bobbitt and others (1994).

Variables

Variables included in the study are reported in Table 10.1. These variables are extracted from the teacher, administrator, and school and school district components of SASS91 and are grouped into three categories: (1) personal characteristics, (2) school characteristics, and (3) teachers' perceptions.

Table 10.1. A Description of Variables

Personal characteristics	
A1	Years in teaching—number of years since first entering teaching (continuous)
A2	Annual salary—base salary for 1990–91 academic year (continuous, 1 = 1,000–20,000; 2 = 20,001–25,000; 3 = 25,001–30,000; 4 = 30,001–35,000; 5 = 35,001 or greater)
A3	Race (dichotomous, 1 = minority, 0 = white)
A4	Background before entering teaching (dichotomous, 1 = education-related jobs, 0 = studying in colleges or having jobs not related to education)
A5	Full-time or part-time (dichotomous, 1 = full-time, 0 = part-time)
A6	Subject matter of undergraduate studies (dichotomous, 1 = sciences, 0 = other)

A7	Having a master's degree—whether having a master's degree (dichotomous, 1 = yes, 0 = no)
A8	Sex (dichotomous, 1 = male, 0 = female)
A9	Level of teaching (dichotomous, 1 = secondary, 0 = elementary)
A10	Bilingual status—whether the teacher is bilingual (dichotomous, 1 = bilingual, 0 = not bilingual)
A11	Number of breaks—number of service breaks of one year or more since entering teaching (continuous)
School characteristics	
B1	Percentage of teachers with less than 3 years of experience—percentage of teachers with less than 3 years of experience in this school (continuous)
B2	Percentage of minority students—percentage of minority students in this school (continuous, 1 = 0–4%, 2 = 5–19%, 3 = 20–49%, 4 = 50–100%)
B3	Number of free lunch students—how many K–12 students receiving free lunches in this school (continuous)
B4	Salary for senior teachers—annual base salary for teachers with a master's degree and 20 years of teaching experience (continuous)
B5	Salary for beginning teachers—annual base salary for teachers with bachelor's degree but no teaching experience (continuous)
B6	Total enrollment (continuous, 1 = 1–149; 2 = 150–299; 3 = 300–499; 4 = 500–749; 5 = 750–1,499; 6 = 1,500 or greater)
B7	Locale (continuous, 1 = rural, 2 = small town, 3 = urban fringe/large town, 4 = central city)
B8	Mentoring program—whether there is a formal program to help beginning teachers (dichotomous, 1 = yes, 0 = no)
B9	Class organization—ways classes are organized (dichotomous, 1 = departmentalized, 0 = other)

	Teachers' perceptions
C1	Teaching having more advantages—teacher's perception that teaching has more advantages than disadvantages (continuous, 1 = strongly disagree to 4 = strongly agree)
C2	Teacher's influence over policy—teacher's perception of his/her influence over school- and teaching-related policy, averaged over 10 items, Cronbach's a = .81 (continuous, 1 = no influence to 6 = complete influence)
C3	School administrators knowing staff's problem (continuous, 1 = strongly disagree to 4 = strongly agree)
C4	Match between expertise and assignment—whether there is a match between main teaching assignment and teacher's perceived best-qualified area of teaching (dichotomous, 1 = match, 0 = not match)
C5	School problems—teacher's perception on the degree to which student deviant behaviors and lack of family support exist, averaged over 21 items with Cronbach's a = .94 (1 = not a problem to 4 = serious)

Data Analysis

Direct discriminant function analyses are conducted to inquire into whether there are differences among the stayers, movers, and leavers in personal characteristics, school characteristics, and their perceptions. If they differ, then the question becomes along which dimension(s) they differ. Discriminant function analysis is a multivariate technique that identifies the combination(s) of variables (i.e., functions) that best separate (i.e., discriminate among) groups.

Results

Table 10.2 reports the intercorrelations of the variables within the three sets so as to assist the reader in interpreting the subsequent analyses where multicollinearity might be an issue. The correlation coefficients are generally low. The results of three discriminant function analyses on personal characteristics, school characteristics, and teachers' perceptions are reported in Table 10.3.

		A1	A2	A3	A4	A5	A6	A7	A8	A9	A10	A11
Personal characteristics												
A1	Years in teaching	1.00										
A2	Annual salary	.54	1.00									
A3	Race	-.03	-.02	1.00								
A4	Background before entering teaching	-.25	-.11	.09	1.00							
A5	Full-time or part-time	.03	.15	.00	-.04	1.00						
A6	Subject matter of undergraduate studies	.05	.05	.02	-.03	.05	1.00					
A7	Having a master's degree	.29	.40	-.03	-.11	.01	.03	1.00				
A8	Sex	.07	.14	-.05	-.09	.02	.15	.08	1.00			
A9	Level of teaching	.02	.06	.05	-.01	.04	.21	.06	.37	1.00		
A10	Bilingual status	-.05	-.01	-.04	.05	.02	-.02	-.07	-.06	-.08	1.00	
A11	Number of breaks	.33	.06	-.05	-.13	-.01	-.04	.06	-.16	-.04	.01	1.00
		B1	B2	B3	B4	B5	B6	B7	B8	B9		
School characteristics												
B1	Percentage of teachers with less than 3-year experience	1.00										
B2	Percentage of minority students	.14	1.00									
B3	Number of free lunch students	.08	.55	1.00								
B4	Salary for senior teachers	-.10	.15	.09	1.00							
B5	Salary for beginning teachers	-.04	.29	.22	.76	1.00						
B6	Total enrollment	-.10	.22	.41	.27	.30	1.00					
B7	Locale	-.02	.43	.30	.33	.34	.32	1.00				
B8	Mentoring program	.10	.16	.11	.09	.14	.15	.11	1.00			
B9	Class organization	-.11	-.04	-.01	.02	-.01	.32	-.03	-.01	1.00		
		C1	C2	C3	C4	C5						
Teachers' perceptions												
C1	Teaching having more advantages	1.00										
C2	Teacher's influence over policies	.26	1.00									
C3	Administrators knowing staff's problems	.19	.38	1.00								
C4	Match between expertise and assignment	-.02	.03	.03	1.00							
C5	School problems	-.22	-.29	-.23	.03	1.00						

Table 10.2. Intercorrelations among the Variables

Chapter Ten

		stayer		mover		leaver		univariate	item to function
		M	SD	M	SD	M	SD	F	correlation
Personal characteristics									
A1	Years in teaching	17.09	9.36	12.13	9.82	13.19	10.46	27.72**	.81
A2	annual salary	3.32	1.37	2.73	1.36	2.81	1.43	19.41**	.68
A3	race	0.10	0.30	0.13	0.34	0.13	0.34	0.96	−.15
A4	background before entering teaching	0.11	0.31	0.80	0.27	0.15	0.36	1.56	.05
A5	full-time or part-time	0.92	0.27	0.90	0.30	0.87	0.34	2.11	.19
A6	subject matter of undergraduate studies	0.06	0.23	0.05	0.22	0.03	0.17	0.74	.10
A7	having a master's degree	0.45	0.50	0.41	0.49	0.47	0.50	0.62	.09
A8	sex	0.29	0.45	0.29	0.44	0.26	0.46	0.18	.01
A9	level of teaching	0.44	0.50	0.43	0.50	0.42	0.50	0.14	.05
A10	bilingual status	0.03	0.16	0.03	0.16	0.02	0.15	0.03	.02
A11	number of breaks	0.43	0.79	0.43	0.74	0.43	0.71	0.00	−.01
	group centroids								
	stayers								.04
	movers								−.60
	leavers								−.47
School characteristics									
B1	Percentage of teachers with less than 3-year experience	11.80	9.77	14.26	11.11	14.24	10.93	6.34**	.55
B2	Percentage of minority students	2.40	1.16	2.83	1.14	2.42	1.16	8.93**	.56
B3	number of free lunch students	202	222	259	239	244	249	5.56**	.52
B4	salary for senior teachers	36,640	7,041	35,247	6,635	35,386	5,949	3.77*	−.43
B5	salary for beginning teachers	21,395	2,980	21,130	3,066	21,049	2,833	1.01	−.22

Table 10.3. Results of Discriminant Function Analyses *(continued on following page)*

		stayer		mover		leaver		univariate	item to function correlation
		M	SD	M	SD	M	SD	F	
B6	total enrollment	3.87	1.26	3.79	1.25	3.73	1.26	0.73	-.18
B7	locale	2.64	1.07	2.74	1.10	2.69	1.07	0.69	.18
B8	mentoring program	0.73	0.44	0.74	0.44	0.60	0.44	3.49*	-.20
B9	class organization	0.45	0.50	0.43	0.50	0.33	0.47	2.17	-.21
	group centroids								
	stayers								-.03
	movers								.46
	leavers								.32
	Teachers' perceptions								
C1	teaching having more advantages	3.54	0.65	3.42	0.78	3.29	0.86	7.99**	.74
C2	teacher's influence over policies	4.41	0.83	4.24	0.86	4.14	1.01	7.57**	.73
C3	administrators knowing staff's problems	3.11	0.90	2.99	0.93	2.84	1.02	5.24**	.60
C4	match between expertise and assignment	0.82	0.39	0.77	0.43	0.81	0.40	1.53	.24
C5	school problems	1.90	0.58	1.98	0.58	1.94	0.51	1.98	-.31
	group centroids								
	stayers								.02
	movers								-.24
	leavers								-.44

$* p < .5; ** p < .01.$

Table 10.3. Results of Discriminant Function Analyses *(continued)*

Personal Characteristics

There is one significant discriminant function to distinguish three groups on personal characteristics: $\chi^2(22) = 88.15, p < .001, R_C = .15$. An examination of group centroids and items to function correlations indicate that this discriminant function separates stayers from movers and leavers on variables of years in teaching and annual salary. Stayers ($M = 17.09$) have taught longer than have movers ($M = 12.13$) and leavers ($M = 13.19$); stayers ($M = 3.32$) have higher salary than do movers ($M = 2.73$) and leavers ($M = 2.81$). Since years in teaching and annual salary are positively correlated ($r = .54$) and are different aspects of the same construct—seniority—this discriminant function is essentially that of seniority. The findings in relation to personal characteristics support previous findings that more experienced teachers and teachers with higher salaries tend to stay in teaching. The three groups do not differ on race, background before entering teaching, full-time or part-time status, subject matter of undergraduate studies, having a master's degree, sex, level of teaching, bilingual status, and number of breaks.

School Characteristics

The discriminant function analysis of three groups on school characteristics yields one significant function, $\chi^2(18) = 55, p < .001, R_C = .12$, which separates stayers from movers and leavers. In comparison to stayers, leavers and movers are in schools that have a higher percentage of teachers with less than three years of teaching experience, a higher percentage of minority students, more students on free lunch, and lower salaries for teachers who have a master's degree and 20 years of teaching experience. This function is a combination of several aspects of school characteristics. First, that movers and leavers are in schools where there is a higher percentage of teachers with less than three years of experience supports the previous finding that teacher attrition occurs early in the professional career. Second, a higher percentage of minority students and more students on free lunch seem to indicate social disadvantage. Therefore, teachers are more likely to move out of or leave teaching from socially disadvantaged schools, a finding that is inconsistent with Heyns's (1988) and Theobald's (1990). Third, in schools where there is a higher salary for teachers with a master's degree and 20 years of experience, teachers are more likely to stay. This points out the importance of constructing a career ladder by having a more differential salary schedule.

Teaching as a careerless profession (Lortie, 1975) seems to be one of the predictors of teachers' moving and leaving behaviors.

Salary for the bachelor's degree holder with no experience, total school enrollment, location of the school, mentoring program, and class organization are predictors of membership neither in the stayers' group nor in the movers' and leavers' group. Among these variables, only mentoring program has a significant univariate F test for three groups. In fact, the second nonsignificant discriminant function, $\chi^2(8) = 15$, $p = .06$, on which the variable mentoring program is heavily loaded, distinguishes stayers ($M = 0.73$) and movers ($M = 0.74$) from leavers ($M = 0.60$). Having a program to help beginning teachers seems to be conducive to teachers' stay in teaching.

Teachers' Perceptions

The final analysis on teachers' perceptions also yields one significant discriminant function, $\chi^2(10) = 32$, $p < .001$, $R_C = .09$, and it separates stayers from movers and leavers. In comparison to leavers and movers, stayers tend to perceive that teaching has more advantages than disadvantages, that they have more influence over school- and teaching-related policies, and that administrators know their problems better. This finding seems to indicate the importance of appreciating intrinsic values of teaching, empowering teachers, and supporting teachers' work from an administrative perspective. Perceptions of match between expertise and teaching assignment and the extent to which school problems exist do not seem to be predictors of group membership.

Discussion

The findings of the study, which is based on a nationally representative sample, both confirm and challenge previous findings. The following findings of the study are consistent with previous ones: First, teachers with less experience tend to move or leave while more experienced teachers tend to stay; second, the amount of salary—in this case annual salary for all teachers and salary for senior members—is positively correlated with teacher retention; third, the appreciation of intrinsic merits of the teaching profession helps teachers remain in teaching; and finally, empowering teachers and letting them have more influence over school and teaching policies are also associated with teacher retention.

The findings of the study also challenge some of the previous findings in the following two aspects. First, this study finds that teachers' moving and leaving behaviors are more associated with poor schools in which there are more students on free lunch and a higher percentage of minority students, and that the locale of the school is not associated with teachers' retention and attrition. The combination of these two findings is contrary to Heyns's (1988) and Theobald's (1990) studies in which they found that teachers tend to leave good schools in wealthy communities. One plausible explanation for the findings of the study is that the school-bus program plays a role in reducing the difference among schools in various localities, and teacher retention and attrition become more associated with characteristics of a particular school than with the general locality of the school. Some qualitative data of future studies will help explain the discrepancy in findings. Second, inconsistent with some of the previous findings, the data of this study indicate that teacher retention and attrition are not associated with the subject matter of teachers' undergraduate studies and the teaching level. The differential salary schedule and incentives for shortage areas (Levin, 1985) seem to have kept more science majors in teaching. Since the issue of science and nonscience majors is usually related to the secondary level, the incentives for science majors appear to have helped close the gap in teacher retention between elementary and secondary teachers.

The findings of the study have policy implications for the issues of teacher retention and attrition in public schools. First, there is an urgent need to build into teaching a career ladder. Teaching is often characterized as "having a flat ladder" or "careerless." Since years in teaching, annual salary for all teachers, and salary for senior teachers are positively associated with teacher retention, it is important not only to raise teachers' salary across the board but also to build a more differential salary schedule. This suggestion is consistent with the human capital theory, which posits that the more a teacher has invested in teaching, the more the teacher tends to stay in teaching. Teaching has been permeated with an egalitarian ethos, a factor that seems to be conducive to teacher attrition.

Second, connected with the suggestion to build into teaching a more differential career ladder is the need to empower teachers. Teachers are traditionally not given much decision power. The educational research and administration communities once tried to provide teachers with "foolproof," prepackaged curriculum as if teachers' thinking and decision are not related to improving teaching quality. The data of the study clearly indicate that teachers who feel having more influence over school and teaching policies are more likely to stay. To empower teachers is one of the ways to improve teacher retention.

Third, the data of the study highlight the importance of paying attention to schools where there are more free-lunch students and a higher percentage of minority students, both of which are indicators of students' poor background. These students are disadvantaged. Their situation is exacerbated by teacher attrition, which not only disrupts the teaching and learning process but also weakens the bond between the teacher and the student. Therefore, special incentives and programs must be provided to teachers working in schools with more disadvantaged students.

Finally, teacher retention is a very complicated issue that involves many factors and processes. The finding that teachers who perceive teaching as having more advantages than disadvantages tend to stay has more implications for recruitment into teacher education programs and hiring into schools; similarly, building a differential professional ladder and empowering teachers have more implications for social and school policies. There is no single solution for the issue of teacher attrition; a multiple-perspective approach to this issue must be in place.

The study is not without its limitations. The major limitation is that the data for this study are cross-sectional. This study inquires into teacher retention and attrition between the 1990-91 and 1991-92 school years. Some of the important issues related to teacher retention and attrition, such as the return of former teachers and teachers' career pattern over a longer period of time, cannot be addressed by using the SASS91 data. The second limitation of the study is that discriminant function analysis is essentially a correlational technique, thus no definitive causality can be inferred from such a technique. However, this does not negate the value of the study because the discriminant function analysis is able to inform us of the pattern in a national setting, and because controlled, experimental approach is almost unrealistic for studying the issue of teacher retention and attrition. The third limitation is that substantively meaningful variables in relation to teacher education programs that these teachers went through are not available in the SASS91 data. Otherwise, it would be interesting to inquire into the association between features of teacher education programs and the career persistency of their graduates. The final limitation is that the data for this study are purely quantitative. Collecting qualitative data in future studies will offer some explanations for the patterns found in the study as well as for the discrepancy between findings of this study and previous ones. All these limitations point out the directions for future studies.

Teacher retention is a very important issue in education. Given the common finding that more academically talented teachers are more likely to leave in the first few years of entering teaching, the issue of teacher retention gains more urgency. To implement the policy suggestions and to staff this nation's schools with a qualified and stable teaching force will make many teachers have a more satisfying career, improve the bonding between students and teachers in schools, and turn teaching into a lifelong professional career.

References

Bacharach, S. B. (1990). The dimensionality of decision participation in educational organizations: The value of a multi-domain evaluative approach. *Educational Administration Quarterly, 26(2),* 126–167.

Billingsley, B. S. (1993). Teacher retention and attrition in special and general education: A critical review of the literature. *Journal of Special Education, 27(2),* 137–174.

Bloland, P. A., & Selby, T. J. (1980). Factors associated with career change among secondary school teachers: A review of the literature. *Educational Research Quarterly, 5(3),* 13–24.

Bobbitt, S. A., Faupel, E., & Burns, S. (1991). *Characteristics of stayers, movers, and leavers: Results from the Teacher Followup Survey: 1988–89.* Washington, DC: National Center for Education Statistics.

Bobbitt, S. A., Leich, M. C., Whitener, S. D., & Lynch, H. R. (1994). *Characteristics of stayers, movers, and leavers: Results from the Teacher Followup Survey: 1991–92.* Washington, DC: National Center for Education Statistics.

Chapman, D. W. (1984). Teacher retention: The test of a model. *American Educational Research Journal, 21(3),* 645–658.

Chapman, D. W., & Green, M. S. (1986). Teacher retention: A further examination. *Journal of Educational Research, 79(5),* 273–279.

Chapman, D. W., & Hutcheson, S. M. (1982). Attrition from teaching careers: A discriminant analysis. *American Journal of Educational Research, 19(1),* 93–105.

Corcoran, T. B., Walker, L. J., & White, J. L. (1988). *Working in urban schools.* Washington, DC: Institute for Educational Leadership.

Darling-Hammond, L. & Wise, A. E. (1983). Teaching Standards, or Standardized Teaching? *Educational Leadership, 41(2),* 66–69.

Dworkin, A. G. (1980). The changing demography of public school teachers: Some implications for faculty turnover in urban areas. *Sociology of Education, 53(2),* 65–73.

Dworkin, A. G. (1985). *When teachers give up: Teacher burnout, teacher turnover, and their impact on children.* Austin, TX: University of Texas,

Hogg Foundation for Mental Health (ERIC Document Reproduction Service No. ED 273 575).

Grant, C. A. (1989). Urban teachers: Their new colleagues and curriculum. *Phi Delta Kappan, 70(10)*, 764–770.

Grissmer, D. W., & Kirby, S. N. (1987). *Teacher attrition: The uphill climb to staff the nation's schools*. Santa Monica, CA: Rand.

Haberman, M. (1987). *Recruiting and selecting teachers for urban schools*. New York: ERIC Clearing House on Urban Education (ERIC Document Reproduction Service No. ED 292 942).

Hanushek, E. A., Kain, J. F., & Rivkin, S. G. (2004). Why public schools lose teachers. *The Journal of Human Resources, 39* (2), 326–354.

Heyns, B. (1988). Educational defectors: A first look at teacher attrition in the NLS-72. *Educational Researcher, 17(3)*, 24–32.

Ingersoll, R. M. (2001). Teacher turnover and teacher shortages: An organizational analysis. *American Educational Research Journal, 38* (3), 499–534.

Ingersoll, R. M. (2002). The teacher shortage: A case of wrong diagnosis and wrong prescription. *NASSP Bulletin, 86* (631), 16–31.

Keith, P. M., Warren, R. D., Dilts, H. E. (1983). Teacher education graduates: Sex, career plans, and preferences for job factors. *Urban Education, 18(3)*, 361–375.

Kelly, S. (2004). An event history analysis of teacher attrition: Salary, teacher tracking, and socially disadvantaged schools. *The Journal of Experimental Education, 72* (3), 195–220.

Kirby, S. N., & Grissmer, D. W. (1993). *Teacher attrition: Theory, evidence, and suggested policy options*. Santa Monica, CA: Rand.

Levin, H. M. (1985). Solving the shortage of mathematics and science teachers. *Educational Evaluation and Policy Analysis, 7(4)*, 371–382.

Liu, X. S., & Meyer, J. P. (2005). Teachers' perceptions of their jobs: A multilevel analysis of the teacher follow-up survey for 1994–95. *Teachers College Record, 107* (5), 985–1003.

Lortie, D. C. (1975). *Schoolteacher: A sociological study*. Chicago: University of Chicago Press.

Metzke, L. K. (1988). A study of the causes of teacher attrition in regular and special education in Wisconsin. (Doctoral dissertation, Marquette University, 1988). *Dissertation Abstracts International, 50*, 42A.

Murnane, R. J., Singer, J. D., & Willett, J. B. (1989). The influences of salaries and "opportunity costs" on teachers' career choices: Evidence from North Carolina. *Harvard Educational Review, 59(3)*, 325–346.

Murnane, R. J., Singer, J. D., Willett, J. B., Kemple, J. J., & Olsen, R. J. (1991). *Who will teach? Policies that matter*. Cambridge, MA: Harvard University.

Schlechty, P. C. & Vance, V. S. (1981). Do academically able teachers leave education? The North Carolina case. *Phi Delta Kappan, 63(2)*, 106–112.

Singer, J. D. (1993). Are special educators' career paths special? Results from a 13-year longitudinal study. *Exceptional Children, 59(3)*, 262–279.

Smith, T. M., & Ingersoll, R. M. (2004). What are the effects of induction and mentoring on beginning teacher turnover? *American Educational Research Journal, 41* (3), 681–714.

Theobald, N. D. (1990). An examination of the influence of personal, professional, and school district characteristics on public school teacher retention. *Economics of Education Review, 9(3)*, 241–250.

SECTION 5

Teacher Preparation

CHAPTER ELEVEN

Improving the Professional Status of Teaching
Perspectives of Future Teachers, Current Teachers, and Education Professors

Jianping Shen and Chia-lin Hsieh

The low professional status of teaching has been a focus of discussion. For example, Goldberg and Renton (1993) indicated that the symptoms of teaching's low status remain prevalent—from inadequate student motivation and complacency to parent dissatisfaction with mediocre performance and society's low regard for teachers. Darling-Hammond (1994), Darling-Hammond and Bransford (2005), Goodlad (1990, 1994), Ornstein (1988), and Pratte and Rury (1991) also analyzed and lamented the low professional status of teaching. Associated with the discussion of the low professional status of teaching are proposals to improve the professional status of teaching. The following is a review of this body of literature.

Literature Review

In the literature there were basically two lines of proposals for improving the professional status of teaching. The first focused on the teacher education program and teacher certification, including suggestions such as increasing the length of teacher training, improving teacher education program quality, and raising teacher certification standards. The other line emphasized the rewards for teaching, including increasing teachers' leadership and extrinsic rewards such as salary. These major ideas for improving the professional status of teaching became the rubrics for organizing the literature review.

To Improve Teacher Education Programs and Certification

To increase the length of training
Many researchers proposed to increase the length of training for teachers (e.g., Holmes Group, 1986; Miller & Silvernail, 1994). The idea usually includes the following elements: an undergraduate major in arts and sci-

ences with an accompanying minor in educational studies, intensive postgraduate year(s) of professional preparation, and finally a clinical master's degree available to interns once they become practicing teachers. It was argued that states should abolish the undergraduate degree in education and make professional teacher education a graduate-level enterprise (e.g., Carnegie Forum on Education and the Economy, 1986; Holmes Group, 1986).

To raise program standards
Requirements for entry into teacher education programs were raised and imposed in a number of states (American Council on Education, 1985). These requirements were intended to upgrade the academic quality of teacher education students (Darling-Hammond & Berry, 1988; Darling-Hammond & Bransford, 2005; Hitz, 2008). The Carnegie Forum on Education and the Economy (1986) suggested that to ensure that teachers receive adequate preparation in their field of study, college faculties and disciplinary societies should undertake a thorough reexamination of undergraduate programs in the arts and sciences to ensure their appropriateness for the preparation of professional teachers. Some researchers and organizations proposed to establish professional development schools that aim to provide new models of teacher education and development by serving as exemplars of practice, builders of knowledge, and vehicles for communicating professional understandings among teacher educators, novices, and veteran teachers (e.g., Darling-Hammond, 2008; Darling-Hammond, 1994; Darling-Hammond & Berry, 1988; Goodlad, 1994; Goodlad & Sirotnik, 1988; Holmes Group, 1986; Levine, 1992; Osguthorpe, 1995).

To raise the exit-level standards
The teaching profession began to engage in serious standard-setting that reflects a growing knowledge base about teaching and a growing consensus about what teachers should be able to do to help all students learn to high levels. The National Education Association and the American Federation of Teachers were among the organizations that enhance reciprocity and make uniform certifying standards among the states. The Carnegie Forum on Education and the Economy (1986) suggested that the National Board for Professional Teaching Standards should be created to establish standards for high levels of competence in the teaching profession, to assess the qualifications of those seeking board certification, and to grant certificates to those who meet the standards. Several national organizations tried to raise the exit-level standards (Interstate New Teacher As-

sessment and Support Consortium, 1991; National Board for Professional Teaching Standards, 1991; National Council for Accreditation of Teacher Education, 1993). Some states, such as Texas, used testing of practicing teachers as a method to improve the quality of the teaching force and, therefore, to raise the status of teaching (Shepard, 1987).

To Improve the Intrinsic and Extrinsic Rewards for Teaching

To increase teachers' leadership and build a career ladder into teaching
Effective teaching research of the late 1960s through the 1970s influenced policymakers and educators to focus almost exclusively on basic skill instruction and specific teaching functions (Rosenshine, 1983). As a consequence, educators failed to extend their thinking about significant teaching goals and, therefore, limited their involvement in key decision-making activities that affected students, schools, and their own professional growth. For this reason the recent restructuring efforts had to convince teachers of their efficacy and responsibility in decision making (Alexander, 2008; Sykes, 1990).

Generally speaking, the argument to increase teachers' leadership is associated with the notion that true professionals are entitled to decision making and leadership. Therefore, the literature on site-based decision making, teacher empowerment, shared leadership, and distributed leadership was consistent with this proposal (e.g., Austin & Reynolds, 1990; Grace, 1995; Harris, Lowery-Moore, & Farrow, 2008; Koster, Dengerink, Korthagen, & Lunenberg, 2008; Lipham, 1991; Rots, Aelterman, Vlerick, & Vermeulen, 2007; Sergiovanni, 1991; Vandenberghe, 1995). For example, Whitaker and Moses (1995) suggested that schools must create a more thoughtful workplace where teachers are empowered to make decisions affecting their work. They suggested further that principals should create the following conditions to empower teachers: (a) letting the teachers make decisions; (b) learning to relinquish control; (c) organizing into teacher teams; (d) coming to grips with empowerment; and (e) getting rid of the hierarchical organizational structure.

Teaching has long been characterized as careerless and flat (e.g., Goodlad, 1984; Lortie, 1975; Shen, 1997; Whitaker & Moses, 1995). Therefore, to build a career ladder in teaching becomes an argument for improving the professional status of teaching. For example, the Holmes Group (1986) proposed a career ladder from instructors, to professional teachers, and to career professionals. The Carnegie Forum on Education and the Economy (1986) and Goodlad (1984) argued for the need to develop a small cadre of teachers who are experienced, effective, and educated at a much higher level.

To increase extrinsic rewards
Teachers' low pay has been characterized as a culprit of the low professional status of teaching. The Carnegie Forum on Education and the Economy (1986) and the Holmes Group (1986) suggested that states and school boards, working closely with teachers, should establish incentive systems that link teachers' compensation to student performance. Several different types of performance-based compensation systems, such as merit and incentive pay, were advanced during the 1980s reform movement (Anderson, 2008; Barber & Klein, 1983; Darling-Hammond & Berry, 1988; Rosenholtz & Smylie, 1984; Shulman, 1987). Associated with the salary was the argument that working conditions for teachers also needed improvement (Gonzalez, Brown, & Slate, 2008; Lieberman & Miller, 1986; Sykes, 1987; Whitaker & Moses, 1995).

Professionalism Issues outside the United States

Improving the status of the teaching profession is an issue in other Western countries as well. For example, Judge (1988) studied public perceptions of the role and status of teachers in the United Kingdom, among other nations. Robinson (1995) examined the status of the teaching profession in England and Wales and proposed an agenda for improving teacher education and the professional status of teaching. Furlong (2008) updated the status of teaching in the twenty-first century. In Australia, Whalley (1986) warned that educational malpractice in the United States may affect legal accountability of Australian teachers. He suggested that teachers should embrace their widening legal responsibility in order to advance professionalism and status in teaching. Sachs and Logan (1990) argued that Australian inservice education policies have unintentionally controlled and deskilled teachers. The authors claimed that teachers' managerial skills are emphasized over curricular and instructional skills, and that teachers' professional development and status suffer consequently.

Research Purposes and Questions

The purpose of this chapter is twofold. First, although we used a set of rubrics to organize the literature review in the foregoing, we did not have any studies that empirically inquire into what the major dimensions of the agenda to improve the professional status of teaching are. Therefore, this study inquired into the dimensionality of the agenda for improving teaching by conducting factor analysis. Second, most of the literature on this topic is produced by education professors, and no studies compare future teachers', current teachers', and education professors' ideas on improving the teaching profession. It is very important for us to be aware of the congruence and/or incongruence among these three groups because the knowledge not only contributes to the literature but also has implications for implementing an agenda to improve the professional status of teaching. As the literature on educational change indicates, an agenda inconsistent with stakeholders' perceptions will encounter resistance in the implementation process (e.g., Cohen, 1990; Fullan, 1993).

Methods

Sample

The data for this chapter were gathered during the Study of the Education of Educators (SEE), which used a purposive, representative sample of 29 institutions across the United States. These 29 institutions were representative in terms of institutional type, geographic and demographic diversity, religious/nonreligious affiliation, and the public/private dimension.

The SEE Faculty Survey questionnaires were mailed to 2,042 faculty members in the 29 institutions; 1,219 returned the questionnaire, yielding a return rate of 59.6%. The Future Teacher Survey questionnaires were sent to 4,644 students at or near the end of their teacher education programs in the 29 institutions; 2,947 returned the questionnaire, resulting in a return rate of 63.5%. The Current Teacher Survey was administered to 994 students in educational administration programs in the 29 institutions; 457 responded, leading to a return rate of 46%. Given the rule of thumb that a response rate of 50% is adequate for analysis and reporting, a response rate of 60% is good, and a response rate of 70% is very good (Babbie, 1989, p. 242); the data collected for this study are satisfactory for analysis. For a detailed discussion of the methodology of SEE, please refer to Goodlad (1990) and Sirotnik (1989).

Instrument

The Future Teacher, Current Teacher, and Faculty Surveys were designed to collect data regarding their biographic and career information and their perceptions of ways to improve the teaching profession, among others. These surveys asked respondents to indicate the extent to which they agreed or disagreed with a list of 20 suggestions for enhancing the status of teaching as a profession. The participants responded on a 7-point Likert scale, with "1" meaning "not at all important" and "7" "extremely important."

Data Analysis

Corresponding to the two purposes of the study, there were two major steps in data analysis. First, a factor analysis was conducted to collapse the items into factors that depict the major dimensions of the agenda for improving the professional status of teaching. After averaging across the items within each factor, ANOVA was then conducted to inquire into whether the three groups were different in the mean of each factor. If the ANOVA indicated that there were statistically significant differences among the three groups, multiple comparisons were employed to inquire into which groups differed from one another.

Results

Results of Factor Analysis

The results of the factor analysis are displayed in Table 11.1. Principal components extraction, eigenvalue greater than 1.0, and varimax rotation were employed to collapse the 20 items into factors. During the first preliminary analysis, a six-factor solution emerged, with the item "clear conceptual and practical argument for why teaching is a profession" being cross-loaded. Therefore, this item was deleted and the analysis was conducted again. The second run resulted in the same factorial structure as the first one. The factors, reported in Table 11.1, explained 60% of the variance.

Table 11.1. Results of Factor Analysis

Item	Loading	Factor
National teacher certification board	.84	Factor 1 Higher national entry, exit, and certification standards
National program exit-level teacher examination	.82	
Require national accreditation with high program standards for all teacher preparing institutions	.73	
Higher program entry-level standards	.58	
Model teacher education programs after other professional training programs in medicine, law, and so forth	.47	

Item	Loading	Factor
Develop leadership roles as an integral part of teaching responsibilities	.82	Factor 2 Improving teacher leadership and career opportunity
Develop participatory management roles as an integral part of teaching responsibilities	.81	
Develop differentiated staffing/career opportunities based upon education plus experience	.75	
Develop a clear, conceptual and practical argument for teaching as part art, part science, and part craft	.62	
Eliminate/phase out undergraduate education majors	.88	Factor 3 Eliminating undergraduate education majors/ courses
Eliminate/phase out undergraduate education courses	.85	
A master's degree in addition to the teaching credential	.81	Factor 4 Lengthening the training
A doctoral degree in addition to the teaching credential	.70	
Five years of university/college preparation	.69	
Develop a small cadre (say 20% of current teacher force) of "professional teachers" with the remaining force at lower level of preparation	.70	Factor 5 Strengthening the professional base
Eliminate "emergency certification" options	.62	
Demonstrable, scientific basis of teaching	.44	
High teacher salaries	.80	Factor 6 Higher salary and improved working condition
Significantly altered working conditions for teachers in schools	.68	

The factor analysis showed that there were six dimensions to the agenda of improving the teaching profession. The following three factors seemed to focus on the program and certification: (1) higher national entry, exit, and certification standards; (2) eliminating undergraduate education majors/courses; and (3) lengthening the training. Two factors appeared to emphasize each of the two types of rewards for teaching: Improving teacher leadership and career opportunity pointed to the intrinsic reward, and higher salary and improved working conditions to the extrinsic reward. There was also a factor focusing on the foundation and organization of the teaching profession—strengthening the professional base.

Results of the ANOVA and Multiple Comparison

The mean and rank for each factor, and the results of ANOVA and multiple comparisons, are displayed in Table 11.2. The ANOVA on each factor was statistically significant at .001 level; Scheffé's multiple range test was conducted and the statistically significant differences at the .05 level are indicated in the table. There were several patterns as displayed in the mean, rank, and the multiple comparison results.

First, there were statistically significant differences among the groups in each of the factors. The multiple comparison tests indicated that, generally speaking, future teachers differed from current teachers and education professors.

Table 11.2. Results of ANOVA and Multiple Comparisons

Factor	Future Teachers (FT)		Current Teachers (CT)		Professors (P)		p	Multiple comparison
	Mean	Rank	Mean	Rank	Mean	Rank		
Higher salary and improved working conditions	5.81	1	5.96	1	6.06	1	< .001	FT < CT, P
Improving teacher leadership and career opportunity	4.90	2	5.45	2	5.36	2	< .001	FT < CT, P
Higher national entry, exit, and certification standards	4.56	3	4.62	3	4.33	4	< .001	FT, CT > P
Strengthening the professional base	3.72	4	4.03	4	4.45	3	< .001	FT, CT < P; FT < CT, P
Lengthening the training	3.30	5	3.72	5	3.88	5	< .001	FT < CT, P
Eliminating undergraduate education majors/courses	2.24	6	2.68	6	2.58	6	< .001	FT < CT, P

Second, when we examined the rank order of the means within each group, the rank ordering was very similar. The Spearman's rank order correlation between future teachers and current teachers was perfect, and those between the professor group and the other two groups were both .94 ($p < .01$). The two factors rated highest by all three groups were (1) higher salary and improved working conditions and (2) improving teacher leadership and career opportunity. They were followed by (3) strengthening the professional base and (4) higher standards for entry, exit, and certification. The two factors rated lowest were (1) lengthening the training and (2) eliminating undergraduate education majors/courses. All three groups seemed to suggest that in order to improve the professional status of teaching, it is most important to improve the extrinsic and intrinsic reward for teaching, and also to raise the standards for entry, exit, and certification. All three groups gave very low ratings to eliminating undergraduate education majors/courses, with the means of the groups ranging from 2.24 to 2.68 on a 7-point Likert scale.

Third, it is interesting to note that except for the case of higher national entry, exit, and certification standards, the means for the group of future teachers were lower than those of the groups of current teachers and education professors. In other words, future teachers seemed to be less confident that these measures would improve the status of teaching, or they perhaps did not consider professional status to be a critical issue at their early stage of professional development.

Discussion

The data analysis shows that the suggestions for improving the status of teaching are clustered around six factors. As to the rank order of the importance of these factors for improving the status of teaching, there is similarity among future teachers, current teachers, and education professors. They all rate increasing the extrinsic and intrinsic reward for teaching—including increasing salaries, improving working conditions, and improving teachers' leadership and career opportunity—as the most important. They also rate programmatic and certification issues—including raising entry/exit level and national certification—as fairly important. However, they feel that eliminating undergraduate education majors/courses is much less important.

Although the three groups are similar in rank ordering the factors, they are different in the ratings they give to each factor. The multiple comparisons indicate that future teachers differ from current teachers and education professors in their perceptions. The general pattern is that teacher candidates rate the factors lower than do current teachers and education professors. These findings have the following implications for the theory and practice of improving the status of teaching.

All three groups agree that raising teachers' salaries and improving teachers' working conditions are the most important for improving the status of teaching. Teaching has been an area where females constitute the majority of the working force. Because of this history, teachers tend to be paid less than those having similar educational experience but working in other professional areas. This raises the issue of whether our society is willing to compensate teachers more. Given the large number of teachers, it is a very difficult decision. Some scholars have argued that a small cadre of 20% of the teaching force should be developed and paid salaries commensurate with other professionals, an idea that teachers' unions strongly oppose. As much literature indicates, the teaching profession is dominated by an egalitarian ethos (Goodlad, 1984; Lortie, 1975).

The three groups feel that improving teachers' leadership and career opportunities are also important for improving the status of teaching. This is consistent with the literature that advocates teacher empowerment and criticizes the careerlessness of the teaching profession (Goodlad, 1984; Lortie, 1975; Shen, 1997; Whitaker & Moses, 1995). However, since leadership and career opportunity are related to the intrinsic reward, and salary and working condition to the extrinsic reward, all three groups seem to suggest that extrinsic reward is more important than the intrinsic one. A materialistic approach to improving the teaching profession is evident.

Enhancing the status of teaching through improving the teacher education program and certification is ranked after improving the extrinsic and intrinsic reward for teaching. All three groups agree that raising entry, exit, and certification standards as well as lengthening the training will improve the status of teaching. However, they agree that eliminating the undergraduate education majors/courses is much less important. Raising entry, exit, and certification standards is consistent with the literature. However, the lack of support for eliminating undergraduate education majors/courses is not consistent with, for example, the Holmes Group's proposal, which argues for conducting all teacher education at the graduate level. It appears that the three groups do not support the pure post-baccalaureate model, according to which teacher education begins after the baccalaureate degree. Rather, they support the model that allows undergraduate education majors/courses and also lengthens the program.

In conclusion, the data collected for the study illustrate that the agenda for improving the professional status of teaching involves many aspects of work. Future teachers, current teachers, and education professors are similar in prioritizing the agenda. They feel that how the work is rewarded, both intrinsically and extrinsically, is more important than how teachers are educated and certified. However, teacher candidates differ from others in that they rate most of these measures to help improve the status of teaching as less important. It is interesting to note that none of the three groups support the Holmes Group's idea of eliminating teacher education at the undergraduate level. When we work on improving the status of teaching, we must take into account future teachers', current teachers', and education professors' perceptions, among others.

The current study raises some interesting questions for further investigations. First, future teachers' means are lower than those of current teachers and education professors. Is this because future teachers do not consider professional status to be a critical issue at their early stage of professional development, or is it because they do not expect any of these measures to be successful, or are there possibly other reasons? Second, current teachers and education professors give similar ratings to lengthening the training and eliminating undergraduate education majors/courses. However, teachers tend to rate education courses poorly and education professors have a vested interest in maintaining teacher education programs. Therefore, do current teachers and education professors have similar or different reasons for their similar ratings? Finally, all three groups indicate that extrinsic rewards are more important than intrinsic rewards for improving the professional status of teaching. A materialistic approach to improving the professional status of teaching is obvious. However, is this a valid approach to improving the status of teaching, and how does the public perceive the approach? In this research area, there are many important questions to be investigated.

Authors' Note

The authors want to thank Dr. John I. Goodlad and the Center for Educational Renewal for making available the data collected during the Study of Education of Educators.

References

Alexander, P. A. (2008). Charting the course for the teaching profession: The energizing and sustaining role of motivational forces. *Learning and Instruction, 18* (5), 483-491.

American Council on Education. (1985). *Recent changes in teacher education programs. Higher education panel report #67.* Washington, DC: Author.

Anderson, S. E. (2008). Teacher career choices: Timing of teacher careers among 1992093 Bachelor's degree recipients. *Postsecondary Education Descriptive Analysis Report. NCES 2008-153.* National Center for Education Statistics. ED501228.

Austin, G., & Reynolds, D. (1990). Managing for improved school effectiveness: An international survey. *School Organisation, 10* (2), 167–178.

Babbie, E. (1989). *The practice of social research.* Belmont, CA: Wadsworth.

Barber, L. W., & Klein, K. (1983). Merit pay and teachers evaluation. *Phi Delta Kappan, 65* (4), 247–251.

Carnegie Forum on Education and the Economy. (1986). *A nation prepared: Teachers for the 21st century.* New York: Author.

Cohen, D. (1990). A revolution in one classroom: The case of Mrs. Oublier. *Educational Evaluation and Policy Analysis, 13* (3), 327–345.

Darling-Hammond, L. (2008). A future worthy of teaching for America. *Phi Delta Kappan, 89* (10), 730–733.

Darling-Hammond, L. (1994). *Professional development schools: Schools for developing a profession.* New York: Teachers College Press.

Darling-Hammond, L., & Berry, B. (1988). *The evolution of teacher policy.* Center for Policy Research in Education. Santa Monica, CA: Rand.

Darling-Hammond, L., & Bransford, J. (2005). *Preparing teachers for a changing world: What teachers should learn and be able to do.* Indianapolis, IN: Jossey-Bass.

Fullan, M. (1993). *Changing forces: Probing the depths of educational reform.* London: Falmer.

Furlong, J. (2008). Making teaching a 21st Century profession: Tony Blair's big prize. *Oxford Review of Education, 34* (6), 727–739.

Goldberg, M., & Renton, A. M. (1993). Heeding the call to arms in "A Nation at Risk." *School Administrator, 50* (4), 16–18, 20–23.

Gonzalez, L., Brown, M., & Slate, J. (2008). Teachers who left the teaching profession: A qualitative understanding. *Qualitative Report, 13* (1), 1–11.

Goodlad, J. I. (1984). *A place called school.* New York: McGraw-Hill.

Goodlad, J. I. (1990). *Teachers for our nation's schools.* San Francisco: Jossey-Bass.

Goodlad, J. I. (1994). *Educational renewal: Better teachers, better schools.* San Francisco: Jossey-Bass.

Goodlad, J. I., & Sirotnik, K. A. (1988). *School-university partnership in action: Partnerships, cases, and concerns*. New York: Teachers College Press.

Grace, G. (1995). *School leadership: Beyond educational management*. London: Falmer.

Harris, S., Lowery-Moore, H., & Farrow, V. (2008). Extending transfer of learning theory to transformative learning theory: A model for promoting teacher leadership. *Theory Into Practice, 47* (4), 318–326.

Hitz, R. (2008). Can the teaching profession be trusted? *Phi Delta Kappan, 89* (10), 746–750.

Holmes Group. (1986). *Tomorrow's teachers: A report of the Holmes Group*. East Lansing, MI: Author.

Interstate New Teacher Assessment and Support Consortium. (1991). *Model standards for beginning teacher licensing and development: A resource for state dialogue*. Washington, DC: Council of Chief State School Officers.

Judge, H. G. (1988). Cross-national perceptions of teachers. *Comparative Education Review, 32* (2), 143–158.

Koster, B., Dengerink, J., Korthagen, F., & Lunenberg, M. (2008). Teacher educators working on their own professional development: Goals, activities and outcomes of a project for the professional development of teacher educators. *Teachers and Teaching: Theory and Practice, 14* (5), 567–587.

Levine, M. (Ed.). (1992). *Professional practice schools: Linking teacher education and school reform*. New York: Teachers College Press.

Lieberman, A., & Miller, L. (1986). School improvement: Themes and variations. In A. Lieberman (Ed.), *Rethinking school improvement: Research, craft, and a concept*. New York: Teachers College Press.

Lipham, J. M. (1991). *Effective principal, effective school*. Reston, VA: National Association of Secondary School Principals.

Lortie, D. C. (1975). *Schoolteacher*. Chicago: University of Chicago Press.

Miller, L., & Silvernail, D. L. (1994). Wells junior high school: Evolution of a professional development school. In L. Darling-Hammond (Ed.), *Professional development schools* (pp. 28–50). New York: Teacher College Press.

National Board for Professional Teaching Standards. (1991). *Toward high and rigorous standards for the teaching*. Detroit, MI: Author.

National Council for Accreditation of Teacher Education. (1993). *NCATE public opinion poll*. Washington, DC: Author.

Ornstein, A. C. (1988). The changing status of the teaching profession. *Urban Education, 23* (3), 261–279.

Osguthorpe, R. T. (Ed.). (1995). *Partner schools: Centers for educational renewal*. San Francisco: Jossey-Bass.

Pratte, R., & Rury, J. L. (1991). Teachers, professionalism, and craft. *Teachers College Record, 93* (1), 59–72.

Robinson, B. (1995). The professional development of teachers in the United Kingdom in the 1990s: Evolution or revolution? *Teacher Education Quarterly, 22* (1), 17–24.

Rosenholtz, S. J., & Smylie, M. A. (1984). Teacher compensation and career ladders. *Elementary School Journal, 85* (2), 149–166.

Rosenshine, B. (1983). Teaching functions in instructional program. *The Elementary School Journal, 83* (4), 335–352.

Rots, I., Aelterman, A., Vlerick, P., & Vermeulen, K. (2007). Teacher education, graduates' teaching commitment and entrance into the teaching profession. *Teaching and Teacher Education: An International Journal of Research and Studies, 23* (5), 543–556.

Sachs, J., & Logan, L. (1990). Control or development? A study of inservice education. *Journal of curriculum studies, 22*, 473–481.

Sergiovanni, T. J. (1991). *The principalship: A reflective practice perspective* (2nd ed.). Boston: Allyn & Bacon.

Shen, J. (1997). How to reduce teacher attrition in public schools: Policy implications from a national study. *Educational Horizons, 76* (1), 33–39.

Shepard, L. A. (1987). *A case study of the Texas teacher study: Technical report*. Los Angeles: University of California.

Shulman, L. S. (1987). Knowledge and teaching: Formulations and the new reform. *Harvard Educational Review, 57* (1), 1–22.

Sirotnik, K. A. (1989). *Studying the education of educators, technical report No. 2*. Seattle, WA: Center for Educational Renewal, University of Washington.

Sykes, G. (1987). Reckoning with the spectre of professionalism. *Educational Researcher, 16* (6), 19–21.

Sykes, G. (1990). Fostering teacher professionalism in schools. In R. F. Elmore and Associates (Eds.), *Restructuring schools: The next generation of education reform* (pp. 59–96). San Francisco: Jossey-Bass.

Vandenberghe, R. (1995). Creative management of a school: A matter of vision and daily interventions. *Journal of Educational Administration, 33* (2), 31–51.

Whalley, P. W. F. (1986). Educational malpractice: American trends and implications for Australian schools. *Bulletin of the Australian College of Education, 12*, 203–209.

Whitaker, K. S., & Moses, C. (1995). Four recommendations for enhancing the professional status of teachers. *The Teacher Educator, 31*, 23–33.

CHAPTER TWELVE

Student Teaching in the Context of a School-University Partnership
A Case Study of a Student Teacher

Jianping Shen

Student teaching is perceived by teacher education students, teachers, and teacher educators as the most influential component of the teacher education program (Conant, 1963; Cruickshank & Armaline, 1986; Goodlad, 1990; Su, 1990; Plourde, 2002a; Wilson, 2006; Wilson, Floden, & Ferrini-Mundy, 2002). There is perhaps more research on student teaching than on any other topics pertaining to teacher education (Lamer & Little, 1986). Among the large body of research literature on student teaching, some research focused on the impact of student teaching on student teachers in terms of their pupil-control orientations, attitudes toward teaching, beliefs in teaching, and so on. These studies reported quite different research findings. Some researchers concluded that after student teaching, student teachers become more authoritarian, rigid, impersonal, bureaucratic, and custodial (e.g., Copeland, 1980; Emans, 1983; Glassberg & Sprinthall, 1980; Jones, 1982; Packard, 1988) as well as less confident (Plourde, 2002b). Some inquirers reported that student teachers become more liberal and confident (Tabachnick & Zeichner, 1984; Zeichner & Grant, 1981). Still other scholars denied the impact of student teaching, sometimes even the impact of the whole professional preparation (Arnstine, 1979; Lortie, 1975).

However, as Zeichner (1986, p. 5) observed, "Studies of the role of student teaching in learning to teach, by any account, have not provided us with much information that is useful for policy decisions related to student teaching programs." Zeichner argued that the failure of studies to attend to the complex, dynamic, and multidimensional reality of student teaching is a major reason for the unsatisfactory state of our knowledge base related to the influence of student teaching on the process of learning to teach. He concluded that the lack of attention to the content and context of student teaching has been the most serious flaw in the research on student teachers. Nonetheless, both the context and content of student teaching influence teacher education students' thinking and reflective process when they learn to teach (Day, Calderhead, & Denicolo, 1993; Mcintyre, Byrd, & Foxx, 1996; Richert, 1987, 1992; Russell & Munby, 1992).

Many years have passed since Zeichner made his comments in 1986. Nevertheless, the problem pointed out by Zeichner remains. For example, Hoy and Woolfolk's experimental study (1990) concluded that student teachers became significantly more custodial in pupil-control orientation, and they became less confident that they could overcome the limitation of their students' home environment and family background. However, student teachers' sense of personal teaching efficacy improved as their sense of general teaching efficacy declined. MacKinnon's study (1989) depicted a similar picture. He found that compliance was, in the eyes of the four student teachers he studied, a taken-for-granted part of being an outsider in someone else's classroom. "Living with conformity" was a fact of life for the student teachers in the eight-week practicum.

It is interesting that Cochran-Smith (1991) reported a different student teaching experience. She found that there was a powerful way for student teachers to learn to reform teaching, or for what she referred to as "teaching against the grain." By placing student teachers in the company of experienced teachers who are themselves struggling to be reformers in their own classrooms and schools, student teachers learn to (a) rethink the language of teaching—a collaborative process of uncovering the values and assumptions implicit in the educational language, (b) pose problems of practice, (c) construct curriculum, and (d) confront the dilemmas of teaching—a process of identifying and wrestling with educational issues that are characterized by equally strong but incompatible and competing claims to justice.

It is clear that Cochran-Smith's research findings are different from Hoy and Woolfolk's and MacKinnon's. Cochran-Smith is a promising advocate of learning to teach against the grain, and Hoy and Woolfolk and MacKinnon are pessimistic critics of student teachers' conformity to their cooperating teachers, of the status quo in the teaching environment, and of becoming more conservative after student teaching. The reason that they came to different conclusions is that their studies were conducted in different contexts. However, the nature of the contexts in which these studies were carried out is not clear, except that in Cochran-Smith's study student teachers were placed with reform-oriented experienced teachers. Although these studies, without being situated in specific contexts, are constructive in terms of illustrating possible images of student teaching, they have limited implications for policy decisions because they do not pinpoint the context and content of student teaching. For example, Hoy and Woolfolk's study begs the following questions: In which context do student teachers become more conservative after experiencing student teaching? What are the activities in the student teaching experience that make them so? The same scrutiny can be applied to other studies on student teaching.

Some studies (Richert, 1987, 1992) indicate that the structure of teacher education programs could facilitate or inhibit future or beginning teachers' learning and reflection. Therefore, it will be interesting to inquire into whether the structure of a school-university partnership in teacher education—a relatively new and developing phenomenon—is beneficial for future teachers. Nonetheless, structure alone might not be sufficient because some studies suggest that teacher knowledge is personal, practical, contextualized, task-specific, and event-structured (Carter, 1992; Yinger & Hendricks-Lee, 1993). It takes carefully coordinated events for future teachers to learn to reflect and to acquire personal, practical, task-specific, and event-structured knowledge (Day, Calderhead, & Denicolo, 1993; Howey, 1996; Russell & Munby, 1992).

This study intended to contribute to our understanding of the context and content of student teaching by exploring a student teacher's field experience in the context of a school-university partnership. The study reported here employed a case study methodology in order to expose the context and content of this student teacher's field experience. The primary data sources included three interviews with the student teacher, observation of her work in the school and two method classes on the university campus, and all of her writings since entering the teacher education program. The interviews and the lesson plan periods between the student teacher and the cooperating teacher were audiotaped and transcribed verbatim. This chapter first contextualizes the informant's field experience, then proceeds to illustrate some features of her student teaching experience, and finally reflects upon her experience.

PDC Program: An Innovative Preservice Teacher Education Program

Since the mid-1980s, there has been a professional development school (PDS) movement within the context of a school-university partnership (e.g., Darling-Hammond, 2005; Goodlad, 1993, 1994; Holmes Group, 1988; Johnston-Parsons, 2000; Levine, 1992; Osguthorpe, 1995; Sirotnik & Goodlad, 1988; Stallings & Kowalski, 1990). PDSs are "teaching schools," analogous to "teaching hospitals" in medicine. They are established to improve the education of prospective and practicing teachers, to strengthen knowledge and practice in teaching, and to strengthen the profession of teaching by serving as models of promising and productive programs for student teaching (Abdal-Haqq, 1989; Schlechty et al., 1988).

In 1988, Puget Sound Professional Development Center (PSPDC, also known as PDC) was created as a consortium of the University of Washington, four middle schools in the Seattle area, and the Washington Office of the Superintendent of Public Instruction. One of the goals of PSPDC was to pilot a middle school preservice teacher education program through the College of Education at the University of Washington. The PDC Middle School Preservice Teacher Education Program is a fifth year program, which enrolled small cohorts of 12, 14, and 15 students for the academic years of 1990–91, 1991–92, and 1992–93 respectively. In contrast to the regular teacher education program, the PDC Middle School Preservice Teacher Education Program has its characteristics in the following three areas (Grossman & McDaniel, 1990; Yerian & Grossman, 1993).

Core Seminar
Four required courses in curriculum and instruction, educational psychology, and educational leadership and policy studies were replaced by a block of courses aimed at middle level preparation of teachers and were taught by an interdisciplinary team of three to five professors (representing the areas of curriculum and instruction, educational psychology, educational leadership and policy studies, and special education), a middle school teacher, and a graduate assistant who also served as a cross-site supervisor. In the fall quarter, when the students were at the university nearly full time, the seminar met twice a week. As the year progressed and the students became more involved with their teaching responsibilities at their school sites, the time commitment to the seminar was reduced. By the third quarter, the seminar format consisted of problem-solving sessions in which student teachers would discuss their day-to-day teaching concerns, reflecting upon their experiences across school sites. In addition to the core seminar, the PDC students attended subject-specific method courses with students from the regular teacher education program.

Field Experience
The four middle schools in the PSPDC, representing four school districts in the Seattle area, provided the field sites for most of the PDC students. In a few cases, students with special certification emphases, such as English as

a Second Language, were placed in non-PDC schools to gain the necessary experience for the certificate. Each student was placed with a cooperating teacher or a teaching team. Planning for the field experience involved the site supervisors, the cooperating teachers, and the seminar teaching team. The school-based members of the planning team coordinated the curriculum activities of the student teachers at the school sites and arranged for the cross-site school visits that occurred during the year. Periodically, the cooperating teachers would meet with the teaching team to discuss seminar and field-related issues.

Onsite Supervision

In a departure from the traditional method of university-based supervision in which one supervisor evaluates a large number of students at various school sites, the site supervisor at each PDC school site was responsible for supervising a group of two to four students who had been placed at that school. Communication among the student teacher, the cooperating teacher, and the site supervisor was facilitated by their informal day-to-day contact, and through formal weekly meetings between the student teacher and the site supervisor. In addition, the site supervisors were responsible for finding alternative placements when the original placement failed. Site supervisors met monthly with the teaching team to plan the curriculum and to share information about supervision.

The Student Teacher, the Cooperating Teacher, and the School

Sara, in her late 30s, was the principal informant for the study. She was a nontraditional teacher education student who had spent ten years in marketing, training employees in product knowledge and sales strategies, and five years as an assistant for a government environmental research project, developing standard operation procedures for chemical processing.

Sara was one of a cohort of fifteen who were admitted to the PDC Middle School Preservice Teacher Education Program for the 1992–93 academic year. However, she started her coursework for the teacher education program in summer 1992. Her coursework for the PDC Middle School Preservice Teacher Education Program was as follows:

Summer 1992	Educational Psychology
Autumn 1992	PDC Core Seminar on Teaching
	Reading in the Elementary School
	Mathematics in the Elementary School

Winter 1993	PDC Core Seminar on Teaching Language Arts in the Elementary School
Spring 1993	PDC Core Seminar on Teaching Science in the Elementary School Social Studies in the Elementary School Physical Education and Health in Schools
Summer 1993	Arts in Child Education Music in Child Education Multiethnic Curriculum and Instruction

As was mentioned in the previous section on field experience, the PDC core seminar gradually led students from the university to the school. When this study was conducted, Sara was a part-time student teacher in the Seattle Middle School, one of the four PDSs in PSPDC.

Sara, among other things, was teaching the social studies/language arts block to the mainstreamed seventh graders. She taught eight to ten periods a week. Her cooperating teacher, Tina (Sara, "S" for student; Tina, "T" for teacher), was a middle-aged woman who was a two-thirds teacher in the Seattle Middle School. Sara perceived that she had a good relationship with her cooperating teacher and claimed that they had the same philosophy of teaching.

Two other persons with whom Sara had frequent contacts in the school were the site supervisor and Steve, one of Sara's classmates in the PDC Middle School Preservice Teacher Education Program. The site supervisor had a weekly meeting with the PDC interns. She also coordinated the student teaching, conducted a final evaluation of student teachers, and made recommendations for licensing. Sara often exchanged ideas with Steve, who had the same experience as Sara. They helped each other emotionally and practiced team-teaching.

The Seattle Middle School is a racially heterogeneous school in a large suburban school district. Of the more than 500 students enrolled in August 1992, 72% were Caucasian, 18% Asian, 6% black, and 2% Hispanic. It had been a professional development school since 1986. More than 80% of the faculty supported the school's involvement in the PDC Middle School Preservice Teacher Education Program. Previous studies (Shen, 1993,1994,1996) revealed that the school teachers' vision of preservice teacher education in the PDS context was comprised of the following elements: (a) student teachers' field experience should be a year-long experience; (b) student teachers' responsibilities should be gradually enlarged, moving from coursework on campus to taking over a classroom completely; (c) student teachers should be matched with cooperating teachers; (d) there should be a site supervisor responsible for coordinating and evaluating student teaching; (e) student teachers should move beyond classroom teaching and become involved in all the work that teaching entails; (f) student teachers should work with a team of teachers and transcend student teachers' preconception regarding teaching; and (g) student teaching should take place in the context of a school-university partnership. These teachers' vision of preservice teacher education in the context of professional development school is largely focused on the socialization of student teachers.

Sara's Early Field Experience: Cross-site Visits

The traditional method of field experience is to place, usually at the end of the program, a teacher education student with a cooperating teacher in a school. One of the shortcomings of the traditional way is that student teachers have limited field experience due to the fact that they are exposed to only one way of teaching. This narrows student teachers' horizons and becomes an impediment to their further professional development. Another shortcoming is that there is not a smooth transition from the campus to the school; all the fieldwork is crammed in the last few months.

The structure of the PSPDC provides student teachers with the opportunity to visit sites other than the one in which they are student teaching. While taking the PDC Core Seminar on Teaching in autumn 1992, Sara was engaged in cross-site visits, and she wrote her reflection entitled "A case of similar objectives or there is more than one way to achieve a goal." What follows are excerpts from her journal:

> One thing is clear about both College Place [a middle school in PSPDC] and [the Seattle Middle School]. Both middle schools are meeting students' needs. What was enlightening was that they had different ways of doing it.... I was very interested in their [College Place Middle School] grading system. Students were all able to achieve B or more through re-testing or negotiation. In line with middle school philosophy, this allows all students to succeed and allows them to learn from their errors. I was impressed with the diversity of the electives. Students were given a wide variety of choices from Quest and Journalism (with a TV studio) to Computer Labs. What excited me most was the use of technology ... integrating real world technology into curriculum.
>
> I enjoyed this exercise [cross-site visit], and I found it to be a learning experience. It gave me a base for comparing and contrasting many theories of middle school philosophy. It reinforces life's lessons that there is no one right way and the value of diversity. I also find it very valuable to see as many methods in action as possible. This creates a greater data base within myself to draw from in the real world of teaching. Methods that are presented visually and

authentically are more likely to be conceptualized in my mind. Now, I have a strong desire to see the other schools in our program.

I enjoyed doing our cross site visits as part of a larger group. It was the first opportunity to get to talk to other interns outside the seminar besides those assigned to our schools. A camaraderie was created that has gotten stronger in time: We found similarities and compassion in our concerns and strength and quality in our differences. Along with that and meeting professionals from other schools, I found that this project had broadened my educational community base.

It is apparent from Sara's writing that she came to realize that there were more ways of educating children. The experience of cross-site visits allowed Sara to move beyond what Lortie (1975) characterized as "apprenticeship of observation"—teaching in the same way as what student teachers learned by observing their own teachers when moving through the educational ladder. College Place Middle School's grading system was not a part of Sara's educational thought when she visited the school. She was impressed by the practice that later became a part of her philosophy of teaching. When she responded to the question regarding her philosophy of teaching during an interview with this author, she observed that "I also believe in correcting errors. All students should have A by correcting what they've done, because there's value in learning from your mistakes." Through activities such as cross-site visits, Sara became identified with a more diversified culture of teaching.

Cross-site visits also provided Sara with the opportunity to share with her counterparts in the teacher education program. The membership in the cohort group, or "camaraderie" in Sara's own word, helped her become socialized into the culture of teaching.

Part-time Teaching Experience

Sara began part-time student teaching in winter 1992, that is, the second quarter of the teacher education program. During the second quarter, she observed many classes taught by different teachers and became an assistant for her present cooperating teacher, Tina.

This study took place during the third quarter of her teacher education program. Most of her work in the school involved teaching the social studies/language arts block to the mainstreamed seventh graders. In addition to this, she also worked on a teaching team for the gifted. By the time Sara was in her third quarter, she was spending more time in the school than on the university campus. She was taking a social studies method course and a science method course on Monday and Wednesday mornings, and Physical Education and Health in Schools on Saturdays. For the rest of the time she worked as an intern in the school. The following are some snapshots to illustrate Sara's teaching experiences.

Russia: A Nine-Week Unit
Sara designed and carried out a nine-week unit on Russia's history and geography by employing a teaching strategy named "jigsaw." Students were divided into six home groups, each home group consisting of four or five students. For each task, such as studying Russia's history, students within a home group decided who would study leadership evolution, domestic policies, foreign policies, literature and art, and so on. The students who studied the same topic formed an expert group. After doing some research work as an expert group, these experts on, for example, Russian foreign policies, returned to their home groups to share what they had learned in the expert group with their friends in home groups. Each member in the home group would share what he/she had learned in different expert groups.

The final product for each home group was to build a timeline of the evolution of leadership in Russia, marking the corresponding foreign policies, domestic policies, literature, and art on the timeline. In the process of building the timeline, all members in the home group contributed their understanding. Each student in the home group had a part of puzzle; the puzzle would not come together if a part of it was missing.

Since this was a social studies class, Sara employed the jigsaw strategy not only to teach Russian history but Russian geography as well. Students were actively engaged in activities. They compiled tables and drew pictures to illustrate Russia's natural resources and climate. Four weeks into the nine-week unit, the class held a conference to report to their parents what they had learned regarding Russia. The conference was successful according to Sara and Tina.

Snapshot Biography
Since Sara was also teaching language arts to the same group, she integrated the social studies class with the language arts class. At the end of the subunit on Russian history, Sara taught students how to write a snapshot biography of one of the Russian leaders. Students were again divided into groups. Each group first decided on whose biography they would write. Then, the group discussed the features of this person's life. These features became chapters in the biography, and each student wrote a chapter. After working on the table of contents and an introduction, and

asking somebody else to write a foreword, each group produced a biography collectively. Each group of students then shared its biography with other groups. By engaging in snapshot biography, students not only acquired knowledge of a historical figure but learned how to write as well.

Lesson Plan Period

Sara and Tina had about four lesson plan periods each week. The lesson plan periods, lasting 35–50 minutes, were between 11:30 AM to 1:30 PM, depending on the daily schedules. The lesson plan period was the time for Sara and Tina to sit down and prepare for the coming days. In all the sessions that the author observed, Sara prepared her lesson plan well. She first talked about her lesson plan and then asked for input from Tina.

When Sara proposed to teach the nine-week unit by employing the jigsaw teaching strategy, she explained to Tina the process of applying this model. During Sara's explanation, Tina probed for clarification regarding the activity of the home group and the expert group. The two questions that Tina asked after Sara finished her introduction were about seating and grading. Sara said the final evaluation would be based on the group's final project rather than on each individual's work, although in the process there would be some formative evaluation of each individual's work. As to the question of seating, Sara said she had not prepared for grouping, so they worked together to put students into home groups. It was apparent from their conversation that Tina had more knowledge of the students' characteristics; she tended to group compatible students together in order for the cooperative learning to take place.

The situation was almost the same when Sara suggested integrating social studies and language arts by engaging students in writing a snapshot biography. The following was the dialogue between Sara and Tina when they discussed the snapshot biography approach for the first time:

> S: After finishing Boris [a biography of Boris Yeltsin], I plan to ask them to write biographies on Russian leaders.
> T: Wait a minute. Having the kids write biographies on various people?
> S: Some of the leaders.
> T: OK.
> S: And I was thinking about only doing Lenin, Stalin, and three current ones, because they'll get more information out of those five than anybody else.
> T: How long are these biographies going to be?
> S: OK. The concept. I don't think I sat down and explained this to you. Am I right?
> T: I don't think so.
> S: OK. And we are doing it in class right now so that I don't have a complete concept of it. Basically, it's called a snapshot biography. Basically they're

gonna produce a book, which means they have to do a table of contents, an introduction, a foreword about the authors, and a timeline and a map. So, they got everything covered. And what we'll be doing is we each pick something significant in that person's life, and write a chapter, and chapters of the whole book come together. So, we're doing one on an Indian doctor in my class. And like one person is writing about her heritage in her early childhood. I am writing about the influences in her life about what made her later become a doctor. Another person is talking about her kind of medical school. The other person is talking about her getting married and working on the Indian reservation. Foreword is written by somebody who is not writing the book. The introduction basically gives you a background, what's going on. The map gives them a concept of where it happened, where this person lived. The timeline gives all the events of that person's life so that you get the whole picture. And the chapters are just snapshots from that, four snapshots or five snapshots, that is more story-like than fact. I mean it's "fact" but you write it in a kind of story-like tone.

T: I'd love to see that product when you get it.
S: I'll have it done next week.
T: Great.
S: I'm kind of enjoying the fact that we're working together and also instead of looking at the whole, we start to look at the specifics about a person, and using our imagination to fill in to make it story-like, do you know what I am saying?
T: I know exactly what you are saying
S: And they come up with a book.
T: The only thing I might recommend, though. These kids have been doing group work for two weeks on the timeline, it might be time to back off a week and have them do something on their own.
S: What we're gonna let them do?
T: I thought it will be the Russian language. I can insert that. It's writing. And it is individual.
S: I would like an extra week to plan the biography. I am only getting it done next week.

It is clear from the above conversation that Sara's blueprint for the teaching unit on snapshot biography was accepted without any challenges from Tina. The concerns Tina expressed during the four lesson plan periods that this author observed were all logistical questions rather than conceptual ones. The cooperating teacher acted as a cooperative figure but not as a friendly critic. It is interesting to note that when Sara introduced the concept of snapshot biography, she mentioned that she was working on a project of the same nature for the social studies course that she was taking in the university.

Social Studies in the Elementary School: The Course Where the Ideas Originate

In the syllabus for "Social Studies in the Elementary School," the instructor stated that one of objectives of the course was the following:

> Students will be able to plan social studies units on important topics featuring these teaching strategies: a. concept formation and classifying; b. jigsaw (a cooperative learning strategy); c. integrating literacy education with social studies education through, for example, biography production.

Corresponding to this objective, three of the six assignments for this course were concept formation lesson plan, jigsaw lesson plan, and team biography. When the instructor assigned the team biography, her wording was almost the same as when Sara introduced the concept of snapshot biography to Tina. The instructor first highlighted what a snapshot biography was and then described the assignment to teacher education students as follows:

> In a snapshot biography, each person takes one piece and writes it independently.... Each of you should pick up one part of her life [Susan LaFlesche Picotte, a native American doctor] and write it up. Together you write an introduction. Somehow, as a group, you should come up with a map, showing where she studied in college and when she practiced medicine and so on. Another is that you together make a timeline. On the timeline, you might include other things that happened, such as the national events and when she died. And a table of contents. These are the parts you have to have. You have to have the introduction, a timeline, a map, and a table of contents that you all work on together. Another thing that you could ask your kids to do, and I would also like you to do is to ask someone to write a foreword for it.

After explaining the components of the assignment, the instructor went on to ask teacher education students to brainstorm about what was involved in the teaching strategy of snapshot biography. The instructor summarized the responses as "reading for information, expository writing, and cooperative skills."

Sara used, in addition to the snapshot biography, the jigsaw lesson plan in her student teaching. In a reflective journal she kept for the social studies course, she wrote the following:

> I have enjoyed the jigsaw lesson development in this class the most. I have finally seen the full value of jigsaw. Teaching my jigsaw has been a joy. At the beginning, the students were resistant to the new process and depending on a group for a final product. [Tina] says that my expectations are what got them

over the hump. Because I believed that they could do it, slowly students started believing that they could do it. Everyday, several students would come in saying, "I'm starting to get it, [Sara]!" The day that the students did their teaching to their [home] groups, I heard students asking great questions and even arguing about unclear facts. The students got very enthusiastic when it came time to build the timeline.... I am looking forward to using this method the way it is meant to be used many times during my teaching career. Thank you, [the name of the instructor], for taking the time to show the value and proper use of this great teaching strategy!

There are perhaps two major reasons for Sara's enthusiasm about jigsaw. First, the jigsaw lesson plan works very well with her students. Second, she can integrate her assignment on campus and internship in the school. This means that if the orientation and specific content of the coursework on campus are compatible with and can be immediately utilized in the internship, Sara will be prone to accept and apply the concepts, such as snapshot biography and, particularly, jigsaw. The relevancy of university coursework to the internship in the school appears to be an important factor in future teachers' learning to teach. A new dimension will be added to this observation if we examine the science method class in which Sara's willingness to accept the approach modeled by the instructor was dramatically reduced.

Science in the Elementary School: Different Reaction from Sara

As the instructor stated, the science method class was hands-on and inquiry-oriented. This author observed two lessons taught by this instructor: one was to ask teacher education students to explain why a small section of trees in Mt. Rainier National Park were dead on the basis of a set of well-prepared pictures and maps. The other was to develop the concept of a circuit by using bulbs, batteries, and wires. The approach of these two classes was the same; therefore, only the circuit class will be described below in detail.

The class comprised of three parts. The instructor first asked the students to write down their own definition of "circuit." Five minutes later, he collected the notes and read them to the whole class. He asked the teacher education students whether their students would understand what a circuit was on the basis of their own definitions. Most of the teacher education students said "No."

The instructor then asked students to work individually to come up with ways they were successful and unsuccessful in making a circuit by using a wire, a battery, and a bulb. The instructor said that this was perhaps the only time they would work individually in this quarter, although the students were sitting in groups. After the students' experiments, the instructor demonstrated four ways to build a circuit with the same three items. He also explained the structure of the bulb, which was crucial for understanding the four possibilities. The instructor also generalized that the direction of the battery did not matter.

He finally gave out Prediction Sheet 1 and asked students to try to determine which of the 12 pictures represented a true circuit. Without his comment on the teacher education students' work on Prediction Sheet 1, the students started to work on Prediction Sheet 2, which contained more complicated circuits. The third part of the class was intended to further develop students' concept of a circuit.

After the class, this author talked with the teaching assistant for this course. He told me that most of the students in this class were not interested because the subject matter was not relevant to the elementary curriculum. This was confirmed to a certain degree when this author interviewed Sara. She said that "science has been a waste of my time. I learned a lot about science, but it's certainly not gonna help me to teach. He has not presented anything that I had not already learned."

The science method course presents an interesting case in contrast to that of the social studies course. Although the general approach of the science method course—hands-on and inquiry-oriented activities—was compatible with Sara's philosophy of teaching and the same as that of the social studies course, the science method course had not impacted Sara to the degree that was intended. This is due to the fact that the subject matter of the science method course was difficult for most of the teacher education students, and the subject matter was perceived by them as irrelevant to the elementary curriculum. In other words, the subject matter per se distracted Sara's attention from the teaching method and philosophy that the instructor tried to model.

If we compare the social studies method course with the science method course, we may see the mechanism with which a course effectively influences a student teacher. Since Sara was teaching social studies in the Seattle Middle School while she took the social studies method course in the university, her teaching in the school was a logical extension of her coursework on the campus. The assignments of the course such as writing a jigsaw lesson plan were interwoven with the internship in the school. Because of the alignment of the work in the two institutions, the jigsaw and snapshot biography teaching strategies achieved the impact that the instructor intended.

In contrast, the science method course did not achieve the effectiveness it intended, although the instructor of the course tried to model an inquiry-oriented, hands-on approach to teaching science. As in the circuit lesson, the instructor was modeling how to help learners to develop a concept of a circuit by engaging them in inquiry. The lesson started with trial-and-error, asking learners to create the simplest circuit by hands-on activities involving a battery, a bulb, and a wire. It ended with predicting more complicated versions of a circuit, and having teacher education students resort to more hands-on activities involving more batteries, bulbs, and wires if they were not sure. However, due to the fact that many teacher education students did not have a correct understanding of the circuit when they came to the class, which was apparent in the definitions they wrote at the beginning of the lesson, the instructor's intention to model a hands-on, inquiry-oriented approach to teaching science was obscured by the overwhelming pressure on the students to acquire the knowledge regarding circuits.

Another factor that influenced the effectiveness of the science method course is that it was not aligned with the internship in the school. Sara was not engaged in teaching science at all. She could not apply what she learned, nor was she required to do so. The lack of immediate urgency regarding her work in the school setting shifted her attention away from the hands-on, inquiry-oriented approach that the instructor was modeling.

Implications of Sara's Case

Sara's case of field experience, which was depicted in the foregoing, has its implications for constructing field experiences in the context of a school-university partnership. It is now common knowledge that "Schools, colleges, and departments of education (SCDEs) alone cannot educate prospective teachers well. Neither can schools. The success of teacher education requires the partnership of schools and universities" (Shen, 1993, p. 27). However, there are more questions than answers as to how to organize the field experience. Although it is not practical to expect a certain structure that is applicable to all settings (Goodlad, 1988, p. 30), an analysis of some of the variables involved in Sara's case may contribute to our understanding of the context and content of the field experience and how they impact future teachers' learning to teach.

The field experience is one of the innovative elements of the PDC Middle School Preservice Teacher Education Program. Sara seemed to enjoy the field experience organized by the program. She liked the PDC core seminar that gradually introduced her to the field. She said that "I would not trade my PDC seminar with anything in the world." She perceived that in the Seattle Middle School, "being a PDS, we [interns] were welcomed by 90% of the staff. We have been able to be a part of the community instead of outsiders visiting." Sara also felt quite comfortable with Tina, as illustrated by what she wrote in her reflective journal:

> My cooperating teacher is a member of the team and is very comfortable working with someone and is comfortable with letting another person teach her class.... My [cooperating] teacher is progressive and loves to try out the ideas I learned from my university classes.

Sara liked to work with the site supervisor and members of her cohort in the PDC Middle School Preservice Teacher Education Program. She told this author the following during an interview:

> Onsite supervision was absolutely the best thing in the world. I never would have made it through this year without her [the site supervisor]. Being assigned to a school as an intern team, and being able to work with other interns in my class was wonderful, emotionally as well as mentally. We worked on special projects together. We helped each other back and forth. We learned a lot about team teaching because of it.

In short, Sara felt satisfied with the arrangement regarding her field experience. She concluded her comment on her field experience with the following observation: "I just think the whole thing was better. We did more work, but I think we got ten times more in-class experience."

Because the PDC Middle School Preservice Teacher Education Program was developed in the context of a school-university partnership, there was a supportive context for the field experience. Sara benefited from this supportive context. Some of the features of this context that Sara perceived as constructive include the following: (a) letting students have early experience to gain exposure to more educational practices, (b) gradually enlarging the field experience, from cross-site visits to part-time student teaching, and finally to full-time student teaching, (c) matching a student teacher with a cooperating teacher, (d) having a cohort in the school in order to ease the transition from the campus to the school, and (e) having an onsite supervisor who bridges the school and the campus and also makes recommendations for licensing.

One conclusion that can be drawn at this point is that the supportive context embedded in the PDC Middle School Preservice Teacher Education helped Sara to ease her transition from the university into the field. During her field experience, there was not the "becoming more conservative" phenomenon as illustrated by Hoy and Woolfolk (1990), nor was there "living with conformity in student teaching" as elaborated by MacKinnon (1989). Therefore, by virtue of constructing field experience in the school-university context, Sara did not have the miserable experience as depicted by MacKinnon (1989) and Hoy and Woolfolk (1990).

On the other hand, although Tina supported Sara's trying out the ideas she learned in the social sciences method, she did not aggressively engage Sara in "teaching against the grain." Whenever Sara proposed an idea to plan a unit or part of a unit, the cooperating teacher asked questions for clarification and tried to help Sara to accommodate the idea into the classroom, but she did not challenge Sara for the underpinnings of teaching strategies such as snapshot biography and jigsaw. There seemed to be a one-way influence from the campus to the school in terms of teaching strategies. The cooperating teacher's role was to provide a laboratory and help the student teacher to experiment, but not to take a more critical stance to challenge Sara and make her more conscious of the underlying assumptions of the teaching strategies. Without such challenges, the student teacher might apply and enjoy such teaching strategies as jigsaw, but she did not necessarily develop an inquiring and reflective attitude toward teaching. Jigsaw and snapshot biography are, after all, two teaching strategies introduced by the social studies course. What is more important is to assimilate the philosophical underpinnings embedded in the strategies.

The nature of Sara's field experience revealed that a supportive structure in the context of a school-university partnership is a necessary but not sufficient condition for a successful field experience. In Sara's case, more attention should be paid to the content involved in the field experience. Several questions deserve our attention in this regard: (a) how should the science method course be reconstructed so as to let the student teacher realize the teaching philosophy that the instructor is modeling? (b) how should the coursework and internship be integrated so that learning to teach becomes less serendipitous? (c) how should the role of the cooperating teacher change from being cooperative to being critical? and (d) how should the context and content of the field experience be constructed to let future teachers not only enjoy practicing certain teaching strategies but begin to develop an inquiring attitude as well? Addressing these questions would require a micromanagement of the content of the field experience within the supportive context of a school-university partnership.

Sara's case of student teaching illustrates the promise and potential of the field experience in the context of a school-university partnership. Without school-university partnerships, many things are left to chance. Because of the inertia in the field, "becoming conservative" and "living with conformity" will occur in many cases. The benefits of the supportive structure, however, make us realize the imperative to pay attention to the content of the field experience. More work is needed to improve the school-university coordination in respect to the content of the field experience so as to help our future teachers learn to teach.

References

Abdal-Haqq, I. (1989). *The nature of professional development schools.* ERIC Document Reproduction Service No. 316 548.

Arnstine, D. (1979). The temporary impact of teacher education. *Journal of Teacher Education, 30* (2), 51–60.

Carter, K. (1992). Creating cases for the development of teacher knowledge. In T. Russell & H. Munby (Eds.), *Teachers and teaching: From classroom to reflection* (pp. 109–123). London: Falmer Press.

Cochran-Smith, M. (1991). Learning to teach against the grain. *Harvard Educational Review, 61*(3), 279–310.

Conant, J. (1963). *The education of American teachers.* New York: McGraw-Hill.

Copeland, W. (1980). Student teachers and cooperating teachers: An ecological relationship. *Theory into Practice, 18* (3), 194–199.

Cruickshank, D., & Armaline, W. (1986). Field experiences in teacher education: Considerations and recommendations. *Journal of Teacher Education, 37* (3), 34–40.

Darling-Hammond, L. (Ed.) (2005). *Professional development schools: Schools for developing a profession.* New York, NY: Teachers College Press.

Day, C., Calderhead, J., & Denicolo, P. (1993). *Research on teacher thinking: Understanding professional development.* London: Falmer Press.

Emans, R. (1983). Implementing the knowledge base: Redesigning the function of cooperating teachers and college supervisors. *Journal of Teacher Education, 43* (3), 14–18.

Glassberg, S., & Sprinthall, N. (1980). Student teaching: A developmental approach. *Journal of Teacher Education, 31* (2), 31, 35–38.

Goodlad, J. I. (1988). School-university partnerships for educational renewal: Rationale and concepts. In K. A. Sirotnik & J. I. Goodlad (Eds.),

School-university partnerships in action: Concepts, cases, and concerns. New York: Teachers College Press.

Goodlad, J. I. (1990). *Teachers for our nation's schools.* San Francisco: Jossey-Bass.

Goodlad, J. I. (1993). School-university partnership and partner schools. *Educational Policy, 7* (1), 24–39.

Goodlad, J. I. (1994). *Educational renewal: Better teachers, better schools.* San Francisco: Jossey-Bass.

Grossman, P., & McDaniel, J. E. (1990). *Breaking boundaries: Restructuring preservice teacher education as a collaborative school/university venture.* Paper presented at the annual meeting of the American Educational Research Association, Boston.

Holmes Group. (1988). *Tomorrow's schools: Principles for the design of professional development schools.* East Lansing, MI: Author.

Howey, K. (1996). Designing coherent and elaborate teacher education program. In J. Sikula, T. J. Buttery, & Y. E. Duyton (Eds.), *Handbook of research on teacher education* (2nd ed.). New York: Macmillan.

Hoy, W. K., & Woolfolk, A. E. (1990). Socialization of student teachers. *American Educational Research Journal, 27* (2), 279–300.

Johnston-Parsons, M. (2000). *Collaborative reform and other improbable dreams: The challenges of professional development schools.* Albany, NY: State University of New York Press.

Jones, D. R. (1982). The influence of length and level of student teaching on pupil control ideology. *High School Journal, 65* (7), 220–225.

Lamer, J. E., & Little, J. W. (1986). Research on teacher education. In M. C. Wittrock (Ed.), *Handbook of Research on Teaching* (3rd ed.). New York: Macmillan.

Levine, M. (Ed.) (1992). *Professional practice schools: Linking teacher education and school reform.* New York, NY: Teachers College Press.

Lortie, D. C. (1975). *Schoolteacher: A sociological study.* Chicago: University of Chicago Press.

MacKinnon, J. D. (1989). Living with conformity in student teaching. *Alberta Journal of Educational Research, 35* (1), 2–19.

Mcintyre, D. J., Byrd, D. M., & Foxx, S. M. (1996). Field and laboratory experiences, In J. Sikula, T. J. Buttery, & Y. E. Duyton (Eds.), *Handbook of research on teacher education* (2nd ed.). New York: Macmillan.

Osguthorpe, R. T. ,Harris, R. C., Harris, M. F., & Black, S. (Eds.) (1995). *Partner schools: Centers for educational renewal.* San Francisco: Jossey-Bass.

Packard, J. S. (1988). The pupil control studies. In N. J. Boyan (Ed.), *Handbook of research and educational administration.* New York: Longman.

Plourde, L. A. (2002a). Elementary science education: The influence of student teaching—Where it all begins. *Education, 123* (2), 253–259.

Plourde, L. A. (2002b). The influence of student teaching on preservice elementary teachers' science self-efficacy and outcome expectancy beliefs. *Journal of Instructional Psychology, 29* (4), 245–53.

Richert, A. E. (1987). *Reflex to reflection: Facilitating reflection in novice teachers.* Unpublished doctoral dissertation, Stanford University.

Richert, A. E. (1992). The content of student teachers' reflections within different structures for facilitating the reflective process. In T. Russell & H. Munby (Eds.), *Teachers and teaching: From classroom to reflection* (pp. 171-191). London: Palmer Press.

Russell, T., & Munby, H. (Eds.) (1992). *Teachers and teaching: From classroom to reflection.* London: Palmer Press.

Schlecty, P. C. (1988). Inventing professional development schools. *Educational Leadership. 46* (3), 28-31.

Shen, J. (1993). *Voices from the field: School-based faculty members' vision of preservice teacher in the context of a professional development school.* Seattle: Occasional Paper No. 16, Center for Educational Renewal, University of Washington.

Shen, J. (1994). Voices from the field: Emerging issues from a school-university partnership. *Metropolitan Universities: An International Forum. 5* (2), 77-85.

Shen, J. (1996). A study of contrast: Visions of preservice teacher education in the context of a professional development school. *The Professional Educator, 18* (2), 45–58.

Sirotnik, K. A., & Goodlad, J. I. (Eds.) (1988). *School-university partnerships in action: Concepts, cases, and concerns.* New York, NY: Teachers College Press.

Stallings, J. A., & Kowalski, T. (1990). Research on professional development schools, In W. R. Houston (Ed.), *Handbook of research on teacher education.* New York, NY: Macmillan.

Su, Z. (1990). Exploring the moral socialisation of teacher candidates. *Oxford Review of Education, 16* (3), 367–391.

Tabachnick, B. R., & Zeichner, K. M. (1984). The impact of the student teaching experience on the development of teacher perspectives. *Journal of Teacher Education, 35* (6), 28–36.

Wilson, E. K. (2006). The impact of an alternative model of student teacher supervision: Views of the participants. *Teaching and Teacher Education, 22* (1), 22–31.

Wilson, S., Floden, R. E., & Ferrini-Mundy, J. (2002). Teacher preparation research: An insider's view from the outside. *Journal of Teacher Education, 53* (3), 190–204.

Yerian, S. Y., & Grossman, P. L. (1993). *Emerging themes on the effectiveness of teacher preparation through professional development schools.* Paper presented at the annual meeting of the American Educational Research Association, Atlanta.

Yinger, R., & Hendricks-Lee, M. (1993). An ecological conception of teaching. *Learning and individual differences,* 5(4), 269-281.

Zeichner, K. M. (1986). Content and contexts: Neglected elements in studies of student teaching as an occasion for learning to teach. *Journal of Education for Teaching, 12* (1), 5–24.

Zeichner, K. M., & Grant, C. A. (1981). Biography and social structure in the socialization of student teachers. *Journal of Education for Teaching, 7* (3), 298–314.

CHAPTER 13

A Study of Contrast

Visions of Preservice Teacher Education in the Context of a Professional Development School

Jianping Shen

Introduction, Literature Review, and Conceptual Framework

The idea of establishing the Professional Development School (PDS) is embedded in two trends. The first of these trends is the movement to reform teacher education. The Holmes Group's *Tomorrow's Teachers* (1986) and *Tomorrow's Schools* (1990), Carnegie Forum's *A Nation Prepared: Teachers for the 21st Century* (1986), and Goodlad's *Teachers for Our Nation's Schools* (1990) have all recommended, among other things, that future teachers be prepared in a PDS to gain hands-on experience and develop professional beliefs, attitudes, and abilities.

The second trend is the school-university partnership movement. School-university partnerships became a popular phenomenon in the mid-1980s. The relationships between schools and universities vary, and the school-university partnerships have different orientations. They can be staff-oriented, student-oriented, task-oriented, or institution-oriented (Su, 1990a). Among these orientations, the institution-oriented school-university partnership focuses on the mutually beneficial relationship between schools and universities with regard to teacher preparation: "For schools to get better, they must have better teachers, among other things. To prepare better teachers (and counselors, special educators, and administrators) universities must have access to school settings exhibiting the very best practices" (Goodlad, 1986, pp. 8–9). The blueprints of the PDS vary in different reports. However, they all emphasize the role of the PDS in preservice teacher education.

More and more research has attested to the importance of student teaching in preservice teacher education programs. Both university faculty members and prospective teachers perceive that among the program segments, student teaching contributes most to one's future career as a teacher (Goodlad, 1990; Su, 1990b; Plourde, 2002a; Wilson, 2006; Wilson, Floden, & Ferrini-Mundy, 2002). However, research indicates that different student teaching experiences can have varying effects on student teachers. Some researchers conclude that after student teaching, student teachers become more authoritarian, rigid, impersonal, bureaucratic, and custodial (e.g., Emans, 1983; Hoy & Woolfolk, 1990; Jones, 1982; Packard, 1988) as well as less confident (Plourde, 2002b). Others report that student teachers become more liberal and confident (e.g., Tabachnick & Zeichner, 1984; Zeichner & Grant, 1981). The contents and contexts of student teaching are major determinants of the effects (Zeichner, 1986). MacKinnon's (1989) case study of four student teachers concludes that living with conformity is a way of life for them in their eight-week practicum, while Cochran-Smith (1991) paints a dramatically different picture—student teachers learn teaching against the grain with reform-minded cooperating teachers. Student teaching as described by MacKinnon and Cochran-Smith will certainly have different effects on student teachers.

Both content and context of student teaching are extremely important in the development of future teachers. This is perhaps one of the reasons why both the recent teacher education reform and the school-university partnership movement came to focus on, among other things, creating the PDS as a context for student teaching. However, to translate the ideas in the literature into practice is very complicated. The dissemination of information cannot guarantee success in educational change (Goodlad, 1975; Sarason, 1990).

In creating a PDS, much of the power for change lies in the hands of street-level bureaucrats (Lipsky, 1969), that is, the school-based faculty members. The rhetoric for establishing a PDS will be filtered by the school-based PDS faculty before it materializes in practice. Only when principals, along with teachers, become responsive to the problems facing their emerging PDS through a continuous process of dialogue, decision, action, and evaluation (Goodlad, 1975), can the new PDS be successfully created. In order to create PDSs successfully, voices of school-based faculty must be heard and taken into account. This study is intended to contribute to this goal.

A review of the major literature on PDS (e.g., Carnegie Forum, 1986; Darling-Hammond, 1989, 1994; Goodlad, 1990, 1993; Goodlad & Soder, 1992; Holmes Group, 1986, 1990; Levine, 1988; Lieberman & Miller, 1990) indicates that as far as preservice teacher education is concerned, the PDS's role is twofold. The first role is that the PDS must be an exemplary setting. Only in such an exemplary setting can student teachers be better educated. The role of PDSs in improving practice and in preparing teachers is analogous to that of teaching hospitals in the medical profession. They are clinical sites where professional standards of practice are developed, refined, and institutionalized; where cohorts of student teachers participate in rigorous induction programs; where both teaching practice and induction are knowledge based. The PDS must also be a self-renewing setting so that it maintains its exemplary status.

The second role of the PDS is reflected in how student teaching is organized. Student teaching is an induction experience to socialize future teachers. The traditional model for organizing student teaching puts student teachers in an apprenticeship situation (Lortie, 1975; Su, 1990b). A student teacher is usually assigned to work solely with one cooperating teacher. In this role, the student teacher is just like an apprentice. Moreover, there is little to suggest that student teaching induces a sense of solidarity with colleagues. Because of the lack of a supportive infrastructure, "the student adjusts his actual methods of teaching, not to the principles which he is acquiring, but to what he sees succeed and fail in an empirical way from moment to moment" (Dewey, 1904, p. 14.). The student teacher becomes an agent for maintaining the status quo after the apprenticeship of student teaching. Therefore, in order to produce better teachers, the PDS must pay attention to socialization, development, and inquiry in student teaching experiences. Student teaching in the PDS, along with the coursework on the university campus, should also help future teachers inquire into schooling and develop professional beliefs, knowledge, and skills.

Difficulties facing the PDS in realizing its role are also identified in the existing literature (Abdal-Haqq, 1991; Case, Norlander, & Reagon, 1993; Darling-Hammond, 1994; Dixon & Ishler, 1992; King & Smith, 1990; Nystrand, 1991; Osguthorpe, 1995; Stoddart, 1993; Winitzky, Stoddart, & O'Keefe, 1992; Zimpher, 1990). The difficulties mentioned in the literature include the following: (a) principals and teachers are overwhelmed by additional work; (b) resources are inadequate; (c) equitable treatment of teachers may be problematic; change to the PDS may divide faculty members into haves and have-nots; and (d) PDSs are innovative; therefore, no single set of standards or attributes exists to characterize effective sites.

The aforementioned models and difficulties are based on the existing literature, almost all of which is authored by university faculty members. Although many university faculty members have been actively involved in creating PDSs, their theorizing may not necessarily be consistent with that of school-based PDS faculty members. The literature written by PDS school-based faculty members is largely concerned with logistics of implementation rather than visions of the PDS (e.g., McDaniel, Rice, & Romerdahl, 1990). Nonetheless, there is always an interaction between teachers and policies. Teachers' beliefs, knowledge, and existing practice are active in this interaction (Cohen & Ball, 1990). This type of interaction also applies to educational administrators (Honig, 2006) and to the school as a whole (Spillane, 2004). We have already learned much from history. The national curriculum reform spurred by the Sputnik launching was unsuccessful behind the classroom door (Goodlad, 1974). Even the California Mathematics Curriculum Framework, which was of small scale and required less organizational change, has not been translated appropriately into classroom use (Cohen, 1990). It is imperative to listen to voices from the field so that preservice teacher education in the PDSs context may proceed successfully.

Research Methodology

The purpose of this study was twofold. The central purpose was to document the school-based PDS faculty members' views on the role of PDSs in preservice teacher education. However, as voices from the field had barely been heard, a second purpose of this study was to identify possible discrepancies between the literature and those voices.

This study addressed the following research questions:

1. What do the PDS's school-based faculty members envision as appropriate preservice teacher education in the PDS context?
2. What, from the school-based faculty members' perspective, are individuals' and the PDS's difficulties in realizing their desirable roles?
3. What is the discrepancy between expectations in the literature and school-based PDS faculty members' vision of preservice teacher education in the PDS context?

This inquiry used a case study methodology, as its central purpose was to generalize to a theoretical framework about school-based faculty members' vision of the PDS's role in preservice teacher education (Yin, 1984, p. 21). The case study approach allowed the gathering of in-depth data on school-based faculty members' vision. In accordance with Cronbach's (1966) admonition that the best case should be selected, the PDS sampled for this study was one of the best in the Puget Sound Professional Development Center (PSPDC), which is a consortium of the University of Washington, four middle schools in the Seattle area, and the Washington Office of the Superintendent of Public Instruction. One of the goals of PSPDC was to pilot a middle school preservice teacher education program through the

College of Education at the University of Washington. Because of the governance structure of the activities pertaining to preservice teacher education in the sampled middle school, seven informants were selected. They were the principal, the teacher leadership coordinator, the site supervisor, three cooperating teachers, and one non-cooperating teacher. The teacher leadership coordinator was responsible for all the renewal efforts in the school, and the site supervisor was in charge of issues related to supervising student teachers. Both the teacher leadership coordinator and the site supervisor were classroom teachers in this school. Five of the informants were female.

The data of this study included one structured interview with each informant. The interview protocol consisted of nine questions, such as "How do you think that student teaching should be organized? (Why?) Have there been any changes in the organization of student teaching in your school since it became a PDS?" The interview protocol was piloted in a PDS that agreed to participate in the study but was not selected because of the sampling strategy. The interviews focused on eliciting school-based faculty members' vision of preservice teacher education in the PDS context. Each interview lasted 40–60 minutes. In addition to the interviews, I observed a weekly meeting among the site supervisor and student teachers. I also collected some documents pertaining to preservice teacher education in the PDS context, such as school newsletters, meeting minutes, reference materials used by cooperating teachers, annual plans and reports, and an ethnographic study report on its becoming a PDS.

The documents were reviewed to gain an insight into this school and its PDS-related activities. The interviews were audiotaped and transcribed verbatim. Three coding systems were developed by a progressive analysis of the data. They are (a) school-based faculty members' vision of how student teaching should be organized in the PDS context, (b) difficulties individuals are facing in realizing their ideal roles in preservice teacher education in the PDS context, and (c) difficulties the school is facing in realizing its ideal role in preservice teacher education in the PDS context. In the second coding system, for example, there are the following codes: LT (lack of time), GT (get tired), MW (matching with student teachers), ES (empty nest-syndrome), I (intrusion), SU (school-university coordination), LI (lack of institutional commitment), LR (lack of resources other than time), and M (miscellaneous).

The coding systems were developed from the interview data. They were gradually developed on the basis of reading the transcribed interview protocols. They were refined with each reading and were finalized after the fourth reading. All the interview data were coded by the final coding systems. As will be described later, decision rules were made to report the findings.

Samples of the data were also coded by a person who was not familiar with the study and was blind to the informants. Cohen's (1960) interrater agreement coefficients were calculated: 0.82 for school-based faculty members' vision of how student teaching should be organized in the context of PDS; 0.74 for difficulties individuals are facing in realizing their ideal roles in preservice teacher education; and 0.76 for difficulties the school is facing in realizing its ideal role in preservice teacher education. Disagreements were resolved by discussion. The results of these analyses revealed both commonalities and discrepancies between voices from the field and the literature.

The Findings

How Student Teaching Should Be Organized

The organization of student teaching is the most important part of the school-based faculty members' view of preservice teacher education. Their views were elicited largely by posing the following question: "How do you think student teaching should be organized?" (it was repeated throughout the transcribed interview protocols). The categories for school-based faculty members' vision of preservice teacher in the PDS context were developed by reviewing the transcribed interview protocol repeatedly and inductively. The categories were codes in the finalized coding system. The decision rule here was to report the visions elaborated by at least four informants. What follows are their visions of how student teaching should be organized.

1. A year-long commitment. All of the seven informants of this study envisioned that student teaching experience should be one year long, with one even arguing for a year and a half. As the site supervisor put it:

> I like the way that we have organized it now and that the student teachers are working with us for at least a year, three quarters for people getting a secondary certificate, four quarters for people getting an elementary certificate. Because they have a chance to work up to full time teaching, they do lots of observation, they work with small groups of students for a while, and gradually taking over the time they work in a classroom. And I really like that. I really like this way.

There was a difference of opinion between the teachers and the administrator on why the student teaching should be one year long. The administrator hoped that the student teachers would become a part of the school faculty and that she could use the services of the student teachers. The teachers emphasized the nature of the teaching job. They wanted student teachers to know all of the work that teaching involves and to strengthen their commitment to teaching. They wanted student teachers to see the entire year-long process, from the beginning to the end of the school year: "There are lots of other things involved than being teaching in the classroom, the end of year grades, and wrap ups, and the activities that go on at the end of the year in Spring." They also wanted student teachers to see the growth of the students during the school year because the best way to organize student teaching is to stage student teachers' responsibilities, to gradually enlarge their responsibilities. This was the second part of school-based faculty members' vision.

2. *Gradually enlarging student teachers' responsibilities.* One of the cooperating teachers summarized her student teaching experience as "just in and out." She took full responsibilities for the classroom two days after she arrived and totally withdrew from the classroom just one month later. The informants talked about the progression in which student teachers move from their seminar classes to taking over a classroom completely. They thought "it's very manageable not only for the cooperating teacher but for the preservice person as well."

In a document circulated among the cooperating teachers, the responsibilities for student teachers are clearly stated. For instance, for the second quarter, "The student teacher is in the classroom 14 hours per week. During this quarter she/he teaches two classes concurrently for at least three weeks and prepares for the full-time commitment in third quarter." Following this statement, there are 11 entries to elaborate on student teachers' responsibilities. In the third quarter, the emphasis is on refining skills and assuming total teaching responsibilities for a minimum of six weeks. Cooperating teachers were informed of the idea of gradually enlarging student teachers' responsibilities, and this idea had become part of their vision for organizing student teaching.

Because the student teachers were involved in their internship in school for one year, the internship progressed in well-organized stages, and the relationship between the student and the cooperating teacher could become more intimate and cordial. Therefore, matching a student teacher with a cooperating teacher became a part of school-based faculty members' vision.

3. *Matching a student teacher with a cooperating teacher*. The conventional way to place a student teacher with a cooperating teacher is merely to make assignments on the basis of subject area and availability of cooperating teachers. According to the informants, better ways to place a student teacher with a cooperating teacher would include the following: student teachers should first pay a visit to the PDS, expressing interest in the one-year program. The student teachers would be received by the teacher leadership coordinator and interviewed by potential cooperating teachers. Would-be cooperating teachers would meet with a number of interns before deciding whether they want to be cooperating teachers and if so, with whom. Student teachers should also have the opportunity to express their preferences. There are several reasons for matching a student teacher with a cooperating teacher, such as to avoid interpersonal conflicts and to optimize student teachers' service and learning opportunities. As a cooperating teacher commented:

> I believe that we need to interview prospective student teachers. There has to be an interview so that you can touch base on your and his strengths.... It gives two people an opportunity to meet and share backgrounds, philosophies, and also that the student teachers might do some observations of some teachers in the classroom, too.... I think the opportunity for them to discuss and share what might be a part of the program for the coming year certainly is important, rather than here is the name, this person is within your subject area, therefore, they should be assigned to you, because that doesn't work. So just because a person is in my particular subject area does not mean that we should match up, that we need to discuss, we need to talk about our goals.

This PDS did not match student teachers with cooperating teachers in the first year. Student teachers were interviewed only by the teacher leadership coordinator. However, starting from the second year, they followed exactly what was described in the foregoing. This idea arose largely from cooperating teachers' personal experience of interacting with student teachers.

4. *A site supervisor responsible for coordinating and evaluating student teaching*. The site supervisor is, in his own words, "a sort of person that they [student teachers and cooperating teachers] can come to ... and talk to ... about things." The informants regarded it "an incredible advantage to be able to have a site supervisor that's on staff, that's here all the time." The site supervisor is the liaison between the student teacher group and the cooperating teacher group. He is familiar with the school, the faculty, and the student teachers. He is on staff and in the school all the time.

Therefore, he can act effectively as a coordinator for the preservice teacher education program in the PDS context.

The site supervisor is also a person who is there when student teachers need someone other than their cooperating teachers to talk to. He brings information from the university to the site and organizes meetings once a week with student teachers to provide a time and place for them to meet as a group. I observed one such weekly meeting. Three student teachers attended. They talked about their teaching experience in the previous week, the somewhat conflicting schedule of internship work in school and coursework on campus, and plans for the weeks to come. They also asked for help in reflecting on their experience and in coordinating the internship and campus coursework. The site supervisor gave them his advice and offered to talk with their cooperating teachers to reschedule their internship work. During the meeting, other student teachers also gave their advice on how to overcome difficulties in the classroom. The meeting lasted about an hour. Throughout the meeting, the site supervisor encouraged the participants to discuss whatever they wished. The meeting ended with a schedule for the site supervisor to observe classes to build up student teachers' internship portfolios. On the way back to the university campus, the student teacher with whom I attended told me that she had found the weekly meeting very helpful.

The site supervisor is also responsible for evaluating student teaching. The State of Washington requires a student teacher evaluation; this evaluation is usually done by persons hired by the university who go from school to school to observe student teachers. They evaluate individual lessons and write recommendations that go into student teachers' files. These evaluators usually bring a checklist and are not familiar with the settings. As illustrated in the following quote, informants argued for having the site supervisor evaluate student teaching:

> The person who is doing the evaluation is on site. It's me. It's not someone who just comes from the University, doesn't know the students, doesn't know the people in the school.... It's a kind of personal connection.... And I think that the student teachers will say that they like that because very often they are having troubles with the classroom students. I probably know that student, you know. And they have experience the day I observe them. Well, we can talk about it right away. It's not like I will disappear and go back to the University. So I think this is one of the main things that I really like. And I would suppose that this is also one of the main things that student teachers like, too.

As illustrated here, the reason for having the site supervisor evaluate student teachers is to have a contextualized evaluation, and to use it as a diagnostic device to improve student teachers' teaching repertoires.

5. *Beyond classroom teaching.* Connected with a year-long commitment and gradual enlargement of student teachers' responsibilities is the idea that the student teacher should move beyond classroom teaching. Cooperating teachers would like to see student teachers take on additional roles, not only to do wrap-ups at the end of the school year and to supervise students' field trips, but also to become more and more visible in other aspects of professional life as well, particularly attending parent meetings.

The administrator would like to see student teachers become more actively involved in all the activities in the building and become a part of the total school, including attending faculty meetings. She also envisioned that "the school district and the school should make a commitment to that individual, to say to that person if you do well in a year and a half, you have a job here or within the school district."

6. *Working with a team of teachers and transcending student teachers' preconceptions regarding teaching.* The conventional way of organizing student teaching is to place a student teacher with one and only one cooperating teacher. The relationship between the student teacher and the cooperating teacher is such that when the student teacher walks into the classroom, the cooperating teacher walks out. This way of organizing student teaching merely reinforces the apprenticeship model and does not help students transcend their preconceptions regarding teaching based on their own educational experiences (Goodlad, 1990, chap. 6).

By contrast, in this PDS context, student teachers are in a more supportive structure and they are encouraged to observe and work with other teachers. The PSPDC encourages student teachers to work with a team of cooperating teachers whenever possible. The teacher leadership coordinator also commented that "generally, what we would like to see them do is work with teams of teachers, although it hasn't always worked that way. Students are encouraged to observe more classes." One cooperating teacher of language arts mentioned that her student teacher was also working with a math teacher and taught math classes.

All three cooperating teachers had a strong desire to encourage student teachers to identify with a more diversified culture of teaching. As one cooperating teacher said,

> I certainly do not want them to copy me. I want them to learn from me. I should be available to them. And I should not tell them what to do. I should let them experience that, and be a shoulder for them. If they come with an

idea, then we talk it through. If they come with a problem, let them solve the problem.

Still another cooperating teacher observed,

> [Part of my responsibilities as a cooperating teacher is] to show one way that you can approach the job, all of the teachers have different styles. It is important that they work with a variety of teachers, and this program is good at that. These student teachers do work with several teachers, to get a feeling about the different ways you can still approach the same situation.

7. *School-university coordination.* The middle school teacher education program was developed jointly by the university and the PDSs. Students enroll concurrently in an integrated core seminar taught by a team composed of professors from curriculum and instruction, special education, and educational psychology, and a teacher from one of the PDSs. There is one doctoral student coordinating the team.

The interview with school-based faculty members revealed a vision of school-university coordination. From the programmatic perspective, the site supervisor observed,

> And I also like the organization that they are doing seminars with the University at the same time, so when they are doing more in the University, they are doing less in the school. And they are sort of switching over until they are doing full-time teaching. We are having now two student teachers right now doing the full-time teaching. And they are totally responsible for the whole day.

Another teacher mentioned the increasing familiarity between faculties of the university and the school and envisioned the probability of increasing school-university coordination. He commented,

> I think as the program has been going longer, the staff over in the University of Washington knows more about the teaching staff here. And just that personal knowledge back and forth is helpful communication. And I think as the staff over there becomes more and more familiar with the staff here, what we are doing here, it will be easier for them to tie in, to train at the U with what's happening here at (the name of the school).

The informants also expressed their vision of school-university coordination from the perspective of what should be improved in this regard. The administrator wanted to know more about the structure of the College of Education so that the school-university coordination would be more effective. One teacher observed that "over there, in the University of Washington, it [the coursework] is not tied directly to real work, real students.

Somewhat theoretical...too theoretical." Although he did not mention directly the idea of school-university coordination, it is obvious that the idea became a part of his vision.

One interesting point found in constructing school-based faculty members' vision of preservice teacher education in the PDS context was that their vision was largely a reflection of what they had already done rather than what they ought to do. This finding will be further elaborated in the discussion section.

Difficulties Facing Individuals and the School in Realizing Ideal Roles in Preservice Teacher Education

The informants were asked two questions about the difficulties they face from the individual and institutional perspectives: (1) "What has made it difficult for you to realize your ideal role in preservice teacher education as a cooperating teacher (or a site supervisor and so on)?" (2) "What has made it difficult for your school to realize its ideal role in preservice teacher education?" Because of the different roles that the several categories of informants played in preservice teacher education in the PDS context, they were facing different difficulties and they viewed these difficulties from different perspectives. Given the nature of the answers to these questions, the decision rule was that the difficulties reported in the following should be elaborated by at least three informants.

The answers to the question on their individual difficulties were coded and sorted into two categories: personal and contextual.

1. *Lack of time.* All informants except for the non-cooperating teacher (who was not asked this question) reported that lack of time was a big issue. One of the cooperating teachers said,

> It's a time commitment. You want to tell them why I did this, or if I would do this once again, these are the things I would change. So every all of that takes time. So it's a big time, the time commitment that you need to share....

The time issue is more serious for the site supervisor and the teacher leadership coordinator. One of them commented,

> It's less difficult now. When I first started doing this, I wasn't allocated a period to do it. And I had to do a lot of juggling within my own classroom.... But now I am allocated one class period.... I do have the allocated time so that we can do the thing we have to do. Well, again, right now I feel like I have time although I do find that sometimes I take time from my own personal part of time to do observations or the other things.

The other also commented that "the district allocated a period of time for me [to fill this role]. So I have been allocated an extra period. It is not nearly enough ..., so that I feel it's a constraint."

2. *Matching with compatible student teachers*. Some cooperating teachers found that it was difficult to match with student teachers. One cooperating teacher described an unhappy experience she went through:

> I would say one year, there was a difficult match, and I felt like I was an ombudsman, trying to be an arbitrator between student teacher and parents, and student teacher and students. Sometimes, in some cases, that was only one situation where it was not a good match, and students had a very difficult time and student teachers had a very difficult time. And there was that added pressure and stress of trying to make everybody happy, trying to have everybody get through this situation. And yeah, that was very difficult. If the match isn't quite right, there is a problem.

The site supervisor and the teacher leadership coordinator also mentioned this difficulty. For them, the difficulty arose from the unavailability of cooperating teachers. They wanted to place student teachers with the best teachers and hoped that the existing cooperating teachers would not burn out.

3. *The empty nest syndrome*. The third personal difficulty is, as a cooperating teacher put it, "the empty nest syndrome." When student teachers assumed total teaching responsibility for a minimum of six weeks at the end of their internship, cooperating teachers felt it was difficult to let their children go. They asked, "Can the students let go of the regular teacher?" One cooperating teacher said, "I am having a hard time letting my children go. I love my classes, and now my student teacher is teaching them, and I am going... [the sentence was incomplete]. They talk about mothers when all the daughters go away to college." Another cooperating teacher talked about her attachment to students in her class.

4. *The need to improve school-university coordination*. Some informants perceived the need to improve school-university coordination as a contextual difficulty. Talking about difficulties in placing "very, very difficult" student teachers with cooperating teachers, the administrator suggested that "the schools and the university need to do a whole lot more cooperating on the selecting [of teacher candidates into the program]." One cooperating teacher also elaborated on the occasional conflicting schedule of the internship in school and the coursework on campus.

Some other personal difficulties mentioned by the informants included tiredness and a feeling of intrusion because somebody was around for the whole year; contextual difficulties included lack of institutional support for cooperating teachers, lack of resources, and so on. The first question on difficulty was focused on individual difficulties; therefore, the contextual difficulties had been mentioned but not elaborated.

The answers to the second question, one discussing the difficulties faced by the PDS, can also be divided into two categories: intra-institutional and inter-institutional. The first three difficulties are intra-institutional, with the last being inter-institutional.

1. *Partial institutional commitment.* Not everyone was involved in pre-service teacher education. Although the faculty of this school voted for continuing to be a PDS (80% of the faculty was supportive of the program), the teacher leadership coordinator perceived that four of them still felt that "not having everybody involved" was a difficulty facing their school. It was reported that some of the faculty members lacked enthusiasm for the PDS program. Part of the reason for the lack of enthusiasm was that there were too many programs going on in the school. This is the second difficulty: competing programs.

2. *Competing programs.* The site supervisor commented that "We have many special programs. And to some people, I think, this [the PDS program] appears to be one more special program in that long list. And because of that, not everybody is working on the same thing and that's difficult." This difficulty was also reflected in the non-cooperating teacher's remarks. She argued that the PDS program was competing for resources with other programs and that "they [the people involved in the PDS program] need to look at the commitment to it, either abandon it or become more involved."

3. *Limited resources of cooperating teachers.* The third difficulty was mentioned particularly by the site supervisor and the teacher leadership coordinator. The site supervisor remarked that "finding cooperating teachers year after year after year is difficult because it requires a big commitment."

4. *Difficulties in placing student teachers.* Connected with the third difficulty is the fourth one: placement of student teachers. This difficulty is twofold. First of all, it was perceived that there were too many student teachers in the building. Second, because it is a year-long program, the limited resources of cooperating teachers had been further depleted.

5. *Lack of inter-institutional coordination.* The difficulty in coordinating between the school and the university was discussed again when talking about the inter-institutional difficulties. One informant regarded the campus coursework as not being tied to the internship work. Another infor-

mant complained about unfamiliarity with and the rigidity of the university.

> I think that part of it is we have never been taught. We participated in what the University is by the fact we went to the University. But we have not been taught what you have to deal with on a daily basis... or the political realities of the College of Education. We don't have a really clear idea about you, and what happens is that does create problems. The reason that creates problems is that we get frustrated because we come up with an idea, it seems incredibly logical to us. And we are met with by the people from the University, they say 'we cannot do that.' It is really frustrating.... By having these relationships with the University, what the individual teachers in the schools are asked is to make changes.... If you draw a picture as to the degree to which schools are changed as opposed to the University... I think you would always see, my conception is, we changed at least twice as much as the University has done.

This inter-institutional difficulty was also expressed in discussing the contextual difficulties facing individuals.

Rhetoric and Voices from the Field: A Contrast

According to the major literature on PDS (Carnegie Forum, 1986; Darling-Hammond, 1989; Goodlad, 1990; Holmes Group, 1986, 1990; Levine, 1988; Lieberman & Miller, 1990), PDSs should be exemplary settings in which the organization of student teaching should pay attention to student teachers' socialization, development, and inquiry.

Comparing voices from the field with the literature, we may find that school-based faculty members' vision of preservice teacher education in the context of a PDS is largely focused on the socialization and development of student teachers. A year-long commitment, gradually enlarging student teachers' responsibilities, matching a student teacher with a cooperating teacher, having a site supervisor, activities beyond classroom teaching, working with a team of teachers, and school-university coordination all pertain to the logistics of socializing and developing student teachers. However, the school-based faculty members did not mention the concept of "cohort group" (Goodlad, 1990, pp. 329,207-211; Su, 1990b)— a group of prospective teachers going through the whole program together which so that each batch can be identified as the class of such and such year. The weekly meeting among student teachers and the site supervisor was an opportunity for student teachers to meet as a cohort group, but the informants of this study justified the weekly meeting from the perspective of facilitating communications between cooperating teachers and student teachers. The concept of cohort group had not become a part of school-based faculty members' vision and, therefore, had not purposefully been institutionalized as a mechanism to strengthen the cohort group in the PDS.

In addition to the absence of the concept of cohort group, there are two significant differences between voices from the field and the literature on PDSs. The first is that the school-based faculty members hardly took into account the idea that student teaching should take place in an exemplary setting. When asked, "What should the PDS be or become so that it can best realize its role in preservice teacher education?" no informants elaborated on the point that it should be an exemplary setting. The issue was intentionally brought up by this author when interviewing one informant, and she interpreted being exemplary as "being realistic." Another informant apparently had difficulties in finding a metaphor to denote what she described; when prodded to give one, she chose "teaching hospital." However, she did not go on elaborating the parallel between teaching hospitals in medicine and professional development schools in education.

There is an assumption underlying voices from the field that once a school has been selected as a PDS, it is exemplary. When one informant discussed how to solve the problem of burn-out among cooperating teachers, she suggested schools take turns in being PDSs. This conception of rotation has the assumption that all schools are exemplary. Still another informant argued that there was no necessary connection between PDS and student teaching. It is clear that school-based faculty members did not have the vision that student teaching should take place in exemplary settings. The lack of this vision of PDSs, evident in the voices from the field, needs attention in order to fulfill the goals of providing exemplary programs for students and of conducting student teaching and inservice teaching in such settings.

The second difference between the rhetoric and voices from the field is that inquiry has been neglected in the informants' vision. Inquiry to strengthen the profession of teaching is one of the goals of the PDS. The PDS must help student teachers inquire into the nature of education, schooling, and teaching as a profession; establish an inquiring attitude; and do so as a natural part of their careers. When asked, "What's your working definition of the concept of PDS?" only one informant mentioned the goal of inquiry to strengthen the profession of teaching. The fact that the school-based faculty members hardly envisioned the role of inquiry in student teaching is due to their conception of the PDS. If the two key elements of exemplary setting and inquiry are missing in the school-based faculty members' vision, and the student teaching is one year long, the image of having student teachers in the school is perhaps very close to that of being an apprentice (Lortie, 1975).

Another interesting finding resulting from contrasting the literature and the school-based faculty members' vision is that the site supervisor's and teacher leadership coordinator's conceptions were closer to the literature, which means that the persons who have more opportunities to work with university people have developed conceptions that are closer to the literature. This finding was confirmed by analyzing informants' answers to the question "How have you shaped your vision of PDSs' role in preservice teacher education?" Three of them, including the site supervisor and the teacher leadership coordinator, identified working with people from the University of Washington as their major source.

Conclusions

This study revealed the discrepancy between voices from the field and the literature. It is clear that the vision of school-based faculty was practice-oriented, that is, their vision consisted largely of what they had done rather than an ideal to be realized. Furthermore, when they were reflecting on difficulties they and their institution were facing in realizing their best roles in preservice teacher education, they talked about the logistics in doing better what they had already done. None of them envisioned the difficulty as being conceptual. There seems to be an inertia in the practice. These findings suggest the importance of interaction between the school faculty and the university faculty so as to develop a shared vision.

In view of the difficulties facing individuals and the school in realizing their perceived roles in preservice teacher education, it is clear that there must be more support within the school for the PDS initiative, and that there also must be more school-university coordination. The idea of simultaneous renewal of schools and universities must be put into practice, because nothing short of simultaneous renewal will succeed. Furthermore, school-university partnership should not be viewed as a strategy for a special short-term project. Rather, it should be perceived as a way of being for both schools and universities.

References

Abdal-Haqq, I. (1991). Professional development schools and educational reform: Concepts and concerns (ERIC Document Reproduction Service No. ED 335 357).

Carnegie Forum on Education and the Economy. (1986). A nation prepared: Teachers for the 21st century. New York: Author.
Case, C. W., Norlander, K. A., & Reagon, T. G. (1993). Cultural transformation in an urban professional development center: Policy implications for school-university collaboration. Educational Policy, 7 (1), 40–60.
Cochran-Smith, M. (1991). Learning to teach against the grain. *Harvard Educational Review, 61* (3), 279–310.
Cohen, D. K. (1990). A revolution in one class-room: The case of Mrs. Oublier. *Educational Evaluation and Policy Analysis, 12* (3), 311–329.
Cohen, D. K., & Ball, D. L. (1990). Relations between policy and practice: A commentary. *Educational Evaluation and Policy Analysis, 12* (3), 249–256.
Cohen, J. (1960). A coefficient of agreement for nominal scales. *Educational and Psychology Measurement, 20* (1), 37–46.
Cronbach, L. J. (1966). The logic of experiments on discovery. In L. S. Shulman & E. R. Keislar (Eds.), *Learning by discovery: A critical appraisal* (pp. 75–92). Chicago: Rand McNally.
Darling-Hammond, L. (1989). Accountability for professional practice. *Teachers College Record, 91* (1), 59–80.
Darling-Hammond, L. (Ed.). (1994). *Professional development schools: Schools for developing a profession.* New York: Teachers College Press.
Dewey, J. (1904). The relation of theory to practice in education. In C. A. McMurry (Ed.), *The relation of theory to practice in the education of teachers* (pp. 9–28), The Third Yearbook of the National Society for the Scientific Study of Education, Part 1. Chicago: University of Chicago Press.
Dixon, P. N., & Ishler, R. E. (1992). Professional development schools: Stages in collaboration. *Journal of Teacher Education, 43* (1), 28–34.
Emans, R. (1983). Implementing the knowledge base: Redesigning the function of cooperating teachers and college supervisors. *Journal of Teacher Education, 34* (3), 14–18.
Goodlad, J. I. (1974). *Looking behind the classroom door.* Worthington, Ohio: Charles A. Jones.
Goodlad, J. I. (1975). *The dynamics of educational change: Toward responsive schools.* New York: McGraw-Hill.
Goodlad, J. I. (1986). Toward a more perfect union. *State Education Leader, 5* (1), 8–9.
Goodlad, J. I. (1990). *Teachers for our nation's schools.* San Francisco: Jossey-Bass.

Goodlad, J. I. (1993). School-university partnerships and partner schools. *Educational Policy, 7* (1), 24–39.

Goodlad, J. I., & Soder, R. (1992). School-university partnership: An appraisal of an idea (Occasional paper No. 15). Seattle: Center for Educational Renewal, University of Washington.

Holmes Group. (1986). Tomorrow's teachers: A report of the Holmes Group. East Lansing, MI: Author.

Holmes Group. (1990). Tomorrow's schools: Principles for the design of professional development schools. East Lansing, MI: Author

Honig, M. I. (2006). *New directions in education policy implementation: Confronting complexity.* Albany, NY: State University of New York Press.

Hoy, W. K., & Woolfolk, A. E. (1990). Socialization of student teachers. *American Educational Research Journal, 27* (2), 279–300.

Jones, D. R. (1982). The influence of length and level of student teaching on pupil control ideology. *High School Journal, 65* (7), 220–225.

King, I. L., & Smith, J. R. (1990). The role of the partnership school in the undergraduate teacher training program at the University of Hawaii (ERIC Document Reproduction Service No. ED 330 643).

Levine, M. (Ed.) (1988). *Professional practice schools: Building a model.* Washington, DC: American Federation.

Lieberman, A., & Miller, L. (1990). Teacher development in professional practice schools. *Teachers College Record, 92* (1), 105–122.

Lipsky, M. (1969). *Toward a theory of street-level bureaucracy.* Madison, WI: University of Wisconsin Press.

Lortie, D. C. (1975). *Schoolteacher: A sociological study.* Chicago: University of Chicago Press.

MacKinnon, J. D. (1989). Living with conformity in student teaching. *Alberta Journal of Educational Research, 35* (1), 2–19.

McDaniel, J. E., Rice, C., & Romerdahl, N. S. (1990). Building teacher leadership in an emerging professional development center. Paper presented at the annual meeting of the American Educational Research Association, Boston, MA.

Nystrand, R. O. (1991). Professional development schools: Toward a new relationship for schools and universities (ERIC Document Reproduction Service No. ED 330 690).

Osguthorpe, R. T., Harris, C. R., Harris, M., and Black, S. (Eds.) (1995) *Partner schools: Centers for educational renewal.* San Francisco, CA: Jossey-Bass.

Packard, J. S. (1988). The pupil control studies. In N. J. Boyan (Ed.). *Handbook of research and educational administration.* New York: Longman.

Plourde, L. A. (2002a). Elementary science education: The influence of student teaching—Where it all begins. *Education, 123* (2), 253–259.

Plourde, L. A. (2002b). The influence of student teaching on preservice elementary teachers' science self-efficacy and outcome expectancy beliefs. *Journal of Instructional Psychology, 29* (4), 245–53.

Sarason, S. B. (1990). *The predictable failure of educational reform: Can we change course before it's too late?* San Francisco: Jossey-Bass.

Spillane, J. P. (2004). *Standards deviation: How schools misunderstand education policy*. Cambridge, MA: Harvard University Press.

Stoddart, T. (1993). The professional development school: Building bridges between cultures. *Educational Policy, 7* (1), 5–23.

Su, Z. (1990a). School-university partnership: Ideas and experiments (1986–1990) (Occasional paper No. 12). Seattle: Center for Educational Renewal, University of Washington.

Su, Z. (1990b). Exploring the moral socialization of teacher candidates. *Oxford Review of Education, 16* (3), 367–391.

Tabachnick, B. R., & Zeichner, K. M. (1984). The impact of the student teaching experience on the development of teacher perspectives. *Journal of Teacher Education, 35* (6), 28–36.

Wilson, E. K. (2006). The impact of an alternative model of student teacher supervision: Views of the participants. *Teaching and Teacher Education, 22* (1), 22–31.

Wilson, S., Floden, R. E., & Ferrini-Mundy, J. (2002). Teacher preparation research: An insider's view from the outside. *Journal of Teacher Education, 53* (3), 190–204.

Winitzky, N., Stoddart, T., & O'Keefe, P. (1992). Great expectations: Emerging professional development schools. *Journal of Teacher Education, 43* (1), 3–18.

Yin, R. K. (1984). *Case study research: Design and methods*. Beverly Hills, CA: Sage.

Zeichner, K. M. (1986). Content and contexts: Neglected elements in studies of student teaching as an occasion for learning to teach. *Journal of Education for Teaching, 12* (1), 5–24.

Zeichner, K. M., & Grant, C. A. (1981). Biography and social structure in the socialization of student teachers. *Journal of Education for Teaching, 7* (3), 298–314.

Zimpher, N. L. (1990). Creating professional development school sites. *Theory into Practice, 29* (1), 42–49.

INDEX

AC (alternative certification). see certification, alternative
achievement, student
and certification, 7–8, 32, 73, 127
  of disadvantaged students, 8, 73–74
  link with teacher preparation, 32, 72–73
  link with teacher qualifications, 7–9, 21, 72–74
  relation to teacher quality, 61
  relation to use of undercertified teachers, 63
  and teacher preparation, 32
  and teacher subject background, 62
achievement gap, 8–9
AC minority teachers. see minority teachers, and AC
ACT scores of new teachers, 65
age of AC teachers, 94–95, 106–7, 111, 118
alternative certification (AC). see certification, alternative
Anderson, R., 62
Ansell, S. E., 8–9, 21, 74
apprenticeship, student teaching as, 201, 214–15
Armour-Thomas, E., 62
assignments, teaching
  in analysis of teacher qualifications, 12
  out-of-field teaching, 5–7
  subject background in, 20, 35–40
  and teacher qualification, 14–17, 19–21
  types of certification in, 38–40
attrition
  and AC, 100, 137
  approaches to studying, 141–44
  characteristics of, 142–43
  conceptualization of study of, 144–46
  factors in, 132–37, 143–44, 149–56
  link with preparation/certification, 128, 132–37
  method of study of, 129–30, 146–49
  and new teachers, 130–31
  rates of, 128
  as result of social learning process, 142
  variables in study of, 145–49
  voluntary vs. involuntary leavers and movers, 146
  see also retention
Australia, 166

Baccalaureate and Beyond Longitudinal Study, 128, 129
Baccalaureate and Beyond Survey, 33, 64, 125
Bailey, C. T., 48
Berliner, D. C., 63
Berry, B., 32, 127
Billingsley, B. S., 145
bivariate approach to studying teacher retention/attrition, 141–44
Blank, R. K., 6
Bobbitt, S. A., 143
Boyd, D., 127
Boykin, A. W., 48
Bransford, J., 163
Brewer, D., 5, 127

California Mathematics Curriculum Framework, 202
career ladder, need for, 153–54, 155, 165–66, 169, 170, 171, 172
career patterns/plans of AC teachers, 98, 100, 108–9, 112

Carnegie Forum on Education and the Economy, 164, 165, 166, 199
certification
    alternative *(see* certification, alternative)
    criticism of policies of, 4
    evolution of, 41
    in high-need schools, 6
    increase in teachers without, 77
    and levels of student poverty, 67–69
    link with attrition, 132–37
    and location, 37, 40, *110*, 117–18
    and location/level, 96–97
    method of study of trends in, 34–35
    and minority student enrollment, 37, 75–85, 97, 99
    of new teachers, 35–36, 39, 41–42, 125
    status of, 41
    and student achievement, 7–8, 32, 73, 127
    in teaching assignments, 5–6, 35–40
    types of, 12, *81 (see also* certification, alternative)
    in urban schools, 7, 21, 37, 40
    see also teacher preparation
certification, alternative (AC)
    and academic qualifications, 32–33, 96, 99, 100, 107–8, *111*, 118–19
    and age of teachers, 94–95, 106–7, *111*, 118
    arguments against, 92, 104, 126–27
    arguments for, 91–92, 104, 115–16, 126
    and attrition, 100, 137
    and career patterns, 98, 100, 108–9, *112*
    and diversity, 91–92, 94–95, 99, 105, 109, *111*, 117, 120
    and educational equity, 100, 106
    and education of teachers, *111*
    and gender, 94, 106, *111*, 117
    impact of policy of, 109–12
    increase in, 91, 104, 115, 125
    lack of information on, 104
    and location/level, *110, 112*
    and math and science teaching force, 96, 108, *112*, 116–20
    methods of studying, 93–94
    and minority student enrollment, *110*
    and minority teachers, 94, 99, 105, 106, 107–12
    percentage of teachers with, 38–40
    policies of, studies on, 92
    as response to teacher shortages, 100
    and student achievement, 63
    and subject background, 96, 108, *112*, 117
    and work experience, 95, 99, 107, *111*, 119
Chapman, D. W., 142
Chen, X., 128
Chmelynski, C., 46
Coble, C. R., 62
Cochran-Smith, M., 31, 34, 179, 200
cohort group, concept of, 213–14
college. *see* education; subject background; teacher preparation
cooperating teacher
    difficulties of in professional development schools, 210–11
    matching *vs.* assigning of, 206
    role of in professional development schools, 194
    core fields, 14–15, 20
    see also mathematics; science
Cronbach, L. J., 202
Cunningham, R. T., 48

Dallas Morning News, 63

Index

Darling-Hammond, L., 8, 30, 32, 61, 100, 127, 128, 163
decision making, 165
  see also empowerment; retention, factors in
degrees earned by teachers, 96, *111*
  see also certification; education; subject background
dichotomous variable, 130
Dill, E. M., 48
diversity in teaching force
  and AC, 91–92, 94–95, 99, 105, 109, *111*, 117, 120
  among new teachers, 51–52
  arguments for, 46–49
  and culturally relevant pedagogy, 48
  and gender, 49, 50, 51, 52
  lack of, 45
  lack of increase in, 51, 54
  method of study of, 49–50
  minority teachers (*see* minority teachers)
  moral imperative for, 47
  and principals, 49
diversity of students, 45–47
Druva, C., 62

education
  of AC teachers, 32–33, 96, 99, 100, 107–8, *111*, 118–19
  degrees earned by teachers, 96
  in retention/attrition, *150, 151*
  see also certification; subject background
education, teacher. *see* teacher preparation
Education Commission of the States, 127
Elementary and Secondary Education Act of 1965, 9
  see also No Child Left Behind (NCLB)
empowerment, 155

  see also decision making; retention, factors in
England, 166

Feistritzer, C. E., 104, 125
Ferguson, P., 63
Ferguson, R., 62
Fetler, M., 32, 127
field experience. *see* student teaching
Floden, R. E., 32, 91
Fries, M. K., 31, 34
Fuller, E. J., 32, 127
Furlong, J., 166

Geis, S., 128
gender
  of AC teachers, 94, 106, *111*, 117
  diversity of in teaching force, 49, 50, 51, 52
  male teachers, distribution of across states, 54, *55*
  of math and science teachers, 117
  in retention/attrition, *150, 151*
  and salary, 172
  of teachers, and minority enrollment, 53–54
Goldberg, M., 163
Goldhaber, D., 5, 127
Goodlad, J. I., 163, 165, 173, 199
GPA of new teachers, 66–67
Green, M. S., 142
Grissmer, D. W., 100, 142
Grossman, P. L., 32, 127

Harris, D., 7
Hawk, P., 62
Henke, R., 128
Heyns, B., 143, 153
Hodgkinson, H., 45
Holmes Group, 165, 166, 172, 173, 199
Hoy, W. K., 179, 180, 194
human capital, 100

human capital theory of occupational choice, 142, 155

Ingersoll, R. M., 6
inquiry, goal of in student teaching, 214–15
Irvine, J. J., 47

jigsaw lesson plan, 189–90
Judge, H. G., 166

Kirby, S. N., 100, 142

Laczko-Kerr, I., 63
Ladd, H., 62
Ladson-Billings, G., 48
Langesen, D., 6
Lankford, H., 127
Lavigne, J. E., 6
leadership, 165, 171, 172
learning. *see* achievement, student
level. *see* location/level
Lewis, L., 3, 5
location/level
    of AC math and science teachers, 117
    and certification, 37, 40, 41, 96–97, *110*, 117
    and gender of teachers, 56
    of highly qualified teachers, 17–18, 63–64
    of minority teachers, 52–53, 106
    and retention/attrition, 155
Logan, L., 166
Lortie, D. C., 142

MacKinnon, J. D., 179, 194, 200
major, college. *see* subject background
mathematics
    and AC, 96, 97–98, 99, 108
    achievement in and teacher background, 7, 62
    achievement in and teacher preparation, 32, 127
    age of teachers in, 118
    gender of teachers in, 117
    minority teachers in, 117
    out-of-field teaching in, 6
    qualifications of teachers in, 7, 14, 15, 16, 21, 32, 62, 127
    subject matter knowledge of teachers in, 5
McCabe, M., 8–9, 21, 74
men, as teachers, 54, *55*
    see also diversity in teaching force; gender
minority student enrollment
    and certification, 37, 75–85, 97, 99
    and competent teachers, 45
    and distribution math and science teachers, 118
    and distribution of highly qualified teachers, 18–19, 21
    and gender of teachers, 53–54
    increase in, 45
    and number of minority teachers in school, 106, *110*
    in retention/attrition, *150, 151,* 153, 155
    and well-qualified teachers, method of studying trends in, 74–75
minority students and culturally relevant pedagogy, 48–49
minority teachers
    and AC, 94, 99, 105, 106, 107–12
    increase in, 51, 52
    lack of information on, 104
    lack of role models for, 46
    location of, 52–53, 106
    in math and science, 117
    and minority student enrollment, 106, *110*
Monk, D. H., 7, 62, 73
Moses, C., 165
M&S. *see* mathematics; science

multivariate approach to studying teacher retention/attrition, 141–42, 144
Murnane, R. J., 141, 142–43

National Assessment of Educational Progress (NAEP), 7, 8
National Postsecondary Student Aid Study (1993), 129
A Nation Prepared (Carnegie Forum), 199
Natriello, G., 99
No Child Left Behind (NCLB), 3, 10, 61
Nye, B., 8, 73

Olson, L., 8, 73
Ornstein, A. C., 163
out-of-field teaching, 5–7
    see also assignments, teaching; certification; subject background

PDC. see Puget Sound Professional Development Center
pedagogy, culturally relevant, 48
perceptions, teachers', in retention/attrition, *150, 152,* 154
personal characteristics in retention/attrition, *150, 151,* 153
Poppink, S., 6
Postsecondary Students Aid Study, 64
poverty level
    and distribution of highly qualified teachers, 64–69
    and retention/attrition, *151,* 156
Pratte, R., 163
principals, 49, 200
professional development schools (PDSs)
    cohort group in, 213–14
    cooperating teacher in, 194, 210–11
    cross-site visits in, 184–85
    description of, 180–82
    difficulties facing, 201, 212–13
    as exemplary setting, 214
    and goal of inquiry, 214–15
    literature on, 200–202
    methods of research on school-based faculty's views on, 202–4
    need for school-university coordination in, 215
    need for support of within school, 215
    need to be responsive to problems in, 200
    and need to listen to school-based faculty, 200
    part-time teaching experience in, 185–88
    power for change in, 200
    rhetoric of *vs.* school-based faculty's experience in, 213–15
    role of in preservice teacher education, 200–201
    school-based faculty's views on, 202–13
    student teaching in, case study on, 182–85
    successful creation of, 200
    as supportive context for field experience, 193, 200
    and university coursework in, 190–92
    visions for, 183–84
    see also student teaching
professionalism of teaching, 163–66, 168–73
PSPDC. see Puget Sound Professional Development Center
Puget Sound Professional Development Center
    case studies of school-based faculty at, 202–13
    case study in student teaching at, 182–95
    core seminar in, 181

field experience in, 181–82
onsite supervision in, 182
see also professional development schools

qualifications, teacher
and AC teachers, 32–33, 96, 99, 100, 107–8, 118–19
and certification, 4
in core fields, 14–15
and distribution of teachers, 6–7, 21
indicators of, 12
and location, 17–18
methods of analysis of, 10–13
and minority student enrollment, 18–19, 21
out-of-field teaching, 5–6 (*see also* assignments, teaching; subject background)
and poverty levels in schools, 64–69
research literature on, 4–9
significance of analysis of, 9–10
and student achievement, 7–9, 21, 72–74
and teaching assignments, 5–6, 14–17, 19–21
see also certification; out-of-field teaching; subject background
Qualities of Effective Teachers (Stronge), 8
quality, teacher, 3

race
and culturally relevant pedagogy, 48–49
in retention/attrition, *150, 151*
see also minority student enrollment; minority teachers
Ravitch, D., 4
Ray, L., 7
reform
failure of, 202

and idea of professional development schools, 199
in student teaching, 179
relative deprivation, 143
remedial courses taken by new teachers, 66
Renton, A. M., 163
retention
approaches to studying, 141–44
conceptualization of study of, 144–46
factors in, 149–56
method of study of, 146–49
as result of social learning process, 142
variables in study of, 145–49
voluntary *vs.* involuntary leavers and movers, 146
see also attrition
Rivers, J., 8, 73
Rury, J. L., 163

Sachs, J., 166
salary
effect of in retention/attrition, *150, 151,* 153, 154, 155
and gender, 172
and status of teaching, 166, *170,* 171, 172
Sanders, W., 8, 73
Sara (case study), 182–95
SAT scores of new teachers, 65
school characteristics in retention/attrition, *150, 151–52,* 153, 155
schools, high-need, 6
schools, inner-city. *see* location/level; schools, urban
schools, rural
effect of AC policy on teacher shortages in, 117
gender of teachers in, 56
qualifications of teachers in, 17–18, 21

Index   225

see also location/level
schools, suburban. see location/level
schools, urban
    certification of teachers in, 7, 21, 37, 40
    impact of AC on, 109, 110, 117
    minority teachers in, 106
    qualifications of teachers in, 17–18
    see also location/level
Schools and Staffing Survey (SASS), 5, 8, 10, 11, 33, 49, 74, 105, 129, 141, 145
school-university partnerships, 199
    see also professional development schools
science
    and AC, 96, 97–98, 99, 108, 116–20
    achievement in and teacher background, 7, 62
    achievement in and teacher preparation, 32, 127
    age of teachers in, 118
    gender of teachers in, 117
    minority teachers in, 117
    qualifications of teachers in, 15, 16–17, 20, 21
    retention/attrition of teachers in, 155
    salary schedule in, 155
    subject matter knowledge of teachers in, 5, 7, 62
science method course, 190–92
Seastrom, M. M., 5, 12, 20
Sergiovanni, T. J., 47
sex. see gender
Shen, J., 6, 7, 33
snapshot biography, 186–89
social studies method course, 189–90, 191–92
standards of teacher preparation, 164–65, 171
status of teaching
    and career opportunity, 165–66, 169, *170*, 171, 172
    and decision making, 165
    and egalitarian ethos, 172
    factors in improving, 165–66, 168–73
    future teachers' views on improving, 171–72, 173
    and leadership, 165, 169, *170*, 171, 172
    materialistic approach to improving, 173
    methods of analysis of, 167–68
    and salary, 166, *170*, 171, 172
    suggestions for improving, 163–66
    symptoms of, 163
    and teacher preparation, 169, *170*, 171, 172
    and working conditions, 171, 172
Stoddart, T., 32, 91
Stronge, J. H., 4, 8
student achievement. see achievement, student
students
    diversity of, 45–47
    minority, 48–49 (see also minority student enrollment)
students, disadvantaged, 8, 73–74
    see also poverty level
student teaching
    as apprenticeship, 201, 214–15
    case study in, 182–95
    content of, 194–95, 200
    context of, 193, 200
    cooperating teachers in, 194, 206, 210–11
    cross-site visits in, 184–85
    difficulties in realizing ideal roles in, 210–13
    effects of on preservice teachers, 179, 195
    evaluations in, 207–8
    goal of inquiry in, 214–15

importance of, 199–200
length of, 204–5
need for site supervisor in, 206–8
organization, faculty views of, 204–10
reform in, 179
research on, 178–80
responsibilities beyond teaching in, suggestions for, 208
school-university coordination in, suggestions for, 209–10
as socialization, 201
student responsibilities in, suggestions for, 205
supportive context for, 193, 194
and teaching philosophies, 184–85, 194
varying effects of, 200
working with a team of teachers in, suggestions for, 208–9
see also professional development schools
Study of the Education of Educators, 167–68
subject background
and AC, 96, 108, *112*, 117
out-of-field teaching, 5–6
and student achievement, 62
in teaching assignments, 20, 35–40
survival. *see* attrition; retention
Swanson, M., 62

Teacher Follow-up Survey, 129, 131, 141, 145
teacher preparation
accountability for, 31–32
debate over need for, 30, 172, 173
decline in, 31
and improving status of teaching, 169, *170*, 171, 172
lack of minority role models in, 46
length of training, 163–64, *170*
link with attrition, 128, 132–37
movement to reform, 199
options for, 30–31
proposal to eliminate courses in, 172, 173
relation to effectiveness, 63, 64
school-university partnerships in, 199 (*see also* professional development schools)
standards of, 164–65, 171
and student achievement, 32, 72–73
student teaching in (*see* professional development schools; student teaching)
views on, 173
visions for in PDS context, 183–84
see also certification; subject background
teachers
deprofessionalization of, 35, 41
diversity of (*see* diversity in teaching force)
teachers, highly qualified
definition of, 62
lack of tracking of, 9
mandate for, 3, 61
and poverty levels in schools, 64–69
see also certification; qualifications, teacher; teacher preparation
teachers, male. *see* diversity in teaching force; gender
teachers, minority. *see* minority teachers
teachers, new
academic preparation of, 65–67
attrition of, 130–31
certification of, 35–36, 39, 41–42, 125

distribution of in relation to poverty levels, 64–69
diversity among, 51–52
use of AC, 125
Teachers for Our Nation's Schools (Goodlad), 199
Teach for America, 127
teaching practices and teacher quality, 4
Theobald, N. D., 143, 153
Third International Mathematics and Science Study, 120
Thoreson, A., 32, 127
Tomorrow's Teachers (Holmes Group), 199

United Kingdom, 166

Wales, 166
Weglinsky, H., 7, 73
Whaley, P. W. F., 166
Whitaker, K. S., 165
Womack, S. T., 63
Woolfolk, A. E., 179, 180, 194
work experience of AC teachers, 95, 99, 107, *111*, 119
working conditions, 166, 171, 172
Wyckoff, J., 127

Zeichner, K. M., 178–79